MAKE FREEZE IT

Taste of Home BOOKS

RDA ENTHUSIAST BRANDS, LLC
MILWAUKEE, WI

Taste of Home

EDITORIAL

Editor-in-Chief Catherine Cassidy
Vice President, Content Operations Kerri Balliet
Creative Director Howard Greenberg

Managing Editor, Print & Digital Books Mark Hagen
Associate Creative Director Edwin Robles Jr.

Editor Christine Rukavena
Art Director Maggie Conners
Layout Designer Nancy Novak
Editorial Production Manager Dena Ahlers
Editorial Production Coordinator Jill Banks
Copy Chief Deb Warlaumont Mulvey
Copy Editors Chris McLaughlin, Mary-Liz Shaw, Dulcie Shoener
Contributing Copy Editors Michael Juley, Kristin Sutter
Business Analyst, Content Tools Amanda Harmatys
Content Operations Assistant Shannon Stroud
Editorial Services Administrator Marie Brannon

Food Editors Gina Nistico; James Schend; Peggy Woodward, RDN
Recipe Editors Sue Ryon (lead); Mary King; Irene Yeh

Test Kitchen & Food Styling Manager Sarah Thompson
Test Cooks Nicholas Iverson (lead), Matthew Hass, Lauren Knoelke
Food Stylists Kathryn Conrad (lead), Leah Rekau, Shannon Roum
Prep Cooks Bethany Van Jacobson (lead), Megumi Garcia, Melissa Hansen
Culinary Team Assistant Megan Behr

Photography Director Stephanie Marchese
Photographers Dan Roberts, Jim Wieland
Photographer/Set Stylist Grace Natoli Sheldon
Set Stylists Melissa Franco, Stacey Genaw, Dee Dee Jacq
Set Stylist Assistant Stephanie Chojnacki

Editorial Business Manager Kristy Martin
Editorial Business Associate Samantha Lea Stoeger
Contributing Editorial Business Assistant Andrea Polzin

BUSINESS

Vice President, Group Publisher Kirsten Marchioli
Publisher Donna Lindskog
General Manager, Taste of Home Cooking School Erin Puariea

TRUSTED MEDIA BRANDS, INC.

President and Chief Executive Officer Bonnie Kintzer
Chief Financial Officer Dean Durbin
Chief Operating Officer Howard Halligan
Chief Marketing Officer C. Alec Casey
Chief Revenue Officer Richard Sutton
Chief Digital Officer Vince Errico
Senior Vice President, Global HR & Communications Phyllis E. Gebhardt, SPHR; SHRM-SCP
General Counsel Mark Sirota
Vice President, Magazine Marketing Christopher Gaydos
Vice President, Operations Michael Garzone
Vice President, Consumer Marketing Planning Jim Woods
Vice President, Digital Content & Audience Development Diane Dragan
Vice President, Financial Planning & Analysis William Houston
Publishing Director, Books Debra Polansky

For other Taste of Home books and products, visit us at tasteofhome.com.

International Standard Book Number: 978-1-61765-549-4
Library of Congress Control Number: 2016930445

Printed in China.
5 7 9 10 8 6 4

Cover Photographer: Grace Natoli Sheldon
Set Stylist: Stacey Genaw
Food Stylist: Leah Rekau

Pictured on front cover:
Simple Creamy Chicken Enchiladas, page 241
Pictured on back cover: Muffin Tin Pizzas, page 176; Butter Pecan Pumpkin Pie, page 225; Stuffed Chicken Rolls, page 160

LIKE US
facebook.com/tasteofhome

TWEET US
@tasteofhome

FOLLOW US
pinterest.com/taste_of_home

SHOP WITH US
shoptasteofhome.com

SHARE A RECIPE
tasteofhome.com/submit

How Cold Is Cold Enough?
Make sure you have a freezer thermometer to track the temperature in your freezer. It should always be 0° or less.

-30 | -20 | -10 | 0 | 10 | 20 | 30 | 40 | 50 | 60 | 70

PAGE 216

PAGE 44

PAGE 173

PAGE 112

CONTENTS

HANDY ICONS

EAT SMART
Lower in calories, fat and sodium

⑤INGREDIENTS
5 ingredients max, plus staples like salt, pepper and oil

SLOW COOKER
Set it and forget it

WANT A QUICK BREAKFAST FOR KIDS? Keep a stash of **Multigrain Waffles**, *page 24*, and spread them with **Strawberry Freezer Jam**, *page 67*.

FREEZER BASICS

Don't let the cold set in. It's essential to use proper containers, pack and store properly, and choose freezer-friendly ingredients to **maximize your deep-freeze potential.**

LABEL EVERYTHING

Keep a marker and freezer labels handy. Jot down the date and contents on each container or freezer bag. Even if you can see what's inside, date it anyway so you won't have to guess how long something's been frozen.

WRAP IT UP

Tightly wrap meats in plastic wrap, then in heavy-duty foil or freezer paper, using freezer tape to seal if necessary. For other foods, use durable, leakproof containers or freezer bags sealed tightly. Press to remove all air. Store raw meats on the bottom shelf to minimize the potential for contamination.

FOLLOW A PLAN

First In, First Out, or FIFO, is a simple practice that's commonly used in restaurants, grocery stores and other food-service industries. It means that you want to use the oldest foods first to ensure timely usage so you waste less.

DO MONTHLY CHECKUPS

Take a minute or two each month to get acquainted with the freezer. Reshuffle items, throw out food that's been frozen too long or use up forgotten treasures, such as the stew your neighbor offered a month ago.

PACK IT FLAT

Always allow hot food to cool to room temperature before freezing; once it's cool, freeze immediately. Freeze foods in a single layer, and stack them after they're frozen.

MAKE SINGLE SERVINGS

A pound of bacon or an entire batch of cookie dough can be too much to thaw at once. Tightly seal small amounts separately; store together in a large container.

Send your recipes!

WHAT'S IN YOUR FREEZER?

Share your favorite freezer recipes at **tasteofhome.com/submit**

STAY ORGANIZED

DIVIDE THE FREEZER INTO ZONES, with areas for veggies, breads, meats, etc., so you always know where to look.

LABEL STRATEGICALLY with masking tape and a permanent marker. Include the date the food went in so you know if it's getting old. Use different-colored markers for different types of food—poultry, seafood, sauces—so you can find what you want at a glance.

COMBINE SIMILAR items. If you have four packages of frozen berries, put them all into one larger plastic bag or an inexpensive plastic basket, then label the bag or basket. Similarly, nuts will stay fresher longer in the freezer. Store all the different bags of nuts in one large zip-top freezer bag.

THAW SAFELY

DEFROSTING IN THE REFRIGERATOR is safe and fuss-free, but it's the slowest method, so plan ahead. Small items, like a pound of ground beef, defrost overnight. Most items take 1 or 2 days. For small beef and pork roasts, allow 3 to 5 hours per pound of meat; for larger cuts, allow 5 to 7 hours. A whole turkey will take 24 hours for every 4 to 5 pounds of weight.

COLD WATER DEFROSTING requires less time than the refrigerator but more attention. Place food in a watertight plastic storage bag; place bag in cold water. Change water every 30 minutes until food is thawed.

MICROWAVE DEFROSTING is suitable for last-minute thawing of small items. Unwrap the food and place it in a microwave-safe dish. Cook the food immediately after defrosting.

USE 'EM OR LOSE 'EM

Even frozen foods don't last forever. The quality may diminish with time. Use this list to keep on course.

FOOD	# OF MONTHS	FOOD	# OF MONTHS
Casseroles	2-3	Cooked Shrimp	3
Soups & Stews	2-3	Ice Cream	2
Uncooked Bacon	1	Cheese, Hard or Soft	6
Uncooked Steak	6-12	Butter	6-9
Uncooked Pork Chops	4-6	Frozen Veggies	8
Ground Beef	4	Baked Pie	1-2
Cooked Chicken Pieces	4	Cheesecake	2-3
Uncooked Chicken Pieces	9	Baked Quick Bread	2-3
Whole Chicken or Turkey	12	Yeast Bread or Rolls	3-6
Cooked Fish	4-6	Baked Cookies	8-12

FREEZE IT BETTER!

USE A THERMOMETER to monitor your freezer. For optimum quality, it should be 0°.

COOL FOOD QUICKLY AND EVENLY before freezing. Transfer hot foods to a shallow pan or several small, shallow containers. Or place the pan in a bowl of ice water. Stir frequently so foods cool faster.

FREEZE A SMALL AMOUNT FIRST if you're not sure that something will freeze well. After it's thawed and reheated (if necessary), decide if the quality is up to your standards.

SEASON SPARINGLY BEFORE FREEZING and add more later if necessary. Spices change flavor during freezer storage.

KEEP THE FREEZER TWO-THIRDS FULL for energy efficiency.

LEAVE SOME SPACE around each package so air can circulate.

MANAGE THE QUANTITIES so whatever is placed in the freezer is frozen solid within 24 hours. Adding a lot of food at once will increase freezing time.

STORE NUTS, FLOUR AND JUICE in the door because it's frequently opened. Save the colder parts of the freezer for other foods.

**APPLE, CHEDDAR &
BACON BREAD PUDDING**
PAGE 22

Breakfast & Brunch

Heat-and-go morning meals make it easy to start the day off right. Here, you'll find quick take-alongs for busy weekdays and cozy casseroles for lazy weekends alike.

Breakfast Biscuit Cups

The first time I made these cups, my husband and his assistant coach came into the kitchen as I pulled the pan from the oven. They devoured the tempting biscuits!

—DEBRA CARLSON
COLUMBUS JUNCTION, IA

PREP: 30 MIN. • **BAKE:** 20 MIN.
MAKES: 8 SERVINGS

- ⅓ **pound bulk pork sausage**
- 1 **tablespoon all-purpose flour**
- ⅛ **teaspoon salt**
- ½ **teaspoon pepper, divided**
- ¾ **cup plus 1 tablespoon 2% milk, divided**
- ½ **cup frozen cubed hash brown potatoes, thawed**
- 1 **tablespoon butter**
- 2 **large eggs**
- ⅛ **teaspoon garlic salt**
- 1 **can (16.3 ounces) large refrigerated flaky biscuits**
- ½ **cup shredded Colby- Monterey Jack cheese**

1. In a large skillet, cook the sausage over medium heat until no longer pink; drain. Stir in the flour, salt and ¼ teaspoon of pepper until blended; gradually add ¾ cup milk. Bring to a boil; cook and stir for 2 minutes or until thickened. Remove from the heat and set aside.

2. In another large skillet over medium heat, cook potatoes in butter until tender. Whisk the eggs, garlic salt and remaining milk and pepper; add to skillet. Cook and stir until almost set.

3. Press each biscuit onto the bottom and up the sides of eight ungreased muffin cups. Spoon the egg mixture, half of the cheese, and sausage into cups; sprinkle with remaining cheese.

4. Bake at 375° for 18-22 minutes or until golden brown. Cool 5 minutes before removing from pan.

FREEZE OPTION *Freeze cooled biscuit cups in a freezer container, separating layers with waxed paper. To use, microwave one frozen biscuit cup on high for 50-60 seconds or until heated through.*

Bacon Vegetable Quiche

The best part about this recipe is you can tailor it to the season and use whatever veggies and cheese you have on hand. I especially love this quiche in spring made with fresh greens and asparagus.

—SHANNON KOENE BLACKSBURG, VA

PREP: 25 MIN. • **BAKE:** 30 MIN.
MAKES: 6 SERVINGS

- 1 **unbaked pastry shell (9 inches)**
- 1 **cup sliced fresh mushrooms**
- 1 **cup chopped fresh broccoli**
- ¾ **cup chopped sweet onion**
- 2½ **teaspoons olive oil**
- 2 **cups fresh baby spinach**
- 3 **large eggs, lightly beaten**
- 1 **can (5 ounces) evaporated milk**
- 1 **tablespoon minced fresh rosemary or 1 teaspoon dried rosemary, crushed**
- ¼ **teaspoon salt**
- ¼ **teaspoon pepper**
- 1 **cup (4 ounces) shredded cheddar cheese**
- 6 **bacon strips, cooked and crumbled**
- ½ **cup crumbled tomato and basil feta cheese**

1. Preheat oven to 450°. Line unpricked pastry shell with a double thickness of heavy-duty foil. Bake for 8 minutes. Remove the foil; bake 5 minutes longer. Reduce oven to 375°.

2. Meanwhile, in a large skillet, saute mushrooms, broccoli and onion in oil until tender. Add spinach; cook until wilted.

3. In a large bowl, whisk eggs, milk, rosemary, salt and pepper. Stir in the vegetables, cheddar cheese and bacon. Pour into crust. Sprinkle with feta cheese.

4. Cover edges loosely with foil. Bake 30-35 minutes or until a knife inserted near the center comes out clean. Let the quiche stand 5 minutes before cutting.

FREEZE OPTION *Cover and freeze unbaked quiche. To use, remove from freezer 30 minutes before baking (do not thaw). Preheat oven to 375°. Place quiche on a baking sheet; cover edges loosely with foil. Bake as directed, increasing time as necessary for a knife inserted near the center to come out clean.*

TOP TIP

Common olive oil works better for cooking at high heat than virgin or extra-virgin oil. These higher grades have ideal flavor for cold foods, but they smoke at lower temperatures.

Jack Cheese Oven Omelet

Although it's easy, the omelet looks impressive. Sometimes I toss in mushrooms and cheddar cheese for a different flavor.

—LAUREL ROBERTS VANCOUVER, WA

PREP: 20 MIN. • **BAKE:** 35 MIN.
MAKES: 6 SERVINGS

- 8 **bacon strips, diced**
- 4 **green onions, sliced**
- 8 **large eggs**
- 1 **cup 2% milk**
- ½ **teaspoon seasoned salt**
- 2½ **cups (10 ounces) shredded Monterey Jack cheese, divided**

1. Preheat oven to 350°. In a large skillet, cook the bacon over medium heat until crisp. Drain, reserving 1 tablespoon drippings. Set bacon aside. Saute onions in drippings until tender; set aside.
2. In a large bowl, beat eggs. Add the milk, seasoned salt, 2 cups of cheese, bacon and the sauteed onions. Transfer to a greased shallow 2-qt. baking dish.
3. Bake, uncovered, for 35-40 minutes or until set. Sprinkle with remaining cheese.

FREEZE OPTION *Freeze unbaked omelet until firm; cover with foil. To use, remove from freezer 30 minutes before baking (do not thaw). Preheat oven to 350°. Bake as directed, increasing time as necessary for a knife inserted near the center to come out clean. Sprinkle with ½ cup cheese.*

Crescent Zucchini Pie

A tender, flaky crust makes this egg-and-zucchini-based pie a special treat rich with delectable cheese, herbs and seasonings.

—ZELDA DEHOEDT CEDAR RAPIDS, IA

PREP: 20 MIN. • **BAKE:** 20 MIN.
MAKES: 6 SERVINGS

- 1 **tube (8 ounces) refrigerated crescent rolls**
- 2 **teaspoons Dijon mustard**
- 4 **cups sliced zucchini**
- 1 **cup chopped onion**
- 6 **tablespoons butter, cubed**
- 2 **large eggs, lightly beaten**
- 1 **cup (4 ounces) shredded part-skim mozzarella cheese**
- 1 **cup (4 ounces) shredded Colby-Monterey Jack cheese**
- 2 **tablespoons dried parsley flakes**
- ½ **teaspoon salt**
- ½ **teaspoon pepper**
- ¼ **teaspoon dried basil**
- ¼ **teaspoon dried oregano**

1. Separate crescent dough into eight triangles and place in a greased 9-in. deep-dish pie plate with points toward the center. Press dough onto the bottom and up the sides of plate to form a crust; seal seams. Spread crust with mustard.
2. In a large skillet, saute the zucchini and onion in butter until tender. In a large bowl, combine the eggs, cheeses, seasonings and the zucchini mixture. Pour into crust.
3. Bake at 375° for 20-25 minutes or until a knife inserted near the center comes out clean. Cover edges loosely with foil if crust browns too quickly.

FREEZE OPTION *Securely wrap and freeze cooled pie in plastic wrap and foil. To use, partially thaw in refrigerator overnight. Remove from refrigerator 30 minutes before baking. Preheat oven to 350°. Unwrap pie; reheat in oven until heated through and a thermometer inserted in center reads 165°.*

Pigs in a Pool

My kids love sausage and pancakes, but making them for breakfast on a busy weekday was out of the question. My homemade version of pigs in a blanket is a great alternative to the packaged kind, and they freeze like a dream.

—**LISA DODD** GREENVILLE, SC

PREP: 45 MIN. • **BAKE:** 20 MIN.
MAKES: 4 DOZEN

- 1 **pound reduced-fat bulk pork sausage**
- 2 **cups all-purpose flour**
- ¼ **cup sugar**
- 1 **tablespoon baking powder**
- 1 **teaspoon salt**
- ½ **teaspoon ground cinnamon**
- ¼ **teaspoon ground nutmeg**
- 1 **large egg, lightly beaten**
- 2 **cups fat-free milk**
- 2 **tablespoons canola oil**
- 2 **tablespoons honey**
  Maple syrup, optional

1. Preheat oven to 350°. Coat mini-muffin cups with cooking spray.

2. Shape sausage into forty-eight ¾-in. balls. Place the meatballs on a rack coated with cooking spray in a shallow baking pan. Bake 15-20 minutes or until cooked through. Drain on paper towels. In a large bowl, whisk the flour, sugar, baking powder, salt and spices. In another bowl, whisk egg, milk, oil and honey until blended. Add to flour mixture; stir just until moistened.

3. Place a sausage ball into each mini-muffin cup; cover with the batter. Bake 20-25 minutes or until lightly browned. Cool for 5 minutes before removing from pans to wire racks. Serve warm with syrup if desired.

FREEZE OPTION *Freeze cooled muffins in resealable plastic freezer bags. To use, microwave each muffin on high for 20-30 seconds or until heated through.*

PER SERVING *4 mini muffins (calculated without syrup) equals 234 cal., 10 g fat (3 g sat. fat), 45 mg chol., 560 mg sodium, 26 g carb., 1 g fiber, 10 g pro.*
Diabetic Exchanges: 1½ starch, 1 medium-fat meat, ½ fat.

Bacon Quiche Tarts

Here's a fun way to make single-serving quiches that people of all ages are sure to enjoy. Flavored with bacon, cheese and veggies, these little bites are just the thing for your next brunch spread.

—**KENDRA SCHERTZ** NAPPANEE, IN

PREP: 15 MIN. • **BAKE:** 20 MIN.
MAKES: 8 SERVINGS

- 6 **ounces cream cheese, softened**
- 5 **teaspoons 2% milk**
- 2 **large eggs**
- ½ **cup shredded Colby cheese**
- 2 **tablespoons chopped green pepper**
- 1 **tablespoon finely chopped onion**
- 1 **tube (8 ounces) refrigerated crescent rolls**
- 5 **bacon strips, cooked and crumbled**

1. In a small bowl, beat cream cheese and milk until smooth. Add the eggs, cheese, green pepper and onion.

2. Separate dough into eight triangles; press onto the bottom and up the sides of greased muffin cups. Sprinkle half of the bacon into cups. Pour egg mixture over bacon; top with remaining bacon.

3. Bake, uncovered, at 375° for 18-22 minutes or until a knife inserted near the center comes out clean. Serve warm.

FREEZE IT

Freeze the cooled baked tarts in a resealable plastic freezer bag. To use, reheat tarts on a baking sheet in a preheated 375° oven.

Better-For-You Buttermilk Pancakes

Top these nutritious flapjacks with whatever fruit you have. My family loves to add fresh blueberries.

—JANET SCHUBERT RIB LAKE, WI

PREP: 15 MIN. • **COOK:** 10 MIN./BATCH
MAKES: 16 PANCAKES

- 1 cup all-purpose flour
- 1 cup whole wheat flour
- 2 tablespoons sugar
- 2 teaspoons baking powder
- 1 teaspoon baking soda
- 2 large egg whites
- 1 large egg
- 2 cups buttermilk
- 2 tablespoons canola oil
  Fresh mixed berries, optional

1. In a bowl, combine first five ingredients. Combine egg whites, egg, buttermilk and oil; stir into dry ingredients just until moist.
2. Pour batter by ¼ cupfuls onto a hot griddle coated with cooking spray. Turn when bubbles just form on top; cook until second side is golden brown. Serve with berries if desired.
FREEZE OPTION *Freeze cooled pancakes between layers of waxed paper in a freezer bag. To use, place pancakes on an ungreased baking sheet, cover with foil and reheat at 375° oven 6-10 minutes. Or, place a stack of three pancakes on a microwave-safe plate and microwave on high for 1¼-1½ minutes or until heated through.*
PER SERVING *2 pancakes (calculated without berries) equals 189 cal., 5 g fat (1 g sat. fat), 29 mg chol., 345 mg sodium, 29 g carb., 2 g fiber, 7 g pro.* **Diabetic Exchanges:** *2 starch, 1 fat.*

Mushroom Quiche Lorraine

I have young children, so a simple dish like this is ideal for our family. My husband's grandmother shared the recipe.

—MICHELLE FINCHER LYMAN, SC

PREP: 15 MIN. • **BAKE:** 30 MIN.
MAKES: 6 SERVINGS

- 1 unbaked pastry shell (9 inches)
- 1 cup sliced fresh mushrooms
- ½ cup chopped green onions
- 2 tablespoons butter
- 4 large eggs
- 1¼ cups half-and-half cream
- ⅛ teaspoon pepper
- 1 cup (4 ounces) shredded Swiss cheese
- 4 bacon strips, cooked and crumbled

1. Line unpricked pastry shell with a double thickness of heavy-duty foil. Bake at 450° for 8 minutes. Remove the foil; bake 5 minutes longer. Remove from the oven; reduce heat to 375°.
2. Meanwhile, in a small skillet, saute mushrooms and onions in butter until tender. In a large bowl, beat the eggs, cream and pepper. Using a slotted spoon, transfer mushrooms and onions to egg mixture. Stir in cheese and bacon.
3. Pour into crust. Cover edges of quiche loosely with foil. Bake for 30-35 minutes or until a knife inserted near the center comes out clean. Let stand for 5 minutes before cutting.
FREEZE OPTION *Cover and freeze unbaked quiche. To use, remove from freezer 30 minutes before baking (do not thaw). Preheat oven to 375°. Place the quiche on a baking sheet; cover edge loosely with foil. Bake as directed, increasing time as necessary for a knife inserted near the center to come out clean.*

FREEZE IT

Securely wrap and freeze cooled quiche in plastic wrap and foil. To use, partially thaw in refrigerator overnight. Remove from refrigerator 30 minutes before baking. Preheat oven to 350°. Unwrap quiche; reheat in oven until heated through and a thermometer inserted in center reads 165°.

Smoked Salmon Quiche

My son fishes for salmon on the Kenai River and smokes much of what he catches. My mom gave this recipe to me because I'm always looking for new ways to cook with salmon. You can use regular cooked salmon, but the smoked flavor can't be beat.

—ROSE MARIE CHERVEN

ANCHORAGE, AK

PREP: 30 MIN.
BAKE: 35 MIN. + STANDING
MAKES: 8 SERVINGS

- 1 sheet refrigerated pie pastry
- 1 cup (4 ounces) shredded reduced-fat Swiss cheese
- 1 tablespoon all-purpose flour
- 3 plum tomatoes, seeded and chopped
- 2 tablespoons finely chopped onion
- 2 teaspoons canola oil
- 3 ounces smoked salmon fillet, flaked (about ½ cup)
- 4 large eggs
- 1 cup whole milk
- ¼ teaspoon salt

1. On a lightly floured surface, unroll pastry. Transfer to a 9-in. pie plate. Trim pastry to ½ in. beyond edge of plate; flute edges. Combine cheese and flour; place in pastry.

2. In a large skillet, saute the tomatoes and onion in oil just until tender. Remove from the heat; stir in salmon. Spoon over cheese mixture.

3. In a small bowl, whisk the eggs, milk and salt. Pour into pastry. Bake at 350° for 35-40 minutes or until a knife inserted near the center comes out clean. Let quiche stand for 15 minutes before cutting.

PER SERVING *1 piece equals 235 cal., 13 g fat (5 g sat. fat), 122 mg chol., 348 mg sodium, 17 g carb., trace fiber, 12 g pro. Diabetic Exchanges: 2 medium-fat meat, 1 starch.*

Peanut Butter & Banana Waffles

Here's a welcome change from your everyday waffles. I like to make big batches up so I can freeze the leftovers and reheat them later for a quick breakfast.

—CHRISTINA ADDISON

BLANCHESTER, OH

PREP: 10 MIN. • **COOK:** 5 MIN./BATCH
MAKES: 16 WAFFLES

- 1¾ cups all-purpose flour
- 2 tablespoons sugar
- 3 teaspoons baking powder
- ¼ teaspoon salt
- ¾ cup creamy peanut butter
- ½ cup canola oil
- 2 large eggs
- 1¾ cups 2% milk
- 1 cup mashed ripe bananas (about 2 medium)

1. In a large bowl, whisk flour, sugar, baking powder and salt. Place peanut butter in another bowl; gradually whisk in oil. Whisk in eggs and milk. Add to dry ingredients; stir just until moistened. Stir in bananas.

2. Bake in a preheated waffle iron according to manufacturer's directions until golden brown.

FREEZE OPTION *Cool waffles on wire racks. Freeze between layers of waxed paper in resealable plastic freezer bags. Reheat waffles in a toaster on medium setting. Or, microwave each waffle on high for 30-60 seconds or until heated through.*

Quiche Pastry Cups

My grandmother used to make "egg cup surprises" on special occasions. The fillings were always a surprise, as she never seemed to use the same ingredients twice. We children had fun guessing what we'd find inside the tender crust.

—DENALEE STANDART

RANCHO MURETA, CA

PREP: 30 MIN. • **BAKE:** 15 MIN.
MAKES: 1½ DOZEN

- 1 package (17.3 ounces) frozen puff pastry, thawed
- 4 large eggs, divided use
- 1 cup plus 2 tablespoons half-and-half cream, divided
- 1 tablespoon minced fresh thyme
- ½ teaspoon salt
- ½ teaspoon pepper
- ¼ teaspoon ground nutmeg
- 1½ cups (6 ounces) shredded Gruyere cheese
- 1½ cups chopped fresh spinach
- 1 medium sweet red pepper, chopped
- 8 bacon strips, cooked and crumbled

1. Preheat oven to 400°. On a lightly floured surface, unfold puff pastry. Roll each sheet into a 12-in. square; cut each into nine squares. Place in ungreased muffin cups, pressing gently onto bottoms and up the sides, allowing corners to point up.
2. In a small bowl, whisk 3 eggs, 1 cup cream, thyme and other seasonings. In another bowl, combine cheese, spinach, red pepper and bacon; divide among the pastry cups. Pour the egg mixture over cheese mixture.
3. In a small bowl, whisk remaining egg with remaining cream; brush over pastry edges. Bake for 15-18 minutes or until golden brown. Remove to wire racks. Serve warm.
FREEZE OPTION *Cover and freeze baked pastries on greased baking sheets until cups are firm. Transfer to resealable plastic freezer bags; return to freezer. To use, reheat frozen pastries on ungreased baking sheets in a preheated 375° oven 17-20 minutes or until heated through.*

EAT SMART
Honey-Oat Granola Bars

My husband and I enjoy these bars every day. It's a basic recipe to which you can add any of your favorites...coconut, different kinds of chips, nuts and dried fruits.

—JEAN BOYCE NEW ULM, MN

PREP: 15 MIN.
BAKE: 15 MIN. + COOLING
MAKES: 3 DOZEN

- 4 cups quick-cooking oats
- 1 cup packed brown sugar
- 1 cup chopped salted peanuts
- 1 cup (6 ounces) semisweet chocolate chips
- ½ cup sunflower kernels
- ¾ cup butter, melted
- ⅔ cup honey
- 1 teaspoon vanilla extract

1. Preheat oven to 350°. In a large bowl, combine oats, brown sugar, peanuts, chocolate chips and sunflower kernels. Stir in butter, honey and vanilla until combined (the mixture will be crumbly). Press mixture into a greased parchment paper-lined 15x10x1-in. baking pan.
2. Bake 15-20 minutes or until browned and bubbly. Cool for 15 minutes on a wire rack; cut into squares. Cool completely before removing from pan.
FREEZE OPTION *Wrap each cooled bar in plastic; freeze until firm. To use, thaw bar at room temperature.*
PER SERVING *1 bar equals 167 cal., 9 g fat (4 g sat. fat), 10 mg chol., 54 mg sodium, 21 g carb., 2 g fiber, 3 g pro.* **Diabetic Exchanges:** *1½ starch, 1½ fat.*

Mushroom Sausage Strata

This delightful casserole is a mainstay for our family's Christmas Day brunch. It's a real plus to be able to put the dish together and freeze it ahead of time!

—**JULIE STERCHI** CAMPBELLSVILLE, KY

PREP: 20 MIN. + CHILLING
BAKE: 35 MIN. + STANDING
MAKES: 8-10 SERVINGS

- 1 **pound bulk pork sausage**
- 10 **slices whole wheat bread, cubed**
- 1 **can (4 ounces) mushroom stems and pieces, drained**
- ½ **cup shredded cheddar cheese**
- ½ **cup shredded Swiss cheese**
- 6 **large eggs**
- 1 **cup 2% milk**
- 1 **cup half-and-half cream**
- 1 **teaspoon Worcestershire sauce**
- ½ **teaspoon pepper**

1. In a large skillet, cook sausage over medium heat until no longer pink; drain. Place the bread cubes in a greased 13x9-in. baking dish. Sprinkle with the sausage, mushrooms and cheeses.

2. In a large bowl, whisk eggs, milk, cream, Worcestershire sauce and pepper; pour mixture over the cheese. Cover dish and refrigerate overnight.

3. Remove from the refrigerator 30 minutes before baking. Preheat the oven to 350°. Bake, uncovered, for 35-45 minutes or until a knife inserted near the center comes out clean.

FREEZE OPTION *After assembling, cover and freeze strata. To use, partially thaw in refrigerator overnight. Remove from refrigerator 30 minutes before baking. Preheat oven to 350°. Bake strata as directed, increasing time as necessary for a knife inserted near the center to come out clean.*

EAT SMART

Banana Blueberry Pancakes

This recipe is a favorite in our home. My kids don't care how healthy it is, but I do!

—KELLY REINICKE
WISCONSIN RAPIDS, WI

PREP: 15 MIN. • **COOK:** 5 MIN./BATCH
MAKES: 14 PANCAKES

- 1 cup whole wheat flour
- ½ cup all-purpose flour
- 2 tablespoons sugar
- 2 teaspoons baking powder
- ½ teaspoon salt
- 1 large egg, lightly beaten
- 1¼ cups fat-free milk
- 3 medium ripe bananas, mashed
- 1 teaspoon vanilla extract
- 1½ cups fresh or frozen blueberries
  Maple syrup, optional

1. In a large bowl, combine the flours, sugar, baking powder and salt. Combine the egg, milk, bananas and vanilla; stir into dry ingredients just until moistened.

2. Pour the batter by ¼ cupfuls onto a hot griddle coated with cooking spray; sprinkle with the blueberries. Turn when bubbles form on top; cook until second side is golden brown. Serve with syrup if desired.

FREEZE OPTION *Freeze cooled pancakes between layers of waxed paper in a resealable plastic freezer bag. To use, place the pancakes on an ungreased baking sheet, cover with foil and reheat in a preheated 375° oven 6-10 minutes. Or, place a stack of three pancakes on a microwave-safe plate and microwave on high for 1¼-1½ minutes or until heated through.*

NOTE *If using frozen blueberries, do not thaw.*

PER SERVING *2 pancakes (calculated without syrup) equals 195 cal., 2 g fat (trace sat. fat), 31 mg chol., 317 mg sodium, 41 g carb., 4 g fiber, 6 g pro.*
Diabetic Exchanges: 1½ starch, 1 fruit.

Breakfast Bundles

Getting kids to eat breakfast is a breeze when you offer them these little bundles of goodness packed with hearty ingredients. The recipe is so simple that kids of all ages can help make them.

—BERNICE WILLIAMS

NORTH AURORA, IL

START TO FINISH: 30 MIN.
MAKES: 2 DOZEN

- ½ cup butter, softened
- 2 tablespoons orange juice concentrate
- 1 large egg
- 1½ cups all-purpose flour
- ⅔ cup sugar
- ½ cup Grape-Nuts cereal
- 1 teaspoon baking powder
- ½ pound bacon strips, cooked and crumbled

1. Preheat oven to 350°. In a bowl, beat the butter and orange juice. Add the egg; mix well. Combine flour, sugar, cereal and baking powder; stir into butter mixture. Fold in bacon.

2. Drop mixture by rounded tablespoonfuls onto ungreased baking sheets. Bake for 11-13 minutes or until edges are light brown. Store in the refrigerator.

FREEZE OPTION *Freeze cooled bundles in resealable plastic freezer bags. To use, bake the bundles on an ungreased baking sheet in a preheated 350° oven until heated through.*

(5) INGREDIENTS

Light 'n' Crispy Waffles

Club soda gives these crisp waffles a light, fluffy texture. With only four ingredients, homemade waffles can't get much easier than this!

—TASTE OF HOME TEST KITCHEN

START TO FINISH: 20 MIN.
MAKES: 12 WAFFLES

- 2 cups biscuit/baking mix
- 2 large eggs, lightly beaten
- ½ cup canola oil
- 1 cup club soda

1. In a large bowl, combine the biscuit mix, eggs and oil. Add club soda and stir until smooth.
2. Bake in a preheated waffle iron according to manufacturer's directions until golden brown.
FREEZE OPTION *Cool waffles on wire racks. Freeze between layers of waxed paper in resealable plastic freezer bags. To use, reheat waffles in a toaster on medium setting. Or, microwave each waffle on high for 30-60 seconds or until heated through.*

Tomato Olive Quiche

Salty, savory olives; two kinds of onions; juicy tomatoes and layers of cheese make this flavorful quiche a dish to remember.

—STEPHANIE PROEBSTING
BARRINGTON, IL

PREP: 30 MIN.
BAKE: 40 MIN. + STANDING
MAKES: 8 SERVINGS

- 1 sheet refrigerated pie pastry
- ¼ cup all-purpose flour
- ½ teaspoon salt
- ½ teaspoon pepper
- 2 medium tomatoes, sliced
- 2 tablespoons olive oil
- 2 large eggs
- 1 cup heavy whipping cream
- 1 cup (4 ounces) shredded sharp cheddar cheese
- 1 can (6 ounces) pitted ripe olives, drained and finely chopped
- ½ cup chopped sweet onion
- 3 green onions, chopped
- 4 slices provolone cheese

1. Unroll pastry into a 9-in. pie plate; flute edges. Line unpricked pastry shell with a double thickness of heavy-duty foil. Bake at 450° for 8 minutes. Remove the foil; bake 5 minutes longer.
2. In a large resealable plastic bag, combine the flour, salt and pepper. Add tomato slices, a few at a time, and shake to coat. In a large skillet over medium heat, cook the tomatoes in oil for 1-2 minutes on each side or until golden brown.
3. In a small bowl, whisk eggs and cream; stir in the cheddar cheese. Sprinkle olives and onions into crust; top with two slices of provolone cheese. Layer with tomatoes and remaining provolone. Pour the egg mixture over the top.
4. Bake at 375° for 40-45 minutes or until a knife inserted near the center comes out clean. Let stand for 10 minutes before cutting the quiche.
FREEZE OPTION *Cover and freeze unbaked quiche. To use, remove from freezer 30 minutes before baking (do not thaw). Preheat oven to 375°. Place on a baking sheet; cover edges loosely with foil. Bake as directed, increasing time as necessary for a knife inserted near the center to come out clean.*

minutes or until apples are tender, stirring occasionally. Cool completely.

2. In a greased 8-in.-square baking dish, layer half of each of the following: bread, bacon, apples and cheese. Repeat the layers. In a large bowl, whisk eggs, milk, cinnamon and salt; pour over the top. Refrigerate dish, covered, for several hours or overnight.

3. Preheat oven to 350°. Remove bread pudding from refrigerator; uncover and let stand while oven heats. Bake 45-55 minutes or until puffed, golden and a knife inserted near the center comes out clean. Let stand 15 minutes before serving.

4. In a microwave-safe bowl, microwave syrup and walnuts until warmed, stirring once. Serve with bread pudding.

FREEZE OPTION *After assembling, cover and freeze bread pudding. To use, partially thaw in refrigerator overnight. Remove from the refrigerator 30 minutes before baking. Preheat oven to 350°. Bake and serve bread pudding with syrup as directed.*

DID YOU KNOW?

Sharp cheddar cheese has been aged longer than regular cheddar. As cheese ages, it loses moisture and its flavor becomes more pronounced. Using aged cheese in a recipe can add complexity and rich flavor, even to humble favorites like casseroles and mac 'n' cheese. It's also great in light cooking because you can get more flavor while using less.

Apple, Cheddar & Bacon Bread Pudding

I first had this dish at a bridal brunch many years ago. It was so delicious that I created my own version, and here's the result. Now I make it all the time!

—**MELISSA MILLWOOD** LYMAN, SC

PREP: 30 MIN. + CHILLING
BAKE: 45 MIN.
MAKES: 9 SERVINGS

- 3 tablespoons butter
- 2 medium apples, peeled and chopped
- ¼ cup packed brown sugar
- 6 cups cubed day-old French bread
- 1 pound bacon strips, cooked and crumbled
- 1½ cups (6 ounces) shredded sharp cheddar cheese
- 5 large eggs
- 2¼ cups 2% milk
- ½ teaspoon ground cinnamon
- ¼ teaspoon salt

SYRUP
- 1 cup maple syrup
- ½ cup chopped walnuts

1. In a large skillet, heat butter over medium heat. Add apples; cook and stir for 2-3 minutes or until crisp-tender. Reduce heat to medium-low; stir in brown sugar. Cook, uncovered, 8-10

Chocolate Chip Pancakes

This recipe is a favorite of mine to make for special occasions like birthdays or holidays. If you want to make it extra special, serve the pancakes with berries or whipped cream—or both.

—LORI DANIELS BEVERLY, WV

PREP: 20 MIN. • **COOK:** 20 MIN.
MAKES: 16 PANCAKES
(1 CUP WHIPPED CREAM)

- ½ **cup heavy whipping cream**
- 1 **tablespoon confectioners' sugar**
- ½ **teaspoon vanilla extract**

BATTER

- 1½ **cups all-purpose flour**
- 3 **tablespoons sugar**
- 1 **teaspoon baking powder**
- ½ **teaspoon baking soda**
- ¼ **teaspoon salt**
- 2 **large eggs**
- 1 **cup milk**
- 1 **cup (8 ounces) sour cream**
- ¼ **cup butter, melted**
- ½ **cup miniature semisweet chocolate chips**

1. In a small bowl, beat cream, confectioners' sugar and vanilla until stiff peaks form. Cover and refrigerate until serving.

2. In a large bowl, combine the flour, sugar, baking powder, baking soda and salt. In another bowl, whisk the eggs, milk, sour cream and butter until blended; stir into the dry ingredients just until moistened. Fold in the chocolate chips.

3. Pour batter by ¼ cupfuls onto a lightly greased hot griddle; turn when bubbles form on top. Cook until second side is golden brown. Serve with the whipped cream.

FREEZE OPTION *Freeze cooled pancakes between layers of waxed paper in a resealable plastic freezer bag. To use, place pancakes on an ungreased baking sheet, cover with foil and reheat in a preheated 375° oven 6-10 minutes. Or, place a stack of three pancakes on a microwave-safe plate and microwave on high for 1¼-1½ minutes or until heated through.*

Multigrain Waffles

These multigrain waffles are crispy, airy and lower in fat, calories and cholesterol than traditional waffles. But they still have all the great taste of the original.

—**BETTY BLAIR** BARTLETT, TN

PREP: 15 MIN. • **COOK:** 5 MIN./BATCH
MAKES: 28 WAFFLES

- 1 **cup all-purpose flour**
- 1 **cup whole wheat flour**
- 1 **cup cornmeal**
- 1 **tablespoon sugar**
- 1 **tablespoon baking powder**
- ¾ **teaspoon baking soda**
- ½ **teaspoon salt**
- 3 **large eggs**
- 4 **large egg whites**
- 3 **cups buttermilk**
- ½ **cup unsweetened applesauce**
- 3 **tablespoons canola oil**
- 2 **tablespoons butter, melted**
  Butter and maple syrup, optional

1. In a large bowl, combine the first seven ingredients. In another bowl, whisk the eggs, egg whites, buttermilk, applesauce, oil and butter; whisk into dry ingredients just until blended.

2. Bake in a preheated waffle iron according to manufacturer's directions until golden brown. Serve with the butter and maple syrup if desired.

FREEZE OPTION *Cool waffles on wire racks. Freeze between layers of waxed paper in a resealable plastic freezer bag. To use, reheat waffles in a toaster on medium setting. Or, microwave each waffle on high for 30-60 seconds or until heated through.*

PER SERVING *2 waffles (calculated without butter and syrup) equals 187 cal., 7 g fat (2 g sat. fat), 52 mg chol., 336 mg sodium, 25 g carb., 2 g fiber, 7 g pro.* ***Diabetic Exchanges: 1½ starch, 1 fat.***

Ham and Cheese Souffle

I like to serve this tasty dish for brunch along with fresh fruit when I'm having guests. Not only is it easy, but everyone enjoys it. Make it the night before; then the next day all you need to do is bake it.

—**AIRY MURRAY** WILLIAMSPORT, MD

PREP: 15 MIN. + CHILLING
BAKE: 40 MIN. + STANDING
MAKES: 8-10 SERVINGS

- 16 **slices white bread (crusts removed), cubed**
- 1 **pound sliced ham, chopped**
- 2 **cups (8 ounces) shredded cheddar cheese**
- 2 **cups (8 ounces) shredded Swiss cheese**
- 5 **large eggs**
- 3 **cups milk**
- 1 **teaspoon ground mustard**
- ½ **teaspoon onion salt**
- 2¼ **cups crushed cornflakes**
- ⅓ **cup butter, melted**

1. In a greased 13x9-in. baking dish, layer half of the bread, ham, cheddar cheese and Swiss cheese. Repeat layers. In a small bowl, whisk the eggs, milk, mustard and onion salt; pour over layered mixture.

2. Cover the dish and refrigerate overnight. Combine cornflakes and butter; sprinkle on top. Bake at 375° for 40 minutes or until a knife inserted near the middle comes out clean. Let stand for 10 minutes before serving.

FREEZE OPTION *Prepare souffle as directed, omitting cornflake mixture. Cover and freeze unbaked souffle. To use, partially thaw in refrigerator overnight. Remove souffle from the refrigerator 30 minutes before baking. Preheat oven to 375°. Prepare cornflake mixture; sprinkle over top. Bake as directed, increasing time as necessary until a knife inserted near the center comes out clean.*

TOP TIP

A thrifty alternative to purchased onion salt is to mix up your own: Just combine 1 teaspoon onion powder with 3 teaspoons of table salt or other fine-grained salt. The ratio works the same for garlic salt, too.

Ham & Collards Quiche

I love quiche and wanted to make something that incorporates my Southern roots, so I came up with this version. With eggs, cheese, ham and nutritious collard greens in a flaky crust, it's a complete meal. Enjoy, everyone!

—BILLIE WILLIAMS-HENDERSON
BOWIE, MD

PREP: 20 MIN.
BAKE: 35 MIN. + STANDING
MAKES: 6 SERVINGS

- 1 **sheet refrigerated pie pastry**
- 2 **cups (8 ounces) shredded Colby-Monterey Jack cheese, divided**
- ¾ **cup cubed fully cooked ham**
- 2 **tablespoons olive oil**
- 1 **cup frozen chopped collard greens, thawed and drained**
- 1 **small onion, chopped**
- 1 **garlic clove, minced**
- ¼ **teaspoon salt**
- ¼ **teaspoon pepper**
- 6 **large eggs**
- 1 **cup 2% milk**

1. Preheat oven to 375°. Unroll pastry sheet into a 9-in. pie plate; flute edge. Sprinkle 1 cup cheese onto bottom of pastry-lined pie plate. Sprinkle with ham.

2. In a large skillet, heat oil over medium-high heat. Add collard greens and onion; cook and stir 5-7 minutes or until the onion is tender. Add garlic; cook 1 minute longer. Stir in salt and pepper. Arrange greens over ham.

3. In a large bowl, whisk the eggs and milk until blended. Pour over top. Sprinkle with remaining cheese.

4. Bake on lower oven rack 35-40 minutes or until a knife inserted near the center comes out clean. Let stand 10 minutes before cutting.

FREEZE OPTION *Cover and freeze unbaked quiche. To use, remove from freezer 30 minutes before baking (do not thaw). Preheat oven to 375°. Place quiche on a baking sheet. Bake as directed, increasing time to 50-60 minutes.*

Whole Wheat Pancakes

These light, fluffy pancakes seem like a treat. Whole wheat flour and toasted wheat germ make them so satisfying.

—**LINE WALTER** WAYNE, PA

START TO FINISH: 25 MIN.
MAKES: 20 PANCAKES

- 2 **cups whole wheat flour**
- ½ **cup toasted wheat germ**
- 1 **teaspoon baking soda**
- ½ **teaspoon salt**
- 2 **large eggs**
- 3 **cups buttermilk**
- 1 **tablespoon canola oil**

1. In a large bowl, combine the flour, wheat germ, baking soda and salt. In another bowl, whisk the eggs, buttermilk and oil. Stir into the dry ingredients just until blended.

2. Pour batter by ¼ cupfuls onto a hot griddle coated with cooking spray; turn cakes when bubbles form on top. Cook until the second side is golden brown.

FREEZE OPTION *Freeze cooled pancakes between layers of waxed paper in a resealable plastic freezer bag. To use, place the pancakes on an ungreased baking sheet, cover with foil and reheat in a preheated 375° oven 6-10 minutes. Or, place a stack of three pancakes on a microwave-safe plate and microwave on high for 45-90 seconds or until all are heated through.*

PER SERVING *2 pancakes equals 157 cal., 4 g fat (1 g sat. fat), 45 mg chol., 335 mg sodium, 24 g carb., 4 g fiber, 9 g pro.* **Diabetic Exchanges:** *1½ starch, 1 fat.*

⑤ INGREDIENTS

Egg Burritos

When I start with a hearty breakfast, I stave off hunger all day. One way to do that is to zap one of these frozen burritos in the microwave. This recipe is my family's favorite combo, but I sometimes choose breakfast sausage instead of bacon.

—**AUDRA NIEDERMAN** ABERDEEN, SD

PREP: 20 MIN. + FREEZING
MAKES: 10 BURRITOS

- 12 **bacon strips, diced**
- 12 **large eggs, lightly beaten**
  Salt and pepper to taste
- 10 **flour tortillas (8 inches)**
- 1½ **cups (6 ounces) shredded cheddar cheese**
- ½ **cup thinly sliced green onions**

1. In a large skillet, cook bacon until crisp; remove to paper towels. Drain, reserving 1-2 tablespoons drippings. Add eggs, salt and pepper to drippings; cook and stir over medium heat until the eggs are completely set.

2. Spoon about ¼ cup of egg mixture down the center of each tortilla; sprinkle with cheese, onions and reserved bacon. Fold bottom and sides of each tortilla over filling. Wrap each in waxed paper and aluminum foil. Freeze for up to 1 month.

TO USE FROZEN BURRITOS
Remove foil. Place the waxed paper-wrapped burritos on a microwave-safe plate. Microwave at 60% power for 1 to 1½ minutes or until heated through. Let stand for 20 seconds.

NOTE *This recipe was tested in a 1,100-watt microwave.*

Ham & Cheese Breakfast Strudels

Golden breakfast strudels are guaranteed to get the morning off to a wonderful start. Assemble them ahead and freeze individually to make any day great.

—**JO GROTH** PLAINFIELD, IA

PREP: 25 MIN. • **BAKE:** 10 MIN.
MAKES: 6 SERVINGS

- 3 tablespoons butter, divided
- 2 tablespoons all-purpose flour
- 1 cup milk
- ⅓ cup shredded Swiss cheese
- 2 tablespoons grated Parmesan cheese
- ¼ teaspoon salt
- 5 large eggs, lightly beaten
- ¼ pound ground fully cooked ham (about ¾ cup)
- 6 sheets phyllo dough (14x9-inch size)
- ½ cup butter, melted
- ¼ cup dry bread crumbs

TOPPING

- 2 tablespoons grated Parmesan cheese
- 2 tablespoons minced fresh parsley

1. In a small saucepan, melt 2 tablespoons butter. Stir in the flour until smooth; gradually add milk. Bring to a boil; cook and stir 2 minutes or until thickened. Stir in cheeses and salt.

2. In a large nonstick skillet, melt the remaining butter over medium heat. Add eggs to pan; cook and stir until almost set. Stir in ham and cheese sauce; heat through. Remove from the heat.

3. Preheat oven to 375°. Place one sheet of phyllo dough on a work surface. (Keep remaining phyllo covered with plastic wrap and a damp towel to prevent it from drying out.) Brush with melted butter. Sprinkle with 2 teaspoons bread crumbs. Fold in half lengthwise; brush again with butter. Spoon ½ cup filling onto phyllo about 2 in. from a short side. Fold side and edges over filling and roll up. Brush with butter. Repeat with the remaining phyllo, butter, bread crumbs and filling.

4. Place on a greased baking sheet; sprinkle each strudel with 1 teaspoon each of cheese and parsley. Bake 10-15 minutes or until golden brown. Serve the strudels immediately.

FREEZE OPTION *After topping strudels with cheese and parsley, freeze unbaked on a waxed paper-lined baking sheet until firm. Transfer to a freezer container; return to freezer. To use, bake strudels as directed, increasing time to 30-35 minutes or until heated through and golden brown.*

Gingerbread Buttermilk Waffles

We created this recipe so folks could enjoy the festive flavor of gingerbread at breakfast. For a pretty look, sprinkle the waffles with confectioners' sugar.

—TASTE OF HOME TEST KITCHEN

START TO FINISH: 30 MIN.
MAKES: 8 WAFFLES

- 1 cup all-purpose flour
- 1½ teaspoons baking powder
- 1 teaspoon ground ginger
- ¾ teaspoon ground cinnamon
- ½ teaspoon baking soda
- ¼ teaspoon salt
- ⅛ teaspoon ground cloves
- ⅓ cup packed brown sugar
- 1 large egg, separated
- ¾ cup buttermilk
- ¼ cup molasses
- 3 tablespoons butter, melted
- ⅛ teaspoon cream of tartar
  Confectioners' sugar, optional

1. In a large bowl, combine the first seven ingredients. In a small bowl, beat the brown sugar and the egg yolk until fluffy; add the buttermilk, molasses and butter. Stir into the dry ingredients just until combined.

2. In another small bowl, beat the egg white and cream of tartar until stiff peaks form. Gently fold into batter. Quickly spoon batter onto a preheated waffle iron. Bake waffles according to manufacturer's directions until golden brown. Sprinkle with confectioners' sugar if desired.

FREEZE OPTION *Cool waffles on wire racks. Freeze between layers of waxed paper in a resealable plastic freezer bag. To use, reheat waffles in a toaster on medium setting. Or, microwave each waffle on high for 30-60 seconds or until heated through.*

APRICOT TURKEY
PINWHEELS
PAGE 38

Entertaining Made Easy

Party prep is a snap when you have a stock of tasty
hors d'oeuvres like these tucked away in the freezer.
Now you can always be ready for guests!

Potato Chip Chicken Strips

This novel recipe is a fast and tasty change from fried chicken.

—**JUDITH LABROZZI** CANTON, OH

PREP: 20 MIN. • **BAKE:** 20 MIN.
MAKES: 10 SERVINGS

- 1 **cup (8 ounces) sour cream**
- ⅛ **teaspoon garlic salt**
- ⅛ **teaspoon onion salt**
- ⅛ **teaspoon paprika**
- 1 **package (12 ounces) potato chips, crushed**
- 2 **pounds boneless skinless chicken breasts, cut into 1-inch strips**
- ¼ **cup butter, melted**
  Salsa, barbecue sauce or sweet-and-sour sauce

1. In a shallow bowl, combine the sour cream and seasonings. Place crushed potato chips in another shallow bowl. Dip the chicken strips in sour cream mixture, then coat with crushed potato chips. Place in a greased 15x10x1-in. baking pan. Drizzle with butter.

2. Bake at 400° for 20-22 minutes or until chicken is no longer pink. Serve with salsa or sauce.

FREEZE OPTION *Transfer cooled chicken strips to a resealable plastic freezer bag; freeze. To use, reheat chicken strips in a greased 15x10x1-in. baking pan in a preheated 400° oven until crisp and heated through.*

Apple-Nut Blue Cheese Tartlets

These appetizers look and taste sophisticated, but they're a cinch to prepare. Fill the phyllo shells, bake when you have the time, and freeze. Then pop them in the oven when you want to impress your guests.

—**TRISHA KRUSE** EAGLE, ID

PREP: 25 MIN. • **BAKE:** 10 MIN.
MAKES: 15 APPETIZERS

- 1 **large apple, peeled and finely chopped**
- 1 **medium onion, finely chopped**
- 2 **teaspoons butter**
- 1 **cup (4 ounces) crumbled blue cheese**
- 4 **tablespoons finely chopped walnuts, toasted, divided**
- ½ **teaspoon salt**
- 1 **package (1.9 ounces) frozen miniature phyllo tart shells**

1. In a small nonstick skillet, saute apple and onion in butter until tender. Remove from the heat; stir in the blue cheese, 3 tablespoons walnuts and salt. Spoon a rounded tablespoonful into each tart shell.

2. Place on an ungreased baking sheet. Bake at 350° for 5 minutes. Sprinkle tarts with the remaining walnuts; bake for 2-3 minutes longer or until lightly browned.

PER SERVING *1 appetizer equals 76 cal., 5 g fat (2 g sat. fat), 7 mg chol., 200 mg sodium, 5 g carb., trace fiber, 3 g pro.* **Diabetic Exchanges:** *1 fat, ½ starch.*

FREEZE IT

Freeze cooled pastries in a freezer container, separating the layers with waxed paper. To use, reheat pastries on a baking sheet in a preheated 350° oven until crisp and heated through.

(5)INGREDIENTS
Caramelized Fennel Tarts

Fennel is a big favorite of mine no matter how it's cooked, but I think it is really amazing sauteed until rich and golden, then baked on top of flaky puff pastry.
—**MARY LISA SPEER** PALM BEACH, FL

PREP: 1 HOUR • **BAKE:** 15 MIN.
MAKES: 2 DOZEN

- 2 **medium fennel bulbs, quartered and thinly sliced**
- 2 **tablespoons olive oil**
- 1½ **teaspoons minced fresh thyme or ½ teaspoon dried thyme**
- 1 **teaspoon balsamic vinegar**
- ¼ **teaspoon salt**
- ⅛ **teaspoon pepper**
- 1 **package (17.3 ounces) frozen puff pastry, thawed**

1. In a large skillet, saute fennel in oil until softened. Reduce the heat to medium-low; cook, uncovered, for 40 minutes or until deep golden brown, stirring occasionally. Stir in the thyme, vinegar, salt and pepper.

2. Unfold each puff pastry sheet onto an ungreased baking sheet. Using a knife, score 1 in. from the edges of each pastry. Spread fennel mixture to within ½ in. of edges.

3. Bake the tarts at 400° for 12-15 minutes or until golden brown. Cut each into 12 pieces.

FREEZE IT

Freeze cooled pastries in a freezer container, separating layers with waxed paper. To use, reheat pastries on an ungreased baking sheet in a preheated 400° oven until crisp and heated through.

Puttanesca Meatball Sliders

Their just-right size and spice set these tender meatballs apart from others you may have tried. Placed on soft dinner rolls and topped with a zesty sauce, these unique sliders quickly win over a crowd.

—**AMY COELER** LEMOORE, CA

PREP: 50 MIN. • **COOK:** 25 MIN.
MAKES: 15 SLIDERS

- 1 can (28 ounces) whole tomatoes, undrained
- 1 medium onion, finely chopped
- 3 tablespoons olive oil
- 2 garlic cloves, minced
- 1 teaspoon crushed red pepper flakes
- ½ teaspoon fennel seed, crushed
- 1 tablespoon chopped capers
- ⅛ teaspoon salt
- ¼ teaspoon pepper

MEATBALLS
- 1 cup shredded Parmesan cheese, divided
- ½ cup panko (Japanese) bread crumbs
- ¼ cup 2% milk
- 1 large egg, beaten
- 2 tablespoons minced fresh parsley
- 1 garlic clove, minced
- ½ teaspoon pepper
- ¼ teaspoon salt
- ½ pound lean ground beef (90% lean)
- ½ pound ground pork
- 1 tablespoon canola oil
- 15 dinner rolls

1. Place tomatoes in a food processor; cover and process until pureed. Set aside. In a large skillet, saute onion in oil until tender. Add the garlic, pepper flakes and fennel; cook for 2 minutes longer. Stir in the tomatoes, capers, salt and pepper. Bring to a boil. Reduce heat; simmer for 15-20 minutes or until thickened, stirring the sauce occasionally.

2. Meanwhile, in a large bowl, combine ½ cup cheese, bread crumbs, milk, egg, parsley, garlic, pepper and salt. Crumble meat over the mixture and mix well. Shape the mixture into fifteen 1½-in. balls.

3. In a large skillet, brown the meatballs in oil; drain. Transfer meatballs to sauce; simmer, uncovered, for 15-20 minutes or until a thermometer reads 160°.

4. Place a meatball on each roll. Top sliders with the sauce and remaining cheese.

FREEZE OPTION *Freeze rolls in resealable freezer bags. Freeze meatball mixture in freezer containers. To use, partially thaw in refrigerator overnight. Microwave meatballs, covered, on high in a microwave-safe dish until heated through, gently stirring and adding a little water if necessary. Place a meatball on each roll and top as directed.*

Green Bean Casserole Stuffed Mushrooms

Green bean casserole is a constant go-to for us, but it needed some updating. Our bite-size version gets fun reactions every time.
—**KAYTIE PICKETT** JACKSON, MS

PREP: 20 MIN. • **BAKE:** 20 MIN.
MAKES: 2½ DOZEN

- **3 turkey bacon strips, diced**
- **1½ teaspoons minced garlic**
- **1 can (14½ ounces) French-style green beans, drained**
- **¾ cup grated Parmesan cheese, divided**
- **¼ cup condensed cream of onion soup, undiluted**
- **¼ cup water**
- **⅛ teaspoon ground nutmeg**
- **⅛ teaspoon pepper**
- **1 cup dry bread crumbs**
- **30 whole baby portobello mushrooms**
- **Cooking spray**
- **1 can (2.8 ounces) French-fried onions**

1. In a small skillet, cook bacon over medium heat until crisp. Add garlic; cook 1 minute longer. Place the green beans, ½ cup of cheese, soup, water, nutmeg, pepper and bacon mixture in a food processor; process until blended. Transfer to a small bowl; fold in bread crumbs.
2. Remove the stems from mushrooms; discard stems or save for another use. Spritz the mushroom caps with cooking spray; place in an ungreased 15x10x 1-in. baking pan, stem side down. Bake caps at 425° for 10 minutes, turning once.
3. Drain liquid from caps; fill with green bean mixture. Top with remaining cheese and fried onions. Bake 8-10 minutes

longer or until mushrooms are tender and the filling is heated through.
FREEZE OPTION *After baking mushroom caps, drain and stuff mushrooms. Cool. Freeze on waxed paper-lined baking sheets until firm. Transfer to resealable plastic freezer bags; return to freezer. To use, bake mushrooms as directed, increasing time as necessary to heat through.*

⑤ INGREDIENTS

Blackberry Brandy Slush

We wanted a grown-up twist on a favorite slushy, so we spiked it with blackberry brandy. Here's a refreshing must-have for your next party.
—**LINDSEY SPINLER** SOBIESKI, WI

PREP: 10 MIN. + FREEZING
MAKES: 28 SERVINGS (1 CUP EACH)

- **8 cups water**
- **2 cups sugar**
- **3 cups blackberry brandy**
- **1 can (12 ounces) frozen lemonade concentrate, thawed**
- **1 can (12 ounces) frozen grape juice concentrate, thawed**
- **14 cups lemon-lime soda, chilled**

1. In a large bowl, stir water and sugar until the sugar is dissolved. Stir in the brandy and fruit juice concentrates. Transfer mixture to freezer containers; freeze overnight.
2. To serve, place about ½ cup brandy mixture in each glass; top with ½ cup soda.

Crispy Baked Wontons

These quick, versatile wontons are great for a savory snack or paired with a bowl of soothing soup on a cold day. I usually make a large batch, freeze half on a floured baking sheet, then store in an airtight container.

—**BRIANNA SHADE** BEAVERTON, OR

PREP: 30 MIN. • **BAKE:** 10 MIN.
MAKES: ABOUT 4 DOZEN

- ½ **pound ground pork**
- ½ **pound extra-lean ground turkey**
- 1 **small onion, chopped**
- 1 **can (8 ounces) sliced water chestnuts, drained and chopped**
- ⅓ **cup reduced-sodium soy sauce**
- ¼ **cup egg substitute**
- 1½ **teaspoons ground ginger**
- 1 **package (12 ounces) wonton wrappers**
  Cooking spray
  Sweet-and-sour sauce, optional

1. In a large skillet, cook the pork, turkey and onion over medium heat until meat is no longer pink; drain. Transfer to a large bowl. Stir in the water chestnuts, soy sauce, egg substitute and ginger.

2. Position a wonton wrapper with one point toward you. (Keep remaining wrappers covered with a damp paper towel until ready to use.) Place 2 heaping teaspoons of filling in the center of wrapper. Fold bottom corner over filling; fold sides toward center over filling. Roll toward the remaining point. Moisten top corner with water; press to seal. Repeat with the remaining wrappers and filling.

3. Place on baking sheets coated with cooking spray; lightly coat the wontons with additional cooking spray.

4. Bake wontons at 400° for 10-12 minutes or until golden brown, turning once. Serve warm with sweet-and-sour sauce if desired.

FREEZE OPTION *Freeze the cooled baked wontons in a freezer container, separating layers with waxed paper. To use, reheat at 400° until crisp.*

PER SERVING *1 wonton (calculated without the sweet-and-sour sauce) equals 38 cal., 1 g fat (trace sat. fat), 5 mg chol., 103 mg sodium, 5 g carb., trace fiber, 3 g pro.*

⑤ INGREDIENTS

Apricot Turkey Pinwheels

I created these unique pinwheels for a football game snack using ingredients I had on hand. They were a huge hit, and I appreciate how quick and easy they are to prepare and serve.

—**MELANIE FOSTER** BLAINE, MN

START TO FINISH: 30 MIN.
MAKES: 16 PINWHEELS

- 1 **sheet frozen puff pastry, thawed**
- ¼ **cup apricot preserves**
- ½ **teaspoon ground mustard**
- ½ **cup shredded Monterey Jack cheese**
- ¼ **pound sliced deli turkey**

1. Unfold the pastry; layer with preserves, mustard, cheese and turkey. Roll up jelly-roll style. Cut into 16 slices. Place cut side down on a parchment paper-lined baking sheet.

2. Bake slices at 400° for 15-20 minutes or until golden brown.

FREEZE OPTION *Freeze cooled appetizers in a resealable plastic freezer bag. To use, reheat the appetizers on a parchment paper-lined baking sheet in a preheated 400° oven until crisp and heated through.*

HAM & BRIE PINWHEELS *Omit mustard. Substitute 4 ounces diced Brie cheese for Monterey Jack and deli ham for the turkey.*

Marmalade Meatballs

I brought this snappy recipe to work for a potluck. I started cooking the meatballs in the morning, and they were ready to eat by lunchtime— when they disappeared fast!

—**JEANNE KISS** GREENSBURG, PA

PREP: 10 MIN. • **COOK:** 4 HOURS
MAKES: ABOUT 5 DOZEN

- 1 **bottle (16 ounces) Catalina salad dressing**
- 1 **cup orange marmalade**
- 3 **tablespoons Worcestershire sauce**
- ½ **teaspoon crushed red pepper flakes**
- 1 **package (32 ounces) frozen fully cooked homestyle meatballs, thawed**

In a 3-qt. slow cooker, combine the salad dressing, marmalade, Worcestershire sauce and pepper flakes. Stir in the meatballs. Cover and cook on low for 4-5 hours or until heated through.

FREEZE OPTION *Freeze cooled meatball mixture in freezer containers. To use, partially thaw in refrigerator overnight. Microwave, covered, on high in a microwave-safe dish until heated through, gently stirring and adding a little water if necessary.*

EASY PARTY MEATBALLS *Omit first four ingredients. Combine 1 bottle (14 ounces) ketchup, ¼ cup A.1. steak sauce, 1 tablespoon minced garlic and 1 teaspoon Dijon mustard in slow cooker; stir in meatballs. Cook as directed.*

Italian Sausage Calzone

My teenage daughter and I have been experimenting in the kitchen to recreate some old-time family dishes. Calzone with spinach and sausage is a favorite. Refrigerated pizza crust makes it easy to prepare one for us or several for a crowd.

—**TERRI GALLAGHER** KING GEORGE, VA

PREP: 20 MIN.
BAKE: 30 MIN. + STANDING
MAKES: 6 SERVINGS

- 1 **tube (13.8 ounces) refrigerated pizza crust**
- 1 **can (8 ounces) pizza sauce**
- 1 **package (10 ounces) frozen chopped spinach, thawed and squeezed dry**
- 1 **pound bulk Italian sausage, cooked and drained**
- 1 **jar (4½ ounces) sliced mushrooms, drained**
- 2 **cups (8 ounces) shredded part skim mozzarella cheese**

1. Unroll pizza dough onto an ungreased baking sheet; pat into a 14x11-in. rectangle. Spread the pizza sauce over one long side of dough to within ½ in. of edges.

2. Layer the spinach, sausage, mushrooms and cheese over sauce. Fold dough over filling; pinch seams to seal.

3. Bake at 400° for 30-35 minutes or until golden brown. Let stand for 10-15 minutes before slicing.

FREEZE OPTION *Freeze cooled unsliced calzone in a resealable plastic freezer bag. To use, place calzone on an ungreased baking sheet, cover with foil and reheat in a preheated 375° oven for 10 minutes. Uncover and bake until heated through.*

FREEZE IT

Prepare croquettes as directed, omitting chilling step. Transfer to waxed paper-lined baking sheets. Prepare butter mixture; drizzle over croquettes. Cover and freeze until firm. Transfer to resealable plastic freezer bags; return to freezer. To use, bake croquettes as directed, increasing time to 20-25 minutes. Serve with dipping sauce.

Bacon-Cheddar Potato Croquettes

Instead of throwing out leftover mashed potatoes, use them to make croquettes. The little baked balls are yummy with ranch dressing, barbecue sauce or Dijon-mayonnaise for dipping.

—**PAMELA SHANK** PARKERSBURG, WV

PREP: 20 MIN. + CHILLING
BAKE: 20 MIN.
MAKES: ABOUT 5 DOZEN

- 4 **cups cold mashed potatoes (with added milk and butter)**
- 6 **bacon strips, cooked and crumbled**
- ½ **cup shredded cheddar cheese**
- 2 **large eggs, lightly beaten**
- ¼ **cup sour cream**
- 1 **tablespoon minced chives**
- ½ **teaspoon salt**
- ¼ **teaspoon pepper**
- 40 **butter-flavored crackers, crushed**
- ¼ **cup butter, melted**
- 1 **teaspoon paprika**
   Barbecue sauce, Dijon-mayonnaise blend or ranch salad dressing

1. In a large bowl, combine first eight ingredients. Shape mixture by tablespoonfuls into balls. Roll each in cracker crumbs. Place on parchment paper-lined baking sheets. Cover and refrigerate for 2 hours or overnight.
2. Combine butter and paprika; drizzle over croquettes. Bake at 375° for 18-20 minutes or until golden brown. Serve with the dipping sauce of your choice.

⑤ INGREDIENTS

Balsamic-Glazed Chicken Wings

Tired of the same ol' buffalo and BBQ sauces? Try spreading your wings with a new balsamic-brown sugar glaze that'll appeal to most any crowd.

—**GRETCHEN WHELAN**
SAN FRANCISCO, CA

PREP: 20 MIN. + MARINATING
BAKE: 25 MIN.
MAKES: ABOUT 1½ DOZEN

- 2 **pounds chicken wings**
- 1½ **cups balsamic vinegar**
- 2 **garlic cloves, minced**
- 2 **teaspoons minced fresh rosemary or ½ teaspoon dried rosemary, crushed**
- ¼ **teaspoon salt**
- ¼ **teaspoon pepper**
- ¼ **cup packed brown sugar**

1. Cut chicken wings into three sections; discard the wing tip sections. In a small bowl, combine the vinegar, garlic, rosemary, salt and pepper. Pour ½ cup marinade into a large resealable plastic bag. Add the chicken; seal bag and turn to coat. Refrigerate for 1 hour. Cover and refrigerate remaining marinade.
2. Drain chicken and discard marinade; place in a greased 15x10x1-in. baking pan. Bake at 375° for 25-30 minutes or until no longer pink, turning pieces every 10 minutes.
3. Meanwhile, combine brown sugar and reserved marinade in a small saucepan. Bring to a boil; cook to reduce liquid by half.
4. Place wings in a large bowl. Pour glaze over wings; toss to coat.
FREEZE OPTION *Cover and freeze cooled wings in freezer containers. To use, partially thaw in refrigerator overnight. Reheat the wings in a foil-lined 15x10x1-in. baking pan in a preheated 325° oven until heated through, covering if necessary to prevent excess browning.*
NOTE *Uncooked chicken wing sections (called wingettes) may be substituted for the whole chicken wings.*

⑤ INGREDIENTS

Mock Champagne

Everyone can join in the toast with this light and refreshing drink. It tastes like champagne, complete with bubbles—but no alcohol!

—**PAM ION** GAITHERSBURG, MD

PREP: 10 MIN. + FREEZING
MAKES: 8 SERVINGS

- 3 **cups white grape juice, divided**
- 2 **cans (12 ounces each) ginger ale, chilled**
- ½ **cup chilled club soda**
  Orange slices and sliced fresh strawberries

1. Pour 2 cups juice into the ice cube trays; freeze until set.
2. Transfer the ice cubes to a pitcher; add remaining juice. Slowly stir in ginger ale and club soda. Garnish with oranges and strawberries. Serve immediately.

Mushroom Palmiers

I found this recipe while working at a small-town museum in West Texas. It was the appetizer for a fundraiser a long, long time ago, but it's still a huge hit at parties.

—**JUDY LOCK** PANHANDLE, TX

PREP: 20 MIN. + COOLING
BAKE: 15 MIN./BATCH
MAKES: 4 DOZEN

- 2 **tablespoons butter**
- ¾ **pound fresh mushrooms, finely chopped**
- 1 **small onion, finely chopped**
- 1 **teaspoon minced fresh thyme or ¼ teaspoon dried thyme**
- ¾ **teaspoon lemon juice**
- ¾ **teaspoon hot pepper sauce**
- ¼ **teaspoon salt**

- 1 **package (17.3 ounces) frozen puff pastry, thawed**
- 1 **large egg**
- 2 **teaspoons water**

1. Preheat oven to 400°. In a large skillet, heat the butter over medium heat. Add mushrooms and onion; cook and stir until tender. Stir in the thyme, lemon juice, hot pepper sauce and salt. Cool completely.
2. Unfold one pastry sheet. Spread half of the mushroom mixture to within ½ in. of edges. Roll up the left and right sides toward the center, jelly-roll style, until rolls meet in the middle. Cut into 24 slices. Repeat with the remaining pastry and mushroom mixture.
3. Place slices on greased baking sheets. In a small bowl, whisk egg and water; brush over the pastries. Bake 15-20 minutes or until golden brown. Serve warm or at room temperature.
FREEZE OPTION *Freeze cooled appetizers in freezer containers, separating layers with waxed paper. To use, preheat oven to 400°. Reheat appetizers on a greased baking sheet until crisp and heated through.*

Artichoke Phyllo Cups

A favorite appetizer that I find addicting is spinach and artichoke dip. So I created a bite-size version to capture the savory richness in a baked phyllo cup.

—**NEEL PATEL** CHAMPAIGN, IL

START TO FINISH: 30 MIN.
MAKES: ABOUT 3½ DOZEN

- 3 packages (1.9 ounces each) frozen miniature phyllo tart shells
- 1 can (14 ounces) water-packed artichoke hearts, rinsed, drained and finely chopped
- ½ cup shredded part-skim mozzarella cheese
- 3 green onions, chopped
- ¼ cup whipped cream cheese
- 2 tablespoons minced fresh parsley
- 2 tablespoons grated Parmesan cheese
- 2 tablespoons sour cream
- 1 tablespoon mayonnaise
- 2 garlic cloves, minced
- ½ teaspoon salt
- ¼ teaspoon pepper

1. Place tart shells on a baking sheet. In a small bowl, combine the remaining ingredients; spoon into tart shells.

2. Bake at 350° for 10-15 minutes or until lightly browned. Serve tarts warm.

FREEZE OPTION *Freeze the cooled baked pastries in freezer containers, separating layers with waxed paper. To use, reheat the pastries on a baking sheet in a preheated 350° oven until heated through.*

are crisp-tender, about 3 minutes. Add chicken; heat through.

2. In a small bowl, combine the cornstarch, water, soy sauce, oil, brown sugar and cayenne until smooth; add to chicken mixture. Bring to a boil. Cook and stir 2 minutes or until thickened; remove from the heat.

3. Spoon ¼ cup chicken mixture on the bottom third of one egg roll wrapper; fold sides toward center and roll tightly. (Keep remaining wrappers covered with a damp paper towel until ready to use.) Place seam side down on a baking sheet coated with cooking spray. Repeat.

4. Spritz tops of egg rolls with cooking spray. Bake at 425° for 10-15 minutes or until rolls are lightly browned.

FREEZE OPTION *Freeze cooled egg rolls in a freezer container, separating layers with waxed paper. To use, reheat on a baking sheet in a preheated 350° oven until the egg rolls are crisp and heated through.*

EFFORTLESS EGG ROLLS *Thaw and chop 1 pound frozen stir-fry vegetable blend; cook in a large skillet with 1 pound bulk pork sausage until meat is no longer pink. Stir in 2 tablespoons of teriyaki sauce. Fill and bake egg rolls as directed.*

DID YOU KNOW?

Green peppers are unripened red, yellow or orange peppers. They're less expensive because they're quicker to get to market. Use the colored peppers in recipes for more sweetness.

Baked Egg Rolls

These egg rolls are low in fat, but the crispiness from baking will fool you into thinking they were fried.

—**BARBARA LIERMAN** LYONS, NE

PREP: 30 MIN. • **BAKE:** 10 MINUTES
MAKES: 8 SERVINGS

- 2 **cups grated carrots**
- 1 **can (14 ounces) bean sprouts, drained**
- ½ **cup chopped water chestnuts**
- ¼ **cup chopped green pepper**
- ¼ **cup chopped green onions**
- 1 **garlic clove, minced**
- 2 **cups finely diced cooked chicken**
- 4 **teaspoons cornstarch**
- 1 **tablespoon water**
- 1 **tablespoon reduced-sodium soy sauce**
- 1 **teaspoon canola oil**
- 1 **teaspoon brown sugar**
  Pinch cayenne pepper
- 16 **egg roll wrappers**
  Cooking spray

1. Coat a large skillet with cooking spray; add the first six ingredients. Cook and stir over medium heat until vegetables

5 INGREDIENTS

Onion Brie Bowl

Golden caramelized onions are paired with buttery, silky Brie in a warm spread. Make sure to have enough bread cubes or crackers to scoop up every gooey bit.

—TASTE OF HOME TEST KITCHEN

PREP: 40 MIN.
BAKE: 25 MIN. + STANDING
MAKES: 18 SERVINGS

- 3 **cups sliced onions**
- 2 **tablespoons canola oil**
- 1 **tablespoon brown sugar**
- 1 **tablespoon balsamic vinegar**
- ½ **teaspoon salt**
- 1 **round loaf sourdough bread (1 pound)**
- 1 **round (8 ounces) Brie cheese**

1. In a large skillet, saute onions in oil until softened. Reduce heat to medium-low; add the brown sugar, vinegar and salt. Cook, stirring occasionally, for 30-35 minutes or until onions are deep golden brown.

2. Cut top third off loaf of bread; hollow out enough bread from the bottom to make room for cheese. Cube removed bread; set aside. Using a knife, make 2-in. cuts into the loaf around edge of bread at 1-in. intervals. Remove rind from cheese; cut cheese in half horizontally. Layer half of the cheese and onions in bread. Repeat layers.

3. Transfer to an ungreased baking sheet. Bake at 350° for 25-30 minutes or until cheese is melted. Let stand for 10 minutes. Serve with bread cubes.

FREEZE OPTION *Cool onion mixture. Assemble the bread, cheese and onion mixture as directed; wrap and freeze. Wrap and freeze bread cubes in a separate freezer container. To use, partially thaw in the refrigerator overnight. Remove from refrigerator 30 minutes before baking. Bake bread bowl as directed, increasing time as necessary until heated through. Serve with bread cubes.*

⑤INGREDIENTS

Gorgonzola Phyllo Cups

You need only a few minutes to put these bites together. The rich Gorgonzola, apple and cranberry combo is especially good in the colder months.

—**TRISHA KRUSE** EAGLE, ID

START TO FINISH: 20 MIN.
MAKES: 2½ DOZEN

- 2 **packages (1.9 ounces each) frozen miniature phyllo tart shells**
- 1⅓ **cups crumbled Gorgonzola cheese**
- ½ **cup chopped apple**
- ⅓ **cup dried cranberries**
- ⅓ **cup chopped walnuts**

1. Preheat oven to 350°. Place tart shells on a 15x10x1-in. baking pan. In a small bowl, mix the remaining ingredients; spoon into tart shells.

2. Bake 6-8 minutes or until the tarts are lightly browned. Serve warm or at room temperature. Refrigerate leftovers.

FREEZE OPTION *Freeze cooled pastries in a freezer container, separating layers with waxed paper. To use, reheat pastries on a greased baking sheet in a preheated 350° oven until crisp and heated through.*

Vanilla-Almond Coffee

Here's a perfect drink for coffee lovers. Instead of buying flavored coffees, I make my own using flavored baking extracts. It's great for adding sweetness to coffee without all the unwanted calories.
—**TINA CHRISTENSEN** ADDISON, IL

START TO FINISH: 5 MIN.
MAKES: 1 POUND

- **1 pound ground coffee**
- **2 tablespoons almond extract**
- **2 tablespoons vanilla extract**

Place coffee in a large jar with a tight-fitting lid. Add the extracts. Cover and shake well. Store in an airtight container in a cool, dark and dry place or in the freezer. Prepare coffee as usual.

Barbecue Glazed Meatballs

Stock your freezer with these meatballs, and you'll always have an appetizer on hand for unexpected guests—or a main dish for anyone.
—**ANNA FINLEY** COLUMBIA, MO

PREP: 30 MIN. • **BAKE:** 15 MIN./BATCH
MAKES: 8 DOZEN

- **2 cups quick-cooking oats**
- **1 can (12 ounces) fat-free evaporated milk**
- **1 small onion, finely chopped**
- **2 teaspoons garlic powder**
- **2 teaspoons chili powder**
- **3 pounds lean ground beef (90% lean)**

SAUCE
- **2½ cups ketchup**
- **1 small onion, finely chopped**
- **⅓ cup packed brown sugar**
- **2 teaspoons liquid smoke, optional**
- **1¼ teaspoons chili powder**
- **¾ teaspoon garlic powder**

1. Preheat oven to 400°. In a large bowl, combine the first five ingredients. Add beef; mix lightly but thoroughly. Shape into 1-in. balls.

2. Place the meatballs on greased racks in shallow baking pans. Bake for 15-20 minutes or until cooked through. Drain meatballs on paper towels.

3. In a Dutch oven, combine sauce ingredients. Bring to a boil over medium heat, stirring constantly. Reduce heat; simmer, uncovered, 2-3 minutes or until slightly thickened. Add meatballs; heat through, stirring gently.

FREEZE OPTION *Freeze cooled meatball mixture in freezer containers. To use, partially thaw in refrigerator overnight. Microwave, covered, on high in a microwave-safe dish until heated through, gently stirring and adding a little water if necessary.*

PER SERVING *1 meatball equals 42 cal., 1 g fat (trace sat. fat), 9 mg chol., 93 mg sodium, 4 g carb., trace fiber, 3 g pro.*

BANANA BERRY
MUFFINS
PAGE 52

Fresh-Baked Breads

From fluffy biscuits and buttery scones to savory dinner loaves and fruit-kissed muffins...delight in the simple pleasure of always having homemade bread at the ready.

⑤ INGREDIENTS

Bacon Crescent Rolls

The mouthwatering aroma of warm bacon in these rolls will draw friends and family to the table. Children love to help with making crescent rolls because they are so easy to assemble and fun to eat.

—JANE NEARING INDIANAPOLIS, IN

START TO FINISH: 25 MIN.
MAKES: 8 SERVINGS

- 1 **tube (8 ounces) refrigerated crescent rolls**
- 6 **bacon strips, cooked and crumbled**
- 1 **teaspoon onion powder**

1. Separate crescent dough into eight triangles. Set aside 1 tablespoon of bacon. Sprinkle onion powder and remaining bacon over triangles; roll up and place point-side down on an ungreased baking sheet. Sprinkle with reserved bacon.
2. Bake rolls at 375° for 10-15 minutes or until golden brown. Serve warm.
FREEZE OPTION *Freeze the cooled rolls in resealable plastic freezer bags. To use, thaw at room temperature or, if desired, microwave each crescent roll on high for 10-15 seconds or until heated through.*

Biscuit Baking Mix

You need just four common pantry staples to put together this versatile mix. Then use it in recipes that call for store-bought baking mix.

—**TAMI CHRISTMAN** SODA SPRINGS, ID

START TO FINISH: 5 MIN.
MAKES: 12 CUPS

- 9 **cups all-purpose flour**
- ¼ **cup baking powder**
- 1 **tablespoon salt**
- 2 **cups shortening**

In a large bowl, mix the flour, baking powder and salt; cut in shortening until the mixture resembles coarse crumbs. Store in an airtight container in a cool dry place or in the freezer for up to 8 months. Use to prepare biscuits or in recipes that call for biscuit/baking mix.

TO PREPARE BISCUITS *Stir 2 cups baking mix with ½ cup half-and-half cream just until moistened. Turn onto a lightly floured surface; knead gently 10 times. Pat or roll out to ½-in. thickness; cut with a 2½-in. biscuit cutter. Place 2 in. apart on an ungreased baking sheet. Bake at 425° for 13-16 minutes or until golden brown. Serve warm. Makes 8 biscuits.*

TOP TIP

Use the homemade Biscuit Baking Mix in these recipes:
Light 'n' Crispy Waffles, page 22;
Buttons and Bows, page 55;
Potluck Taco Casserole, page 125.

Cherry Chip Scones

These buttery scones, dotted with dried cherries and white chips, are so sweet and flaky that sometimes I even serve them for dessert.

—**PAM BROOKS** SOUTH BERWICK, ME

PREP: 15 MIN. • **BAKE:** 20 MIN.
MAKES: 8 SERVINGS

- 3 **cups all-purpose flour**
- ½ **cup sugar**
- 2½ **teaspoons baking powder**
- ½ **teaspoon baking soda**
- 6 **tablespoons cold butter**
- 1 **cup (8 ounces) vanilla yogurt**
- ¼ **cup plus 2 tablespoons milk, divided**
- 1⅓ **cups dried cherries**
- ⅔ **cup white baking chips**
   Coarse sugar, optional

1. Preheat oven to 400°. In a large bowl, combine flour, sugar, baking powder and baking soda. Cut in butter until the mixture resembles coarse crumbs. Combine yogurt and ¼ cup milk; stir into crumb mixture just until moistened. Knead in cherries and chips.

2. On a greased baking sheet, pat dough into a 9-in. circle. Cut into eight wedges; separate wedges. Brush with remaining milk. If desired, sprinkle with sugar. Bake 20-25 minutes or until golden brown. Serve warm.

FREEZE OPTION *Freeze cooled scones in resealable plastic freezer bags. To use, thaw at room temperature or, if desired, microwave each scone on high for 20-30 seconds or until the scones are heated through.*

CRANBERRY CHIP SCONES *Substitute dried cranberries for the cherries. Use white or semisweet chips.*

BLUEBERRY CHIP SCONES *Substitute dried blueberries for the cherries.*

20-25 minutes or until a toothpick comes out clean. Cool for 5 minutes before removing from pans to wire racks. Serve warm.

FREEZE OPTION *Freeze cooled muffins in resealable plastic freezer bags. To use, thaw at room temperature or, if desired, microwave each muffin on high for 20-30 minutes or until the muffin is heated through.*

Parmesan Italian Loaf

This is one of my favorite breads to use with spaghetti, make bologna sandwiches, or anything. And it smells so delicious while it's baking!

—**JAMI BLUNT** HARDY, AR

PREP: 10 MIN. • **BAKE:** 3 HOURS
MAKES: 1 LOAF (1½ POUNDS, 16 SLICES)

- 1 **cup water (70° to 80°)**
- 2 **tablespoons plus 1½ teaspoons butter, softened**
- 1 **tablespoon honey**
- ⅔ **cup grated Parmesan cheese**
- 1½ **teaspoons garlic powder**
- ¾ **teaspoon salt**
- 3 **cups bread flour**
- 2¼ **teaspoons active dry yeast**

In bread machine pan, place all ingredients in order suggested by manufacturer. Select basic bread setting. Choose crust color and loaf size if available. Bake loaf according to the bread machine directions (check after 5 minutes of mixing; add 1 to 2 tablespoons of water or flour if needed).

FREEZE OPTION *Securely wrap and freeze cooled loaf in foil and place in resealable plastic freezer bag. To use, thaw the loaf at room temperature.*

Banana Berry Muffins

My original version of this recipe called for Raisin Bran, but one day I used bran flakes with added blueberries because it was what I had on hand. I liked the muffins even better, so now I always make them this way.

—**ALYCE WYMAN** PEMBINA, ND

PREP: 20 MIN. • **BAKE:** 20 MIN./BATCH
MAKES: 1½ DOZEN

- 4 **cups bran flakes**
- ½ **cup buttermilk**
- ½ **cup butter, softened**
- 1 **cup sugar**
- 2 **large eggs**
- 1½ **cups mashed ripe bananas (about 3 medium)**
- 1 **teaspoon vanilla extract**
- 1½ **cups all-purpose flour**
- 1½ **teaspoons baking powder**
- ½ **teaspoon salt**
- ¼ **teaspoon baking soda**

- 1 **cup fresh or frozen blueberries**
- ⅓ **cup finely chopped pecans**
- ⅓ **cup packed brown sugar**
- ¾ **teaspoon ground cinnamon**

1. In a large bowl, combine bran flakes and buttermilk; set aside.
2. In another large bowl, cream butter and sugar until light and fluffy. Beat in eggs, one at a time, beating well after each addition. Beat in the bananas and vanilla (mixture will appear curdled).
3. Combine the flour, baking powder, salt and baking soda; gradually stir into the creamed mixture just until moistened. Stir in the bran mixture. Fold in the blueberries. Fill greased or paper-lined muffin cups three-fourths full.
4. Combine the pecans, brown sugar and cinnamon; sprinkle over the batter. Bake at 350° for

Onion French Loaves

I often bake French bread to serve with soup. For variety and to copy another bread I had tasted, I added dried minced onion to my usual recipe and created these tasty loaves.

—RUTH FUELLER

BARMSTEDT, GERMANY

PREP: 25 MIN. + RISING • **BAKE:** 20 MIN.
MAKES: 2 LOAVES (¾ POUND EACH)

- 1 **cup water (70° to 80°)**
- ½ **cup dried minced onion**
- 1 **tablespoon sugar**
- 2 **teaspoons salt**
- 3 **cups bread flour**
- 2¼ **teaspoons active dry yeast**
- 1 **tablespoon cornmeal**
- 1 **large egg yolk, lightly beaten**

1. In bread machine pan, place the first six ingredients in order suggested by the manufacturer. Select dough setting (check the dough after 5 minutes of mixing; add 1 to 2 tablespoons of water or flour if needed).

2. When the cycle is completed, turn dough onto a lightly floured surface. Cover and let dough rest for 15 minutes. Divide dough in half. Roll each portion into a 15x10-in. rectangle. Roll up jelly-roll style, starting with a long side; pinch seams to seal. Pinch ends to seal; tuck under.

3. Sprinkle the cornmeal onto a greased baking sheet. Place loaves on pan. Cover and let rise in a warm place until doubled, about 30 minutes. Brush with egg yolk. Make ¼-in.-deep cuts 2 in. apart in each loaf.

4. Bake the loaves at 375° for 20-25 minutes or until golden brown. Remove from pan to a wire rack.

FREEZE OPTION *Securely wrap and freeze the cooled loaves in heavy-duty foil. To use, place a foil-wrapped loaf on a baking sheet and reheat in a 450° oven for 10-15 minutes. Carefully remove foil; return to oven for a few minutes to crisp the crust.*

Rosemary Flatbreads

My family likes pizza crust made with this recipe. But with touches of olive oil and fresh herbs, it becomes an irresistible flatbread.

—SUE BROWN WEST BEND, WI

PREP: 40 MIN. + RISING • **BAKE:** 10 MIN.
MAKES: 6 SERVINGS

- 1 package (¼ ounce) active dry yeast
- ¼ cup plus ⅓ cup warm water (110° to 115°), divided
- ½ teaspoon honey
- 2 cups all-purpose flour, divided
- 1 tablespoon olive oil
- 1 teaspoon minced fresh rosemary
- ½ teaspoon kosher salt

TOPPING

- 1 tablespoon olive oil
- 1 teaspoon minced fresh rosemary
- ½ teaspoon kosher salt

1. In a small bowl, dissolve the yeast in ¼ cup warm water; stir in honey. Add ¼ cup flour; mix until almost smooth. Let stand 30 minutes or until bubbly.

2. Place the remaining flour, the remaining warm water, oil, rosemary and salt in a food processor; add yeast mixture. Process until dough forms a ball. Process 1 minute more to knead dough, pulsing as needed.

3. Transfer to a greased bowl, turning once to grease the top. Cover with plastic wrap and let dough rise in a warm place until doubled, about 1 hour.

4. Punch down dough. Turn onto a lightly floured surface; divide and shape dough into six balls. On greased baking sheets, pat each ball into a 5-in. circle. For topping, brush tops with oil; sprinkle with rosemary and salt. Bake for 8-12 minutes or until golden brown. Serve warm.

FREEZE OPTION *Freeze the cooled flatbreads in a resealable plastic freezer bag. To use, thaw flatbreads at room temperature or, if desired, microwave each flatbread on high 10-15 seconds or until heated through.*

Buttons and Bows

Biscuit mix hurries along these nutmeg-spiced buttons and bows that continue to be a Saturday morning favorite at our house. Serve these sugar-coated treats with hot coffee for dunking.

—**MARCIE HOLLADAY** IRVING, TX

PREP: 20 MIN. • **BAKE:** 10 MIN.
MAKES: 1 DOZEN BUTTONS AND BOWS

- 2 **cups biscuit/baking mix**
- 2 **tablespoons plus ¼ cup sugar, divided**
- 1 **teaspoon ground nutmeg**
- ⅛ **teaspoon ground cinnamon**
- 1 **large egg, beaten**
- ⅓ **cup 2% milk**
- ¼ **cup butter, melted**

1. In a large bowl, combine the biscuit mix, 2 tablespoons sugar, nutmeg and cinnamon. Combine the egg and milk; stir into the dry ingredients just until moistened.

2. Turn onto a heavily floured surface; knead 5-6 times. Roll out to ¼-in. thickness. Cut with a floured 2½-in. doughnut cutter; set centers aside for buttons.

3. For bows, twist each circle to form a figure eight; place on a greased baking sheet. Bake at 400° for 8-10 minutes or until golden brown. Place buttons on another greased baking sheet. Bake for 6-7 minutes.

4. Brush tops of the buttons and bows with butter; sprinkle with remaining sugar. Remove from pans to wire racks. Serve warm.

FREEZE IT

Freeze cooled biscuits in resealable plastic freezer bags, putting the bows in one bag and buttons in another. To use, place bows on one baking sheet and buttons on another. Heat in a preheated 350° oven 6-8 minutes for bows and 2-4 minutes for buttons or until heated through.

Zucchini-Chocolate Chip Muffins

Whenever I make these muffins, I freeze several. As I'm leaving for work in the morning, I take one out of the freezer to enjoy at the office with a cup of coffee.

—JANET PIERCE DECORI ROCKTON, IL

PREP: 20 MIN. • **BAKE:** 20 MIN.
MAKES: ABOUT 1 DOZEN

- 1½ cups all-purpose flour
- ¾ cup sugar
- 1 teaspoon baking soda
- 1 teaspoon ground cinnamon
- ½ teaspoon salt
- 1 large egg, lightly beaten
- ½ cup canola oil
- ¼ cup milk
- 1 tablespoon lemon juice
- 1 teaspoon vanilla extract
- 1 cup shredded zucchini
- ¼ cup miniature semisweet chocolate chips
- ¼ cup chopped walnuts

1. In a bowl, combine flour, sugar, baking soda, cinnamon and salt. Beat the egg, oil, milk, lemon juice and vanilla; stir into the dry ingredients just until moistened. Fold in zucchini, chocolate chips and walnuts. Fill greased or paper-lined muffin cups two-thirds full.
2. Bake at 350° for 20-25 minutes or until a toothpick comes out clean.
FREEZE OPTION *Freeze cooled muffins in resealable plastic freezer bags. To use, thaw at room temperature or, if desired, microwave each muffin on high for 20-30 seconds or until heated through.*

Key Lime Bread

I first tasted this deliciously different bread at a friend's house, and she shared the recipe with me. It's so easy to make and absolutely yummy!

—JOAN HALLFORD
NORTH RICHLAND HILLS, TX

PREP: 15 MIN.
BAKE: 50 MIN. + COOLING
MAKES: 2 LOAVES (16 SLICES EACH)

- ⅔ cup butter, softened
- 2 cups sugar
- 4 large eggs
- 2 tablespoons grated lime peel
- 2 tablespoons Key lime juice
- 1 teaspoon vanilla extract
- 3 cups all-purpose flour
- 3 teaspoons baking powder
- 1 teaspoon salt
- 1 cup milk
- 1 cup chopped walnuts
GLAZE
- ⅔ cup confectioners' sugar
- 1 to 2 tablespoons Key lime juice

1. Preheat oven to 350°. In a large bowl, cream the butter and sugar until light and fluffy. Beat in eggs. Beat in lime peel, juice and vanilla. Combine flour, baking powder and salt; gradually add to creamed mixture alternately with the milk, beating well after each addition. Fold in walnuts.
2. Transfer the mixture to two greased 9x5-in. loaf pans. Bake the bread for 50-55 minutes or until a toothpick inserted in the center comes out clean. Cool for 10 minutes before removing the loaves from pans to wire racks.
3. Combine confectioners' sugar and enough lime juice to achieve desired consistency; drizzle over warm bread. Cool completely.

FREEZE IT

Do not make glaze. Securely wrap cooled loaves in plastic wrap and foil, then freeze. Thaw at room temperature. Make and add glaze as directed.

Banana Wheat Bread

A subtle banana flavor comes through in this moist whole wheat loaf. Flecked with poppy seeds, the sweet slices are wonderful warm or toasted and spread with butter.

—**LOUISE MYERS** POMEROY, OH

PREP: 15 MIN. • **BAKE:** 4 HOURS
MAKES: 1 LOAF
(1½ POUNDS, 16 SLICES)

- ¾ cup water (70° to 80°)
- ¼ cup honey
- 1 large egg, lightly beaten
- 4½ teaspoons canola oil
- 1 medium ripe banana, sliced
- 2 teaspoons poppy seeds
- 1 teaspoon salt
- ½ teaspoon vanilla extract
- 1¾ cups bread flour
- 1½ cups whole wheat flour
- 2¼ teaspoons active dry yeast

In bread machine pan, place all ingredients in order suggested by manufacturer. Select basic bread setting. Choose crust color and loaf size if available. Bake according to bread machine directions (check dough after 5 minutes of mixing; add 1 to 2 tablespoons of water or flour if needed).

FREEZE OPTION *Securely wrap and freeze cooled loaf in foil and place in resealable plastic freezer bag. To use, thaw loaf at room temperature.*

NOTE *We recommend you do not use a bread machine's time-delay feature for this recipe.*

Grandma's Orange Rolls

Our children and grandchildren love these fine-textured sweet rolls. We have our own orange, lime and grapefruit trees, and it's such a pleasure to go outside and pick fruit to use in our recipes!

—**NORMA POOLE** AUBURNDALE, FL

PREP: 20 MIN. + RISING
BAKE: 20 MIN.
MAKES: 2½ DOZEN

- 1 **package (¼ ounce) active dry yeast**
- ¼ **cup warm water (110° to 115°)**
- 1 **cup warm 2% milk (110° to 115°)**
- ¼ **cup shortening**
- ¼ **cup sugar**
- 1 **teaspoon salt**
- 1 **large egg, lightly beaten**
- 3½ **to 3¾ cups all-purpose flour**

FILLING
- 1 **cup sugar**
- ½ **cup butter, softened**
- 2 **tablespoons grated orange peel**

GLAZE
- 1 **cup confectioners' sugar**
- 4 **teaspoons butter, softened**
- ½ **teaspoon lemon extract**
- 4 **to 5 teaspoons 2% milk**

1. In a large bowl, dissolve the yeast in water. Add the milk, shortening, sugar, salt, egg and 3 cups flour. Beat until smooth. Stir in enough remaining flour to form a soft dough.

2. Knead on a lightly floured surface until smooth and elastic, about 6-8 minutes. Place in a greased bowl, turning once to grease top. Cover and let rise in a warm place until doubled, about

1 hour. Meanwhile, in a small bowl, combine the filling ingredients; set aside.

3. Punch dough down; divide in half. Roll each half into a 15x10-in. rectangle. Spread half of filling on each rectangle. Roll up jelly-roll style, starting with a long end. Cut each into 15 rolls.

4. Place, cut side down, in two greased 11x7-in. baking pans. Cover and let rise until doubled, about 45 minutes.

5. Bake at 375° for 20-25 minutes or until lightly browned. In a small bowl, combine the confectioners' sugar, butter, extract and enough milk to achieve the desired consistency; spread over warm orange rolls.

FREEZE OPTION *Cover and freeze unrisen rolls. To use, thaw in refrigerator overnight. Let rise, covered, in a warm place until doubled, about 1½ hours. Bake and frost rolls as directed.*
MAKE-AHEAD CINNAMON ROLLS *For filling, substitute 1 cup packed brown sugar for the sugar and 2 teaspoons ground cinnamon for the orange peel. In glaze, substitute vanilla extract for lemon extract.*

TOP TIP

If you find it hard to slice cinnamon roll dough with a knife, try dental floss. Place a piece under the rolled dough, 1 inch from the end. Bring the floss up around the dough and cross it over the top to slice neatly through. Repeat at 1-inch intervals.

Tropical Muffins

I entered these muffins at our county fair and won the grand champion award for baked goods. They're so moist, they don't even need butter.

—SYLVIA OSBORN CLAY CENTER, KS

PREP: 20 MIN. • **BAKE:** 25 MIN.
MAKES: ABOUT 1 DOZEN

- ¼ **cup butter, softened**
- ½ **cup sugar**
- 1 **large egg**
- 1 **cup (8 ounces) sour cream**
- 1½ **teaspoons rum extract**
- 1½ **cups all-purpose flour**
- 1 **teaspoon baking powder**
- ½ **teaspoon baking soda**
- ½ **teaspoon salt**
- 1 **can (8 ounces) crushed pineapple, drained**
- ½ **cup flaked coconut**
- ⅓ **cup chopped pecans**

1. In a large bowl, cream the butter and sugar until light and fluffy. Beat in the egg, sour cream and extract. Combine the flour, baking powder, baking soda and salt; stir into the creamed mixture just until moistened. Fold in the pineapple, coconut and pecans.

2. Fill greased or paper-lined muffin cups two-thirds full. Bake at 375° for 22-25 minutes or until a toothpick comes out clean. Cool the muffins for 5 minutes before removing from pan to a wire rack.

FREEZE OPTION *Freeze the cooled muffins in resealable plastic freezer bags. To use, thaw at room temperature or, if desired, microwave each one on high for 20-30 seconds or until heated through.*

⑤ INGREDIENTS

Cheesy Garlic Bread

Crispy cheese bread smothered in homemade garlic topping adds zip to meals. I am always sure to come home with an empty plate when I take it to gatherings.

—JUDY SKAAR PARDEEVILLE, WI

PREP: 10 MIN. + FREEZING
BAKE: 20 MIN.
MAKES: 12-15 SERVINGS

- 1½ **cups mayonnaise**
- 1 **cup (4 ounces) shredded sharp cheddar cheese**
- 1 **cup thinly sliced green onions with tops**
- 3 **garlic cloves, minced**
- 1 **loaf French bread (about 20 inches), halved lengthwise**
- ⅓ **cup minced fresh parsley, optional**
  Paprika, optional

1. Mix mayonnaise, cheese, onions and garlic; spread on bread halves. If desired, sprinkle with parsley and paprika. Wrap each half in foil. Freeze for up to 3 months.

2. Unwrap the garlic bread and place on a baking sheet. Bake at 400° for 20-25 minutes or until topping is puffed but not brown.

Orange Banana Nut Bread

I like this recipe because the orange juice gives the banana bread such a unique flavor. And the loaf stays tender even after it's been frozen.

—BARBARA ROETHLISBERGER

SHEPHERD, MI

PREP: 15 MIN.
BAKE: 50 MIN. + COOLING
MAKES: 2 LOAVES

- 1½ **cups sugar**
- 3 **tablespoons canola oil**
- 2 **large eggs**
- 3 **medium ripe bananas, mashed (about 1¼ cups)**
- ¾ **cup orange juice**
- 3 **cups all-purpose flour**
- 1½ **teaspoons baking powder**
- 1½ **teaspoons baking soda**
- ½ **teaspoon salt**
- 1 **cup chopped walnuts**

1. In a bowl, combine the sugar, oil and eggs; mix well. Stir in the bananas and the orange juice. Combine the dry ingredients; add to banana mixture, beating just until moistened. Stir in the walnuts. Pour into two greased 8x4-in. loaf pans.

2. Bake loaves at 325° for 50-60 minutes or until a toothpick inserted near the center comes out clean. Cool for 10 minutes; remove from pans to a wire rack to cool completely.

FREEZE OPTION *Securely wrap and freeze cooled loaves in plastic wrap and foil. To use, thaw bread at room temperature.*

Delicious Pumpkin Bread

An enticing aroma wafts through my house when tender, cake-like pumpkin bread is in the oven. I bake extra loaves for holiday gifts that my friends wait for eagerly every year.

—LINDA BURNETT PRESCOTT, AZ

PREP: 15 MIN.
BAKE: 50 MIN. + COOLING
MAKES: 5 MINI LOAVES (8 SLICES EACH)

- 5 large eggs
- 1¼ cups canola oil
- 1 can (15 ounces) solid-pack pumpkin
- 2 cups all-purpose flour
- 2 cups sugar
- 2 packages (3 ounces each) cook-and-serve vanilla pudding mix
- 1 teaspoon baking soda
- 1 teaspoon ground cinnamon
- ½ teaspoon salt

1. In a large bowl, beat the eggs. Add oil and pumpkin; beat until smooth. Combine the remaining ingredients; gradually beat into pumpkin mixture.

2. Pour batter into five greased 5¾x3x2-in. loaf pans. Bake at 325° for 50-55 minutes or until a toothpick inserted near the center comes out clean. Cool for 10 minutes before removing the loaves from pans to wire racks to cool completely.

FREEZE OPTION *Securely wrap and freeze the cooled loaves in plastic wrap and foil. To use, thaw at room temperature.*

NOTE *Bread may also be baked in two greased 8x4x 2-in. loaf pans for 75-80 minutes.*

Chocolate Toffee Biscuits

These sweet and crunchy biscuits would be perfect with your morning cup of coffee. They're so quick and easy to assemble, and delicious to eat any time of day.

—WENDY WEATHERALL CARGILL, ON

START TO FINISH: 25 MIN.
MAKES: 1½ DOZEN

- 2 **cups all-purpose flour**
- ¼ **cup sugar**
- 3 **teaspoons baking powder**
- ¼ **teaspoon baking soda**
- ½ **cup cold butter, cubed**
- ¾ **cup milk**
- ¼ **cup semisweet chocolate chips**
- ¼ **cup English toffee bits or almond brickle chips**

TOPPING
- 1 **teaspoon butter, melted**
- 1 **teaspoon sugar**

1. In a large bowl, combine the flour, sugar, baking powder and baking soda. Cut in butter until the mixture resembles coarse crumbs. Stir in milk just until moistened. Fold in the chocolate chips and toffee bits.

2. Drop by 2 tablespoonfuls 2 in. apart onto ungreased baking sheets. Brush with the melted butter; sprinkle with sugar. Bake biscuits at 425° for 13-15 minutes or until golden brown. Serve warm.

FREEZE OPTION *Freeze the cooled biscuits in resealable plastic freezer bags. To use, heat in a preheated 350° oven for 15-20 minutes.*

**DIJON VEGGIES
WITH COUSCOUS**
PAGE 80

Sides & More

Quickly pull together a flavorful meal with the colorful sides you'll find here. Plus, discover fresh ways to extend summer's bounty with pickles, jams, pestos and herb butters.

Texas Garlic Mashed Potatoes

These creamy mashed potatoes get their flavor burst from garlic and caramelized onions. They're fine with just about any meal.

—**RICHARD MARKLE** MIDLOTHIAN, TX

PREP: 20 MIN. • **COOK:** 30 MIN.
MAKES: 6 SERVINGS

- 1 whole garlic bulb
- 1 teaspoon plus 1 tablespoon olive oil, divided
- 1 medium white onion, chopped
- 4 medium potatoes, peeled and quartered
- ¼ cup butter, softened
- ¼ cup sour cream
- ¼ cup grated Parmesan cheese
- ¼ cup 2% milk
- ½ teaspoon salt
- ¼ teaspoon pepper

1. Remove papery outer skin from garlic bulb (do not peel or separate cloves). Cut top off of the garlic bulb. Brush top with 1 teaspoon oil. Wrap bulb in heavy-duty foil. Bake at 425° for 30-35 minutes or until softened.

2. Meanwhile, in a large skillet over low heat, cook the onion in remaining oil for 15-20 minutes or until golden brown, stirring occasionally. Transfer to a food processor. Cover and process until blended; set aside.

3. Place the potatoes in a large saucepan and cover with water. Bring to a boil. Reduce the heat; cover pan and cook for 15-20 minutes or until tender. Drain. Place potatoes in a large bowl. Squeeze softened garlic into bowl; add the butter, sour cream, cheese, milk, salt, pepper and onion. Beat until mashed.

FREEZE OPTION *Place cooled mashed potato mixture in a freezer container and freeze. To use, partially thaw in refrigerator overnight. Microwave, covered, on high in a microwave-safe bowl until heated through, stirring twice and adding a little milk if necessary.*

Strawberry Freezer Jam

A dear friend gave this recipe to me when we lived in Germany. It's even good on ice cream!

—MARY JEAN ELLIS INDIANAPOLIS, IN

PREP: 40 MIN. + FREEZING
MAKES: 4½ PINTS

- 2 **quarts fresh strawberries**
- 5½ **cups sugar**
- 1 **cup light corn syrup**
- ¼ **cup lemon juice**
- ¾ **cup water**
- 1 **package (1¾ ounces) powdered fruit pectin**

1. Wash and mash the berries, measuring out enough mashed berries to make 4 cups; place in a large bowl. Stir in sugar, corn syrup and lemon juice. Let stand for 10 minutes.

2. In a Dutch oven, combine strawberry mixture and water. Stir in pectin. Bring to a full rolling boil over high heat, stirring constantly. Boil mixture 1 minute, stirring constantly. Remove from heat; skim off the foam on top.

3. Pour into jars or freezer containers, leaving ½-in. of headspace. Cover and let stand overnight or until set, but not longer than 24 hours. Refrigerate up to 3 weeks or freeze up to 12 months.

(5) INGREDIENTS
Basil Butter

I make this tasty butter in summer and freeze it for later use. When I saute veggies in it, the basil tastes garden-fresh. It's also wonderful on top of grilled meats, tossed into pasta and spread over bread.
—**EMILY CHANEY** PENOBSCOT, ME

PREP: 15 MIN. + CHILLING
MAKES: 1 CUP

- 1½ **cups loosely packed fresh basil leaves**
- 1 **cup butter, softened**
- 1 **teaspoon seasoned pepper**
- 1 **teaspoon lemon juice**
- ½ **teaspoon garlic salt**

1. Place the basil in a food processor; pulse until chopped. Add the remaining ingredients; process until blended.
2. Transfer to a sheet of plastic wrap; shape mixture into a log. Refrigerate up to one week or wrap securely and freeze for longer storage. Unwrap log and slice off desired portions.

HOW TO

HOW TO SHAPE & FREEZE HERB BUTTER

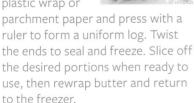

Place butter on plastic wrap or parchment paper and press with a ruler to form a uniform log. Twist the ends to seal and freeze. Slice off the desired portions when ready to use, then rewrap butter and return to the freezer.

Sausage Stuffing Muffins

Here's a clever new take on stuffing. You can also bake the stuffing in a greased baking dish if you want a more traditional presentation.
—**TRICIA BIBB** HARTSELLE, AL

PREP: 45 MIN. • **BAKE:** 20 MIN.
MAKES: 1½ DOZEN

- 1 **pound bulk pork sausage**
- 4 **celery ribs, chopped**
- 2 **medium onions, chopped**
- ¼ **cup butter, cubed**
- 1 **package (14 ounces) crushed corn bread stuffing**
- 2 **medium apples, peeled and chopped**
- 1 **package (5 ounces) dried cranberries**
- 1 **cup chopped pecans**
- 1 **teaspoon salt**
- 1 **teaspoon pepper**
- 2 **to 3 cups reduced-sodium chicken broth**
- 2 **large eggs**
- 2 **teaspoons baking powder**

1. Preheat oven to 375°. In a large skillet, cook sausage over medium heat until no longer pink; drain. Transfer to a large bowl; set aside.
2. In same skillet, saute celery and onions in butter until tender. Transfer to bowl; add stuffing, apples, cranberries, pecans, salt and pepper. Stir in enough broth to reach the desired moistness. Whisk eggs and baking powder; add to stuffing mixture.
3. Spoon into 18 greased muffin cups. Bake 20-25 minutes or until lightly browned. Cool for 10 minutes. Run a knife around edges of muffin cups to loosen. Serve immediately.
FREEZE OPTION *Freeze cooled stuffing muffins in resealable plastic bags. To use, partially thaw in refrigerator overnight. Place muffins on greased baking sheets, cover with foil and reheat in a preheated 375° oven for 6-10 minutes or until heated through.*

Freezer Salsa

Kids in the home economics class at the school where I teach were making this salsa, and it smelled so good that I got the recipe. It's a great way to use up that extra garden produce.

—DEANNA RICHTER ELMORE, MN

PREP: 25 MIN.
COOK: 45 MIN. + COOLING
MAKES: 10 CUPS

- 8 cups diced seeded peeled tomatoes (about 10 large)
- 2 medium green peppers, chopped
- 2 large onions, chopped
- 2 jalapeno peppers, seeded and finely chopped
- ¾ cup tomato paste
- ⅔ cup condensed tomato soup, undiluted
- ½ cup white vinegar
- 2 tablespoons sugar
- 2 tablespoons salt
- 4½ teaspoons garlic powder
- 1 tablespoon cayenne pepper

1. In a Dutch oven or large saucepan, combine all the ingredients. Bring to a boil. Reduce heat; simmer, uncovered, for 45 minutes, stirring often.

2. Pour into small freezer containers. Cool to room temperature, about 1 hour. Cover and freeze for up to 3 months. Stir before serving.

NOTE *Wear disposable gloves when cutting hot peppers; the oils can burn skin. Avoid touching your face.*

EAT SMART

Barley Corn Salad

A great alternative to pasta salads, this fresh, fast dish adds summery flavor to barley and sweet corn. Take it to your next get-together and see how fast it disappears!

—**MARY ANN KIEFFER** LAWRENCE, KS

PREP: 15 MIN. + CHILLING
MAKES: 6 SERVINGS

- 2 cups cooked medium pearl barley
- 2 cups frozen corn, thawed
- ½ cup chopped sweet red pepper
- ½ cup chopped green pepper
- 3 green onions, chopped
- 1 tablespoon minced fresh cilantro
- 2 tablespoons lemon juice
- 2 tablespoons canola oil
- ½ teaspoon salt
- ½ teaspoon dried thyme
- ⅛ teaspoon pepper

In a large bowl, combine the first six ingredients. In a jar with a tight-fitting lid, combine lemon juice, oil, salt, thyme and pepper; shake well. Drizzle over the salad and toss to coat. Cover dish and refrigerate for at least 2 hours before serving.

FREEZE OPTION *Prepare salad without the onions and cilantro. Transfer to freezer containers; freeze. To use, thaw completely in refrigerator. Gently stir in onions, cilantro and a little oil if necessary.*

PER SERVING *⅔ cup equals 163 cal., 5 g fat (trace sat. fat), 0 chol., 201 mg sodium, 29 g carb., 4 g fiber, 3 g pro.* **Diabetic Exchanges:** *1½ starch, 1 vegetable, 1 fat.*

Squash au Gratin

This fabulous-tasting dish has an awesome aroma when baking. Roast a chicken alongside and you'll have your whole meal ready to go.

—DEBORAH WILLIAMS PEORIA, AZ

PREP: 20 MIN. • **BAKE:** 55 MIN.
MAKES: 9 SERVINGS

> 5½ cups thinly sliced peeled butternut squash
> ½ teaspoon salt
> ¼ teaspoon pepper
> ⅛ teaspoon ground nutmeg
> 2 tablespoons olive oil, divided
> 1 cup heavy whipping cream
> 2 medium tart apples, peeled and thinly sliced
> 1 cup (4 ounces) crumbled Gorgonzola cheese

1. In a large bowl, combine the squash, salt, pepper, nutmeg and 1 tablespoon oil; toss to coat. Transfer to a greased 11x7-in. baking dish; pour cream over top.
2. Cover and bake at 325° for 30 minutes. In a small bowl, toss apples in remaining oil. Spoon over squash. Bake, uncovered, for 25-30 minutes or until the squash is tender. Sprinkle with cheese; bake 3-5 minutes longer or until cheese is melted.

FREEZE OPTION *Before adding cheese, cool baked casserole; cover and freeze. To use, partially thaw in refrigerator overnight. Remove from dish refrigerator 30 minutes before baking. Preheat oven to 325°. Reheat casserole, increasing the time as necessary for a thermometer inserted in center to read 165°. Sprinkle with cheese and bake until melted.*

FREEZE IT

Reserving pecans for later, freeze cooled pilaf in a freezer container. To use, partially thaw in refrigerator overnight. Microwave, covered, on high in a microwave-safe dish until heated through, adding 2-3 tablespoons water to moisten. Toast pecans; add to pilaf.

Pecan Rice Pilaf

This is one of my stand-by side dishes, which can complement most meat and meatless entrees. It's special enough for company, yet quick enough for weeknights.

—JACQUELINE OGLESBY
SPRUCE PINE, NC

PREP: 15 MIN. • **COOK:** 20 MIN.
MAKES: 9 SERVINGS

> 1 cup chopped pecans
> 5 tablespoons butter, divided
> 1 small onion, chopped
> 2 cups uncooked long grain rice
> 1 carton (32 ounces) chicken broth
> 3 tablespoons minced fresh parsley, divided
> ½ teaspoon salt
> ¼ teaspoon dried thyme
> ⅛ teaspoon pepper
> 1 cup shredded carrots

1. In a large saucepan, saute pecans in 2 tablespoons butter until toasted; remove from the pan and set aside.
2. In the same pan, saute onion in remaining butter until tender. Add the rice; cook and stir for 3-4 minutes or until the rice is lightly browned. Stir in the broth, 2 tablespoons parsley, salt, thyme and pepper. Bring to a boil. Reduce heat; cover and simmer for 10 minutes.
3. Add the carrots; simmer for 3-5 minutes longer or until rice is tender. Stir in toasted pecans and remaining parsley. Fluff with a fork.

(5) INGREDIENTS

Freezer Sweet Corn

With this preparation the corn stays crisp-tender, so I can enjoy it any time of the year. I got the recipe from my daughter's mother-in-law, who lives on a farm in Iowa.

—**JUDY OUDEKERK** ST. MICHAEL, MN

PREP: 30 MIN. • **COOK:** 15 MIN.
MAKES: 3 QUARTS

- **4 quarts fresh corn (cut from about 20 ears)**
- **1 quart hot water**
- **⅔ cup sugar**
- **½ cup butter, cubed**
- **2 teaspoons salt**

In a stockpot, combine all the ingredients; bring to a boil. Reduce the heat; simmer, uncovered, 5-7 minutes, stirring occasionally. Transfer to large shallow containers; cool, stirring occasionally. Freeze corn in resealable plastic freezer bags or freezer containers, allowing headspace for expansion.

Tortellini Bake

Summer in New Hampshire brings plenty of fresh zucchini and squash. One year when I had so much that I was searching for different ways to prepare it, I came up with this recipe. Serve it as a side dish or on its own as a light meal.

—**DONALD ROBERTS** AMHERST, NH

PREP: 20 MIN. • **BAKE:** 20 MIN.
MAKES: 6-8 SERVINGS

- **1 package (10 ounces) refrigerated cheese tortellini**
- **1 tablespoon olive oil**
- **1 small zucchini, diced**
- **1 yellow squash, diced**
- **1 onion, diced**
- **1 sweet red pepper, diced**
- **1 teaspoon dried basil**
- **½ teaspoon pepper**
- **½ teaspoon salt**
- **1 cup (4 ounces) shredded part-skim mozzarella cheese**
- **1 cup half-and-half cream**

1. Cook tortellini according to package directions. Meanwhile, heat the oil in a skillet; cook zucchini, squash, onion, red pepper and seasonings until vegetables are crisp-tender.
2. Drain tortellini and rinse in hot water; combine with vegetables, mozzarella and cream in a 1½-qt. baking dish.
3. Bake, uncovered, at 375° for 20 minutes or until mixture is heated through.

FREEZE OPTION *Cool unbaked casserole; cover and freeze. To use, partially thaw in refrigerator overnight. Remove from refrigerator 30 minutes before baking. Preheat oven to 375°. Bake the casserole as directed, increasing time as necessary to heat through and for a thermometer inserted in center to read 165°.*

TOP TIP

I made this recipe using two yellow squash, a green pepper and a red onion. I also used a pre-made Alfredo sauce. The family loved it, as did I. I am trying to increase the amount of veggies we eat, and this recipe is great for that!

—**RIVERSONG** TASTEOFHOME.COM

Favorite Cheesy Potatoes

My kids, husband and nephews all love these potatoes. I make a large batch in disposable pans and serve them at get-togethers. The holidays aren't the same without them.
—**BRENDA SMITH** CURRAN, MI

PREP: 30 MIN. • **BAKE:** 45 MIN.
MAKES: 12 SERVINGS (⅔ CUP EACH)

- 3½ **pounds potatoes (about 7 medium), peeled and cut into ¾-inch cubes**
- 1 **can (10½ ounces) condensed cream of potato soup, undiluted**
- 1 **cup French onion dip**
- ¾ **cup 2% milk**
- ⅔ **cup sour cream**
- 1 **teaspoon minced fresh parsley**
- ¼ **teaspoon salt**
- ¼ **teaspoon pepper**
- 1 **package (16 ounces) process cheese (Velveeta), cubed**
  Additional minced fresh parsley

1. Preheat oven to 350°. Place potatoes in a Dutch oven; add water to cover. Bring to a boil. Reduce heat; cook, uncovered, 8-12 minutes or until tender. Drain. Cool slightly.

2. In a large bowl, mix soup, onion dip, milk, sour cream, parsley, salt and pepper; gently fold in potatoes and cheese. Transfer to a greased 13x9-in. baking dish.

3. Bake, covered, 30 minutes. Uncover; bake 15-20 minutes longer or until heated through and cheese is melted. Just before serving, stir to combine and sprinkle with additional parsley. (Potatoes will thicken upon standing.)

FREEZE OPTION *Cover and freeze unbaked casserole. To use, partially thaw in refrigerator overnight. Remove dish from refrigerator 30 minutes before baking. Preheat oven to 350°. Cover casserole with foil; bake as directed, increasing covered time to 1¼-1½ hours or until heated through and a thermometer inserted in center reads 165°. Uncover; bake 15-20 minutes longer or until lightly browned. Just before serving, stir to combine and, if desired, sprinkle with additional parsley.*

Freezer Cucumber Pickles

When I first started to make these crunchy pickles, I wasn't sure that freezing cucumbers would actually work. To my surprise, they came out perfectly. Now I share them with friends and neighbors.

—CONNIE GOENSE

PEMBROKE PINES, FL

PREP: 20 MIN. + FREEZING
MAKES: 10 PINTS

- 4 pounds pickling cucumbers, sliced
- 8 cups thinly sliced onions (about 8 medium)
- ¼ cup salt
- ¾ cup water
- 4 cups sugar
- 2 cups cider vinegar

1. Rinse ten 2-cup plastic containers and lids with boiling water. Dry thoroughly. Divide the cucumbers, onions, salt and water between two large bowls. Let stand at room temperature 2 hours. Do not drain.

2. Add 2 cups sugar and 1 cup vinegar to each bowl; stir until sugar is dissolved. Transfer to prepared containers, leaving 1-in. headspace for expansion; freeze up to 6 months.

3. Thaw pickles in refrigerator 8 hours before using. Serve within 2 weeks after thawing.

Tangy Baked Seven Beans

Everyone needs a go-to side dish for school events, picnics and potlucks. Here's mine. Freeze any leftovers for future outings.

—ROD LUNDWALL TOOELE, UT

PREP: 30 MIN. • **BAKE:** 1 HOUR
MAKES: 18 SERVINGS (¾ CUP EACH)

- 1 **pound bacon strips, chopped**
- 1 **large onion, chopped**
- 1 **large sweet yellow pepper, chopped**
- 1 **large sweet red pepper, chopped**
- 6 **garlic cloves, minced**
- 1 **teaspoon ground chipotle pepper**
- ½ **teaspoon pepper**
- 2 **cans (15 ounces each) pork and beans**
- 1 **can (16 ounces) butter beans, rinsed and drained**
- 1 **can (16 ounces) kidney beans, rinsed and drained**
- 1 **can (15½ ounces) black-eyed peas, rinsed and drained**
- 1 **can (15 ounces) garbanzo beans or chickpeas, rinsed and drained**
- 1 **can (15 ounces) pinto beans, rinsed and drained**
- 1 **can (15 ounces) black beans, rinsed and drained**
- 2 **bottles (18 ounces each) barbecue sauce**
- ⅓ **cup cider vinegar**
- 1 **tablespoon liquid smoke, optional**

1. Preheat oven to 350°. In an ovenproof Dutch oven, cook bacon over medium heat until crisp, stirring occasionally. Remove with a slotted spoon; drain on paper towels. Cook and stir onion, yellow pepper, red pepper, garlic, chipotle pepper and pepper in bacon drippings until vegetables are tender. Remove from heat.

2. Add the beans and cooked bacon to Dutch oven; stir in barbecue sauce, vinegar and, if desired, liquid smoke.

3. Bake, covered, 1 to 1¼ hours or until heated through.

FREEZE OPTION *Freeze cooled beans in freezer containers. To use, partially thaw in the refrigerator overnight. Heat through in a saucepan, stirring occasionally, adding a little water if necessary.*

(5) INGREDIENTS

Asparagus with Dill Butter

This is simple, yet elegant enough to serve at a dinner party. The lemon juice gives it a tangy zip.

—MILDRED SHERRER FORT WORTH, TX

PREP: 10 MIN. + FREEZING
MAKES: RECIPE WILL SEASON ABOUT 4 POUNDS OF ASPARAGUS

- ½ **cup butter, softened**
- ¼ **cup snipped fresh dill**
- 1½ **teaspoons lemon juice**
  Cooked fresh asparagus spears

In a small bowl, combine butter, dill and lemon juice; mix until well blended. Form into a log. (If necessary, refrigerate until mixture is firm enough to shape easily.) Wrap log in plastic wrap; freeze until firm. When ready to serve, slice butter ¼ in. thick and top hot asparagus.

Slow-Roasted Tomatoes

I love tomatoes, and these are healthy and versatile. You can use them in sandwiches, omelets and on top of broiled chicken.

—JULIE TILNEY DOWNEY, CA

PREP: 20 MIN.
BAKE: 3 HOURS + COOLING
MAKES: 4 CUPS

- **20 plum tomatoes (about 5 pounds)**
- **¼ cup olive oil**
- **5 teaspoons Italian seasoning**
- **2½ teaspoons salt**

1. Cut the tomatoes into ½-in. slices. Brush with oil; sprinkle with Italian seasoning and salt.
2. Place on racks coated with cooking spray in foil-lined 15x10x1-in. baking pans. Bake, uncovered, at 325° for 3 to 3½ hours or until the tomatoes are deep brown around the edges and shriveled. Cool tomatoes for 10-15 minutes. Serve warm or at room temperature.
3. Store in an airtight container in the refrigerator for up to 1 week or freeze tomatoes for up to 3 months. Bring tomatoes to room temperature before using.

Herby Mashed Potatoes

Round out any meal with these delightful potatoes. A bit of cottage cheese adds to the creamy texture.

—SANDI GUETTLER BAY CITY, MI

START TO FINISH: 30 MIN.
MAKES: 6 SERVINGS

- **2 pounds Yukon Gold potatoes, peeled and cubed**
- **⅔ cup 4% cottage cheese**
- **⅓ cup shredded cheddar cheese**
- **2 teaspoons butter**
- **2 teaspoons snipped fresh dill or ½ teaspoon dill weed**
- **½ teaspoon salt**

1. Place the potatoes in a large saucepan and cover with water; bring to a boil over medium-high heat. Cook for 10-15 minutes or until tender; drain.
2. Transfer to a large bowl. Add the cheeses, butter, dill and salt; beat until smooth and fluffy.
FREEZE OPTION *Place cooled potato mixture in a freezer container and freeze. To use, partially thaw in refrigerator overnight. Microwave, covered, on high in a microwave-safe bowl until heated through, stirring twice and adding a little milk or cream if necessary.*
PER SERVING *⅔ cup equals 147 cal., 4 g fat (3 g sat. fat), 16 mg chol., 346 mg sodium, 22 g carb., 1 g fiber, 6 g pro.* **Diabetic Exchanges:** *1½ starch, 1 fat.*

Spinach Pesto

Serve this vibrant pesto on pasta, pizza, sandwiches and more. If you don't have fresh oregano on hand, you can omit it.

—SUSAN WESTERFIELD

ALBUQUERQUE, NM

START TO FINISH: 15 MIN.
MAKES: 2 CUPS

- 2 cups fresh baby spinach
- 2 cups loosely packed basil leaves
- 1 cup grated Romano cheese
- 2 tablespoons fresh oregano
- 2 teaspoons minced garlic
- ½ teaspoon salt
- ½ cup chopped walnuts, toasted
- 1 tablespoon lemon juice
- 2 teaspoons grated lemon peel
- 1 cup olive oil
  Hot cooked pasta

1. Place the first six ingredients in a food processor; cover and pulse until chopped. Add the walnuts, lemon juice and peel; cover and process until blended. While processing, gradually add oil in a steady stream.

2. Serve the desired amount of pesto with pasta. Transfer the remaining pesto to ice cube trays. Cover and freeze for up to 1 month.

TO USE FROZEN PESTO *Thaw in the refrigerator for 3 hours. Serve with pasta.*

Scalloped Sweet Corn Casserole

This is my Grandma Ostendorf's corn recipe I grew up enjoying. Now a grandmother myself, I serve this comfy, delicious side as a family classic.

—LONNIE HARTSTACK CLARINDA, IA

PREP: 25 MIN. • **BAKE:** 50 MIN.
MAKES: 8 SERVINGS

- 4 **teaspoons cornstarch**
- ⅔ **cup water**
- ¼ **cup butter, cubed**
- 3 **cups fresh or frozen corn**
- 1 **can (5 ounces) evaporated milk**
- ¾ **teaspoon plus 1½ teaspoons sugar, divided**
- ½ **teaspoon plus ¾ teaspoon salt, divided**
- 3 **large eggs**
- ¾ **cup 2% milk**
- ¼ **teaspoon pepper**
- 3 **cups cubed bread**
- 1 **small onion, chopped**
- 1 **cup Rice Krispies, slightly crushed**
- 3 **tablespoons butter, melted**

1. Preheat oven to 350°. In a small bowl, mix cornstarch and water until smooth. In a large saucepan, heat the butter over medium heat. Stir in the corn, evaporated milk, ¾ teaspoon sugar and ½ teaspoon salt; bring just to a boil. Add the cornstarch mixture; return to a boil, stirring constantly. Cook and stir for 1-2 minutes or until thickened; cool slightly.
2. In a large bowl, whisk eggs, milk, pepper and the remaining sugar and salt until blended. Stir in bread, onion and corn mixture. Place the mixture in a greased 8-in. square or 1½-qt. baking dish.
3. Bake, uncovered, 40 minutes. In a small bowl, toss the Rice Krispies with melted butter; sprinkle over casserole. Bake 10-15 minutes longer or until golden brown.
FREEZE OPTION *Cool unbaked casserole, reserving the Rice Krispies topping for baking; cover and freeze. To use, partially thaw in refrigerator overnight. Remove dish from refrigerator 30 minutes before baking. Preheat oven to 350°. Bake casserole as directed, increasing time as necessary to heat through and for a thermometer inserted in the center to read 165°.*

⑤ INGREDIENTS

Tarragon Butter

Tarragon is a native herb of central Asia and was brought to Spain by the Moors. It has been an important ingredient to French cooking since the 16th century.

—TASTE OF HOME TEST KITCHEN

PREP: 5 MIN. + CHILLING
MAKES: ½ CUP

- ½ **cup butter, softened**
- ¼ **cup minced fresh tarragon**
- ⅛ **teaspoon lemon juice**
  Dash salt and pepper

In a small bowl, beat all the ingredients with a fork or whisk until well blended. Shape into a log; wrap in plastic wrap. Refrigerate for a week or freeze for several months. Slice log and use on fish, poultry, vegetables, pasta and bread.

container. To use, partially thaw in refrigerator overnight. Microwave, covered, on high in a microwave-safe dish until heated through, adding 2-3 tablespoons water to moisten.

PER SERVING *1 cup equals 182 cal., 5 g fat (1 g sat. fat), 0 chol., 388 mg sodium, 29 g carb., 3 g fiber, 6 g pro.* **Diabetic Exchanges:** *1½ starch, 1 vegetable, 1 fat.*

⑤INGREDIENTS
Zesty Tomatoes

I love having pints of these spicy tomatoes in the freezer to use in place of canned stewed tomatoes with green chilies in my favorite recipes. Beside, home-grown food is always much better than any you can buy in the store.

—CATHY HARDIN SANTA MONICA, CA

PREP: 15 MIN.
COOK: 45 MIN. + COOLING
MAKES: 5 PINTS

- 12 **medium tomatoes**
- 3 **green peppers, chopped**
- 2 **large onions, chopped**
- 1 **cup water**
- 3 **garlic cloves, minced**
- 2 **to 4 jalapeno peppers, seeded and chopped**
- 1½ **teaspoons salt**

1. Scald, peel and chop the tomatoes; place in a kettle. Add remaining ingredients.
2. Cook, uncovered, over medium heat for 45 minutes, stirring often. Cool slightly; pack into freezer containers. Freeze up to 8 months.
NOTE *Wear disposable gloves when cutting hot peppers; the oils can burn skin. Avoid touching your face.*

EAT SMART
Dijon Veggies with Couscous

Coated in a tangy Dijon sauce, tasty veggies and fluffy couscous make for a delightful side.

—JULIANA DUMITRU
FAIRVIEW PARK, OH

PREP: 20 MIN. • **BAKE:** 20 MIN.
MAKES: 6 SERVINGS

- ½ **pound medium fresh mushrooms, quartered**
- 1 **medium zucchini, halved lengthwise and sliced**
- 1 **medium sweet red pepper, cut into 1-inch pieces**
- ¼ **cup dry red wine or reduced-sodium chicken broth**
- 3 **tablespoons Dijon mustard**
- 2 **tablespoons olive oil**
- 2 **garlic cloves, minced**
- 1 **teaspoon prepared horseradish**
- ½ **teaspoon salt**
- ¼ **teaspoon pepper**
- 1 **cup water**
- 1 **cup uncooked couscous**

1. Place an 18x12-in. piece of heavy-duty foil on a large baking sheet; set aside.
2. In a large bowl, combine the mushrooms, zucchini and red pepper. Combine wine, mustard, oil, garlic, horseradish, salt and pepper; drizzle over vegetables. Toss to coat; transfer to baking sheet. Top with a second large piece of foil. Bring edges of foil pieces together; crimp to seal, forming a large packet.
3. Bake at 350° for 20-25 minutes or until the vegetables are tender. Open foil carefully to allow steam to escape.
4. Meanwhile, in a small saucepan, bring water to a boil. Stir in couscous. Remove from the heat; cover and let stand for 5-10 minutes or until the water is absorbed. Fluff with a fork. Transfer the couscous and vegetables to a large serving bowl; toss to combine.
FREEZE OPTION *Freeze cooled couscous mixture in a freezer*

Salsa Verde

The tomatillos I grew last year were so abundant that I had enough to eat fresh and freeze some for future gatherings. I like to add an extra zip by juicing fresh lime into the salsa .
—**KIM BANICK** SALEM, OR

PREP: 15 MIN. • **BAKE:** 35 MIN.
MAKES: 2 CUPS

- 2 **pounds medium tomatillos (about 16), husks removed and halved**
- 2 **large sweet onions, coarsely chopped (about 4 cups)**
- 2 **serrano peppers, seeded and chopped**
- 6 **garlic cloves, peeled and halved**
- ¼ **cup olive oil**
- ⅓ **to ½ cup water**
- ½ **cup chopped fresh cilantro**
- 2 **tablespoons lime juice**
- 1 **teaspoon salt**

1. Preheat oven to 425°. In a large bowl, toss the tomatillos, onions, peppers and garlic with oil. Divide mixture between two 15x10x1-in. baking pans. Roast 35-40 minutes or until lightly browned, stirring occasionally. Cool slightly.

2. Process tomatillo mixture in a food processor until smooth, adding enough water to reach desired consistency. Add the remaining ingredients; pulse just until combined.

FREEZE OPTION *Freeze cooled salsa in freezer containers. To use, thaw salsa completely in refrigerator.*

NOTE *Wear disposable gloves when cutting hot peppers; the oils can burn skin. Avoid touching your face.*

DID YOU KNOW?

If you grow cilantro, you can also harvest its seeds, known as coriander. Let the seeds mature from green to brown, then cut heads with a few inches of stem and hang to dry. Gently loosen the seeds and store in a covered jar.

Freezer Coleslaw

Loaded with crunch, this sweet-tart slaw can be made ahead for a family gathering. There's no mayonnaise in the dressing, so it's perfect to take to a picnic.

—DONNA SASSER HINDS
MILWAUKIE, OR

PREP: 25 MIN. + FREEZING
MAKES: 10 SERVINGS

- 1 medium head cabbage (about 2 pounds), shredded
- 1 teaspoon salt
- 2 cups sugar
- 1 cup cider vinegar
- ¼ cup water
- 1 teaspoon celery seed
- 1 teaspoon mustard seed
- 1 large carrot, shredded
- ½ cup finely chopped green pepper

1. In a large bowl, combine cabbage and salt; let stand for 1 hour.

2. In a large saucepan, combine the sugar, vinegar, water, celery seed and mustard seed. Bring to a boil; boil for 1 minute. Remove from the heat; cool.

3. Add the carrot, green pepper and vinegar mixture to the cabbage mixture; stir to combine. Transfer to large freezer bags; seal and freeze for up to 2 months.

4. Remove from the freezer 2 hours before serving. Serve with a slotted spoon.

Swiss Sweet Onion Casserole

I think this is a perfect side dish for barbecued chicken or ribs. Sweet onions are available most of the year, so don't substitute another type of onion. The dish will not be as fantastic.

—MADELINE ETZKORN BURIEN, WA

PREP: 30 MIN. • **BAKE:** 1 HOUR
MAKES: 6 SERVINGS

- ½ cup uncooked long grain rice
- 8 cups sliced sweet onions
- 2 tablespoons butter
- 1 cup (4 ounces) shredded Swiss cheese
- ½ cup half-and-half cream
- ½ teaspoon salt
- ⅛ teaspoon ground nutmeg

1. Cook rice according to the package directions.

2. In a large skillet, saute onions in butter until tender. Remove from the heat; stir in the cooked rice, cheese, cream, salt and nutmeg. Pour into a greased 8-in. square baking dish.

3. Bake, uncovered, at 325° for 1 to 1¼ hours or until mixture is golden brown.

FREEZE OPTION *Cool unbaked casserole; cover and freeze. To use, partially thaw dish in refrigerator overnight. Remove from refrigerator 30 minutes before baking. Preheat oven to 325°. Bake casserole as directed, increasing time as necessary to heat through and for a thermometer inserted in the center to read 165°.*

Tart Cranberry Butter

One of my favorite toppings for toast is this tart spread. It's also great spooned over poultry—and ice cream! When I give the jars away as gifts, I've always gotten positive comments.

—CAROL STUDEBAKER

GLADSTONE, MO

PREP: 5 MIN.
COOK: 30 MIN. + CHILLING
MAKES: 5 CUPS

- 10 **cups fresh or frozen cranberries**
- ⅔ **cup apple juice**
- ½ **to ¾ cup sugar**
- 1 **cup maple syrup**
- ½ **cup honey**
- ½ **teaspoon ground cinnamon**

1. In a saucepan over medium heat, bring the cranberries, apple juice and sugar to a boil. Cook 10-15 minutes or until all berries have popped, stirring occasionally. Remove from heat; cool slightly. Process in batches in a blender or food processor until smooth.

2. Return cranberry mixture to the saucepan; add remaining ingredients. Bring to a boil over medium heat. Reduce the heat; simmer, uncovered, 10 minutes or until thickened, stirring occasionally. Cover and chill for 8 hours or overnight. Store the mixture in an airtight container in the refrigerator up to 1 week or freeze up to 3 months.

**HEARTY BUTTERNUT
SQUASH SOUP**
PAGE 93

Heartwarming Soups

Nothing says love like a piping hot homemade soup, and the 25+ offerings in this chapter are guaranteed to nourish, satisfy and warm you up from head to toe.

Upstate Minestrone

If you love vegetables, you'll find this minestrone especially satisfying. Keep the recipe in mind to make and freeze when you have a bounty of fresh garden produce.

—**YVONNE KRANTZ** MT. UPTON, NY

PREP: 25 MIN.
COOK: 1½ HOURS
MAKES: 8 SERVINGS

- 1 **pound Italian sausage links, cut into ½-inch slices**
- 1 **tablespoon olive oil**
- 1 **cup finely chopped onion**
- 1 **cup sliced fresh carrots**
- 1 **garlic clove, finely minced**
- 1 **teaspoon dried basil**
- 2 **cups shredded cabbage**
- 2 **small zucchini, sliced**
- 2 **cans (10½ ounces each) condensed beef broth, undiluted or 3 beef bouillon cubes plus 1½ cups water**
- 1 **can (14½ ounces) diced tomatoes, undrained**
- 1 **teaspoon salt**
- ¼ **teaspoon pepper**
- 1 **can (15½ ounces) great northern beans, rinsed and drained**
  Minced fresh parsley

1. In a Dutch oven, brown the sausage in oil. Add the onion, carrots, garlic and basil; cook for 5 minutes. Stir in the cabbage, zucchini, broth, tomatoes, salt and pepper.

2. Bring to a boil. Reduce heat; cover and simmer for 1 hour. Add beans; cook 20 minutes longer. Garnish with parsley.

FREEZE OPTION *Freeze cooled soup in freezer containers. To use, partially thaw soup in refrigerator overnight. Heat through in a saucepan, stirring occasionally and adding a little broth or water if necessary.*

Fiesta Turkey Tortilla Soup

I'm just amazed when I can pull together such a delicious soup in less than half an hour.

—**AMY MCFADDEN** CHELSEA, AL

START TO FINISH: 25 MIN.
MAKES: 8 SERVINGS

- 4 **cans (14½ ounces each) chicken broth**
- 3 **cups shredded cooked turkey or rotisserie chicken**
- 1 **can (15 ounces) black beans, rinsed and drained**
- 1 **can (15¼ ounces) whole kernel corn, drained**
- ½ **cup medium salsa**
- 5 **corn tortillas (6 inches), cut into ¼-inch strips**
- ¼ **cup chopped fresh cilantro**
  Additional salsa, optional

1. In a Dutch oven, combine first five ingredients; bring to a boil. Reduce heat; simmer for 10 minutes, stirring occasionally.

2. Meanwhile, spread tortilla strips in a single layer on a baking sheet. Bake at 400° 4-6 minutes or until golden brown and crisp.

3. Stir cilantro into the soup. Top each serving with tortilla strips. If desired, serve with additional salsa.

Rustic Italian Tortellini Soup

This soup is quick to fix on a busy night and full of healthy, tasty ingredients. The recipe originally called for spicy sausage links, but I've found that turkey sausage, or even plain ground turkey breast, is just as good.

—TRACY FASNACHT IRWIN, PA

PREP: 20 MIN. • **COOK:** 20 MIN.
MAKES: 6 SERVINGS (2 QUARTS)

- ¾ pound Italian turkey sausage links, casings removed
- 1 medium onion, chopped
- 6 garlic cloves, minced
- 2 cans (14½ ounces each) reduced-sodium chicken broth
- 1¾ cups water
- 1 can (14½ ounces) diced tomatoes, undrained
- 1 package (9 ounces) refrigerated cheese tortellini
- 1 package (6 ounces) fresh baby spinach, coarsely chopped
- 2¼ teaspoons minced fresh basil or ¾ teaspoon dried basil
- ¼ teaspoon pepper
- Dash crushed red pepper flakes
- Shredded Parmesan cheese, optional

1. Crumble the sausage into a Dutch oven; add onion. Cook and stir over medium heat until meat is no longer pink. Add the garlic; cook for 1 minute longer. Stir in the broth, water and tomatoes. Bring to a boil.
2. Add the tortellini; return to a boil. Cook for 5-8 minutes or until almost tender, stirring occasionally. Reduce heat; add the spinach, basil, pepper and pepper flakes. Cook 2-3 minutes longer or until spinach is wilted and tortellini are tender. Serve with cheese if desired.

FREEZE OPTION *Place individual portions of cooled soup in freezer containers and freeze. To use, partially thaw in refrigerator overnight. Heat through in a saucepan, stirring occasionally and adding a little broth if necessary.*
RUSTIC ITALIAN RAVIOLI SOUP *Substitute ravioli for the tortellini.*

EAT SMART ⑤**INGREDIENTS**

Spicy Pumpkin & Corn Soup

Here's a seriously quick dish that can satisfy a hungry household in 20 minutes. My family loves a hot pan of corn bread alongside it.

—HEATHER ROREX WINNEMUCCA, NV

START TO FINISH: 20 MIN.
MAKES: 8 SERVINGS

- 1 can (15 ounces) solid-pack pumpkin
- 1 can (15 ounces) black beans, rinsed and drained
- 1½ cups frozen corn
- 1 can (10 ounces) diced tomatoes and green chilies
- 2 cans (14½ ounces each) reduced-sodium chicken broth
- ¼ teaspoon pepper

In a large saucepan, mix all ingredients. Bring to a boil. Reduce the heat; simmer, uncovered, for 10-15 minutes or until slightly thickened, stirring occasionally.

FREEZE OPTION *Freeze cooled soup in freezer containers. To use, partially thaw in refrigerator overnight. Heat through in a saucepan, stirring occasionally and adding a little broth if necessary.*
PER SERVING *¾ cup equals 100 cal., trace fat (trace sat. fat), 0 chol., 542 mg sodium, 20 g carb., 5 g fiber, 6 g pro.* **Diabetic Exchange:** *1 starch.*

Turkey Nacho Soup

We like our soup spicy hot, so we tend to use all three tablespoons of jalapenos. But you don't have to. Loaded with turkey, beans, corn and tomatoes, it'll keep you warm .

—**BRENDA KRUSE** AMES, IA

PREP: 20 MIN. • **COOK:** 30 MIN.
MAKES: 7 SERVINGS

- 1 **medium onion, chopped**
- 1 **tablespoon olive oil**
- 1 **can (14½ ounces) chicken broth**
- 2 **to 3 tablespoons diced jalapeno pepper**
- 3 **teaspoons ground cumin**
- 1½ **teaspoons chili powder**
- ¼ **teaspoon salt**
- ¼ **teaspoon cayenne pepper**
- 3 **cups cubed cooked turkey**
- 1 **can (15 ounces) black beans, rinsed and drained**
- 1 **can (10 ounces) diced tomatoes and green chilies, undrained**
- 1½ **cups frozen corn**
  Sour cream, crushed tortilla chips, shredded cheddar cheese and sliced ripe olives, optional

1. In a large saucepan, saute onion in oil until tender. Stir in the broth, jalapeno, cumin, chili powder, salt and cayenne. Add the turkey, black beans, tomatoes and corn.

2. Bring to a boil. Reduce heat; cover and simmer for 20-30 minutes to allow flavors to blend. Garnish with sour cream, chips, cheese and olives if desired.

FREEZE OPTION *Place individual portions of cooled soup in freezer containers and freeze. To use, partially thaw in refrigerator overnight. Heat through in a saucepan, stirring occasionally and adding a little broth if necessary.*

NOTE *Wear disposable gloves when cutting hot peppers; the oils can burn skin. Avoid touching your face.*

DID YOU KNOW?

Beans are an economical source of protein that can help stretch or replace the meat in a recipe. Dried beans roughly double in volume when cooked. If you'd like to cook your own to use in a recipe, start with 3/4 to 1 cup of dried beans for each 15 ounce can.

EAT SMART

Zesty Hamburger Soup

When it's a soup day, turn to the simple, satisfying one here. Zip from the jalapenos and green chilies will perk you right up.

—**KELLY MILAN** LAKE JACKSON, TX

START TO FINISH: 30 MIN.
MAKES: 10 SERVINGS (3¾ QUARTS)

- 1 pound ground beef
- 2 cups sliced celery
- 1 cup chopped onion
- 2 teaspoons minced garlic
- 4 cups water
- 2 medium red potatoes, peeled and cubed
- 2 cups frozen corn
- 1½ cups uncooked small shell pasta
- 1 tablespoon pickled jalapeno slices
- 4 cups V8 juice
- 2 cans (10 ounces each) diced tomatoes with green chilies
- 1 to 2 tablespoons sugar

1. In a Dutch oven, cook beef, celery and onion over medium heat until meat is no longer pink. Add garlic; cook 1 minute longer. Drain. Stir in the water, potatoes, corn, pasta and jalapeno.

2. Bring to a boil. Reduce heat; cover and simmer 10-15 minutes or until pasta is tender. Stir in the remaining ingredients and heat through.

PER SERVING *1½ cups equals 221 cal., 5 g fat (2 g sat. fat), 22 mg chol., 548 mg sodium, 33 g carb., 4 g fiber, 13 g pro.* **Diabetic Exchanges:** *2 vegetable, 1½ starch, 1 lean meat.*

FREEZE IT

Cool soup and transfer to freezer containers. Freeze up to 3 months. To use, thaw in the refrigerator overnight. Transfer to a saucepan. Cover and cook over medium heat until heated through.

Crab Bisque

I love to try new recipes. Bisques are rich, creamy soups. Tasty chunks of crab and corn make this one hearty.

—**SHERRIE MANTON** FOLSOM, LA

START TO FINISH: 25 MIN.
MAKES: 10 SERVINGS

- 1 **celery rib, thinly sliced**
- 1 **small onion, chopped**
- ½ **cup chopped green pepper**
- 3 **tablespoons butter**
- 2 **cans (14¾ ounces each) cream-style corn**
- 2 **cans (10¾ ounces each) condensed cream of potato soup, undiluted**
- 1½ **cups milk**
- 1½ **cups half-and-half cream**
- 2 **bay leaves**
- 1 **teaspoon dried thyme**
- ½ **teaspoon garlic powder**
- ¼ **teaspoon white pepper**
- ⅛ **teaspoon hot pepper sauce**
- 3 **cans (6 ounces each) crabmeat, drained, flaked and cartilage removed**

In a large saucepan, saute celery, onion and green pepper in the butter until tender. Add the next nine ingredients; mix well. Stir in crab; heat through. Discard the bay leaves.

FREEZE OPTION *Freeze the cooled soup in freezer containers. To use, partially thaw in refrigerator overnight. Heat through in a saucepan, stirring occasionally.*

EAT SMART

Apple Squash Soup

I add a little ginger and sage to apples and squash in a creamy soup that my family loves when autumn rolls around.

—**CRYSTAL RALPH-HAUGHN**
BARTLESVILLE, OK

PREP: 10 MIN. • **COOK:** 35 MIN.
MAKES: 5 SERVINGS

- 2 **tablespoons butter**
- 1 **large onion, chopped**
- ½ **teaspoon rubbed sage**
- 1 **can (14½ ounces) chicken or vegetable broth**
- 2 **medium tart apples, peeled and finely chopped**
- ¾ **cup water**
- 1 **package (12 ounces) frozen cooked winter squash, thawed**
- 1 **teaspoon ground ginger**
- ½ **teaspoon salt**
- ½ **cup fat-free milk**

1. In a large saucepan, heat butter over medium-high heat. Add onion and sage; cook and stir 2-4 minutes or until tender. Add broth, apples and water; bring to a boil. Reduce heat; simmer, covered, 12 minutes.

2. Add squash, ginger and salt; return to a boil. Reduce heat; simmer, uncovered, 10 minutes to allow flavors to blend. Remove from heat; cool slightly.

3. Process in batches in a blender until smooth; return to pan. Add milk and heat through, stirring occasionally (do not allow to boil).

FREEZE OPTION *Freeze cooled soup in freezer containers. To use, partially thaw soup in refrigerator overnight. Heat through in a saucepan, stirring occasionally and adding a little broth if necessary.*

PER SERVING *1 cup equals 142 cal., 6 g fat (3 g sat. fat), 13 mg chol., 647 mg sodium, 22 g carb., 2 g fiber, 3 g pro.* ***Diabetic Exchanges:*** *1 starch, 1 fat, ½ fruit.*

Mom's Chicken Noodle Soup

My mother was a pastor's wife, and she did a lot of cooking for potlucks. This recipe's one she created herself. Now I frequently serve it to my own family.

—MARLENE DOOLITTLE
STORY CITY, IA

PREP: 30 MIN. • **COOK:** 55 MIN.
MAKES: 6 SERVINGS

- 1 **broiler/fryer chicken (3 to 4 pounds), cut up**
- 2 **quarts water**
- 1 **medium onion, chopped**
- 2 **teaspoons chicken bouillon granules**
- 2 **celery ribs, diced**
- 2 **medium carrots, diced**
- 2 **medium potatoes, peeled and cubed**
- 1½ **cups fresh or frozen cut green beans**
- 1 **teaspoon salt**
- ¼ **teaspoon pepper**

NOODLES
- 1 **cup all-purpose flour**
- 1 **large egg, lightly beaten**
- ½ **teaspoon salt**
- 1 **teaspoon butter, softened**
- ¼ **teaspoon baking powder**
- 2 **to 3 tablespoons milk**

1. In a Dutch oven, cook chicken in water; cool slightly. Remove chicken from bones; discard bones. Skim fat from broth. Cut the chicken into bite-size pieces; add to broth with the remaining ingredients except noodles. Bring to a boil. Reduce the heat and simmer soup, uncovered, for 50-60 minutes or until the vegetables are tender.

2. Meanwhile, for the noodles, place flour in a small bowl and make a well in the center. Stir together remaining ingredients; pour into the well. Working the mixture with hands, form dough ball. Knead for 5-6 minutes.

3. Cover and let rest 10 minutes. On a floured surface, roll dough into a square, ¹⁄₁₆ to ⅛ in. thick, and cut into ¼-in.-wide strips. Cook noodles in boiling salted water for 2-3 minutes or until done. Drain and add to the soup just before serving.

FREEZE OPTION *Freeze uncooked noodles on waxed paper-lined baking sheets until firm. Transfer to freezer bags; return to freezer. Prepare soup as directed, reserving potatoes for later. Freeze cooled soup in freezer containers. To use, partially thaw in refrigerator overnight. Place potatoes in a small saucepan; add water to cover. Simmer 10-15 minutes or until tender. Drain. Meanwhile, cook noodles as directed; drain. Transfer soup and potatoes to a Dutch oven. Heat through. Just before serving, add noodles.*

TOP TIP

Sometimes I use canned or boxed stock instead of water if I have it on hand. About half an hour before the soup is done, add a whole bag of French-style green beans. Sometimes I put rice in the soup if I have it left over from another meal. If you are adding rice, add it when you add the green beans.

—CJPASEK TASTEOFHOME.COM

Hearty Butternut Squash Soup

A delicious combination of squash, meat, beans and veggies really make my go-to autumn soup. It's so full of goodness.

—JAYE BEELER GRAND RAPIDS, MI

PREP: 20 MIN. • **COOK:** 40 MIN.
MAKES: 12 SERVINGS (4½ QUARTS)

- 1 **pound bulk Italian sausage**
- 1 **medium onion, chopped**
- 1 **medium sweet red pepper, chopped**
- 4 **garlic cloves, minced**
- 1 **large butternut squash (about 5 pounds), peeled, seeded and cut into 1-inch pieces**
- 1 **package (16 ounces) frozen corn, divided**
- 4 **cups water**
- 1 **tablespoon chicken base**
- 2 **cans (15½ ounces each) great northern beans, rinsed and drained**
- 2 **cans (14½ ounces each) fire-roasted diced tomatoes, undrained**
- 1 **teaspoon salt**
- ¼ **teaspoon pepper**
  Heavy whipping cream and minced fresh parsley, optional

1. In a stockpot, cook sausage, onion and red pepper over medium heat 9-11 minutes or until the meat is no longer pink and onion is tender, breaking up sausage into crumbles. Add garlic; cook 1 minute longer. Remove with a slotted spoon; discard drippings.

2. Add squash, 1½ cups corn, water and chicken base to same pan; bring to a boil. Reduce heat; simmer, covered, 15-20 minutes or until squash is tender.

3. Remove soup from heat; cool slightly. Process in batches in a blender until smooth. Return to pot. Add beans, tomatoes, salt, pepper, sausage mixture and remaining corn; heat through. If desired, drizzle servings with cream and sprinkle with parsley

FREEZE OPTION *Freeze the cooled soup in freezer containers. To use, partially thaw soup in refrigerator overnight. Heat through in a saucepan, stirring occasionally and adding a little water if necessary.*

Sunday Cassoulet

Wine lends a warm background flavor to a new take on a traditional French stew. With 10 servings, it's great when you're expecting guests.

—**LYNN STEIN** JOSEPH, OR

PREP: 25 MIN. • **COOK:** 40 MIN.
MAKES: 10 SERVINGS (4 QUARTS)

- 1 pork tenderloin (1 pound), cut into ½-inch pieces
- 1 pound smoked turkey kielbasa, cut into ½-inch pieces
- 1 tablespoon olive oil
- 3 medium carrots, chopped
- 1 large onion, cut into wedges
- 4 garlic cloves, minced
- 2 cans (14½ ounces each) no-salt-added stewed tomatoes, cut up
- 1 can (14½ ounces) reduced-sodium chicken broth
- 3 teaspoons herbes de Provence
- 1½ teaspoons garlic powder
- 1½ teaspoons dried basil
- ½ teaspoon dried oregano
- ¼ teaspoon pepper
- 4 cans (15½ ounces each) great northern beans, rinsed and drained, divided
- ¾ cup white wine or additional chicken broth, divided

1. In a Dutch oven coated with cooking spray, saute pork and kielbasa in the oil until lightly browned; drain. Add carrots and onion; saute 4 minutes longer. Add the garlic; cook for 1 minute longer. Stir in the tomatoes, broth and seasonings. Bring to a boil. Reduce heat; cover and simmer for 10 minutes.

2. Place one can of beans in a food processor; add ¼ cup wine or broth. Cover and process until pureed. Stir into meat mixture. Stir in the remaining beans and wine or broth. Bring to a boil. Reduce heat; simmer, uncovered, for 8-10 minutes or until meat and vegetables are tender.

FREEZE OPTION *Freeze cooled cassoulet in freezer containers. To use, partially thaw in refrigerator overnight. Heat through in a saucepan, stirring occasionally and adding a little broth or water if necessary.*
NOTE *Look for herbes de Provence in the spice aisle.*

Southwest Turkey Soup

Ground turkey and a handful of other ingredients are all that's required for a satisfying bowl. Spiced with salsa, green chilies and chili powder, it's perfect on busy winter weeknights.

—**GENISE KRAUSE** STURGEON BAY, WI

START TO FINISH: 30 MIN.
MAKES: 6 SERVINGS (2½ QUARTS)

- 1 **pound ground turkey**
- 1 **tablespoon olive oil**
- 2 **cans (16 ounces each) kidney beans, rinsed and drained**
- 2 **cans (14½ ounces each) chicken broth**
- 2 **cups frozen corn**
- 1 **cup salsa**
- 1 **can (4 ounces) chopped green chilies**
- 1 **to 2 tablespoons chili powder**
  Sour cream and minced fresh cilantro

1. In a Dutch oven, cook turkey in the oil over medium heat until meat is no longer pink; drain.
2. Add the beans, broth, corn, salsa, chilies and chili powder. Bring to a boil. Reduce the heat; cover and simmer the chili for 10-15 minutes to allow flavors to blend. Serve with sour cream and cilantro.

FREEZE OPTION *Before adding sour cream and cilantro, cool the soup. Freeze soup in freezer containers up to 3 months. To use, partially thaw soup in refrigerator overnight. Heat through in a saucepan, stirring occasionally and adding a little broth or water if necessary. Serve with sour cream and cilantro.*

Good-for-You Split Pea Soup

When I have leftover ham in the fridge, I always like to make this soup. Just throw the ingredients in the slow cooker, turn it on and dinner is done.

—PAMELA CHAMBERS
WEST COLUMBIA, SC

PREP: 15 MIN. • **COOK:** 8 HOURS
MAKES: 8 SERVINGS

- 1 package (16 ounces) dried green split peas, rinsed
- 2 cups cubed fully cooked ham
- 1 large onion, chopped
- 1 cup julienned or chopped carrots
- 3 garlic cloves, minced
- ½ teaspoon dried rosemary, crushed
- ½ teaspoon dried thyme
- 1 carton (32 ounces) reduced-sodium chicken broth
- 2 cups water

In a 4- or 5-qt. slow cooker, combine all ingredients. Cover and cook on low for 8-10 hours or until peas are tender.

FREEZE OPTION *Freeze cooled soup in freezer containers. To use, thaw overnight in the refrigerator. Heat through in a saucepan over medium heat, stirring occasionally.*
PER SERVING *1 cup equals 260 cal., 2 g fat (1 g sat. fat), 21 mg chol., 728 mg sodium, 39 g carb., 15 g fiber, 23 g pro. Diabetic Exchanges: 2½ starch, 2 lean meat.*

Slow Cooker Turkey Chili

I love a recipe you can prepare in the morning and have a wholesome dinner ready when you get home in the evening. Make a big batch to freeze!

—TERRI CRANDALL GARDNERVILLE, NV

PREP: 30 MIN. • **COOK:** 7¼ HOURS
MAKES: 8 SERVINGS (2¾ QUARTS)

- 2 tablespoons olive oil
- 1½ pounds ground turkey
- 1 medium onion, chopped
- 2 tablespoons ground ancho chili pepper
- 1 tablespoon chili powder
- 1½ teaspoons salt
- 1½ teaspoons ground cumin
- 1½ teaspoons paprika
- 2 cans (14½ ounces each) fire-roasted diced tomatoes, undrained
- 1 medium sweet yellow pepper, chopped
- 1 medium sweet red pepper, chopped
- 1 can (4 ounces) chopped green chilies
- 1 garlic clove, minced
- 1 cup brewed coffee
- ¾ cup dry red wine or chicken broth
- 1 can (16 ounces) kidney beans, rinsed and drained
- 1 can (15 ounces) white kidney or cannellini beans, rinsed and drained
  Sliced avocado and chopped green onions

1. In a large skillet, heat oil over medium heat. Add turkey and onion; cook and stir for 8-10 minutes or until meat is no longer pink, breaking up turkey into crumbles.
2. Transfer to a 5-qt. slow cooker; stir in seasonings. Add the tomatoes, sweet peppers, chilies and garlic; stir in coffee and wine.
3. Cook, covered, on low for 7-9 hours. Stir in beans; cook 15-20 minutes longer or until heated through. Top servings with avocado and green onions.

FREEZE IT

Freeze cooled chili in freezer containers. To use, partially thaw in refrigerator overnight. Heat through in a saucepan, stirring occasionally and adding broth or water if necessary.

Sausage Tortellini Soup

I'm always searching for new and different soup recipes. I came across one in an old church cookbook and changed a few ingredients to suit my family's tastes. Now it's a favorite of ours, and friends ask for the recipe.

—HEATHER PERSCH

HUDSONVILLE, MI

PREP: 15 MIN. • **COOK:** 30 MIN.
MAKES: 10 SERVINGS (2½ QUARTS)

- 1 **pound bulk Italian sausage**
- 2 **cups water**
- 2 **cups chopped cabbage**
- 1 **can (14½ ounces) Italian stewed tomatoes, undrained and cut up**
- 1 **can (14½ ounces) beef broth**
- 1 **can (10½ ounces) condensed French onion soup**
- 1 **package (9 ounces) refrigerated cheese tortellini**
- ½ **cup grated Parmesan cheese**

In a large saucepan, cook the sausage over medium heat until no longer pink; drain. Stir in the water, cabbage, tomatoes, broth and soup. Bring to a boil. Reduce heat; simmer, uncovered, for 8 minutes. Stir in tortellini; cook 7-9 minutes longer or until pasta is tender. Sprinkle with cheese.

FREEZE OPTION *Before adding cheese, freeze cooled soup in freezer containers. To use, partially thaw in refrigerator overnight. Heat through in a saucepan, stirring occasionally and adding a little broth, water or milk if necessary. Serve with the cheese.*

Quinoa Turkey Chili

This heart-healthy chili is not only tasty; it's a vitamin and protein powerhouse! Quinoa and beans are a nutritious way to stretch a half-pound of turkey.

—**SHARON GILJUM** ARLINGTON, VA

PREP: 40 MIN. • **COOK:** 35 MIN.
MAKES: 9 SERVINGS (2¼ QUARTS)

- 1 **cup quinoa, rinsed**
- 3½ **cups water, divided**
- ½ **pound lean ground turkey**
- 1 **large sweet onion, chopped**
- 1 **medium sweet red pepper, chopped**
- 4 **garlic cloves, minced**
- 1 **tablespoon chili powder**
- 1 **tablespoon ground cumin**
- ½ **teaspoon ground cinnamon**
- 2 **cans (15 ounces each) black beans, rinsed and drained**
- 1 **can (28 ounces) crushed tomatoes**
- 1 **medium zucchini, chopped**
- 1 **chipotle pepper in adobo sauce, chopped**
- 1 **tablespoon adobo sauce**
- 1 **bay leaf**
- 1 **teaspoon dried oregano**
- ½ **teaspoon salt**
- ¼ **teaspoon pepper**
- 1 **cup frozen corn, thawed**
- ¼ **cup minced fresh cilantro**

1. In a large saucepan, bring quinoa and 2 cups water to a boil. Reduce heat; cover and simmer for 12-15 minutes or until water is absorbed. Remove from heat; fluff with a fork and set aside.
2. Meanwhile, in a large saucepan coated with cooking spray, cook turkey, onion, red pepper and garlic over medium heat until meat is no longer pink; drain. Add the spices and cook 2 minutes longer.
3. Add the black beans, tomatoes, zucchini, chipotle pepper, adobo sauce, bay leaf, oregano, salt, pepper and the remaining water. Bring to a boil. Reduce heat; cover and simmer for 30 minutes. Stir in the corn and the quinoa; heat through. Discard the bay leaf; stir in the minced cilantro.
FREEZE OPTION *Freeze the cooled chili in freezer containers.*

To use, partially thaw in refrigerator overnight. Heat through in a saucepan, stirring occasionally and adding a little broth or water if necessary.
NOTE *Look for quinoa in the cereal, rice or organic food aisle.*
PER SERVING *1 cup equals 264 cal., 5 g fat (1 g sat. fat), 20 mg chol., 514 mg sodium, 43 g carb., 9 g fiber, 15 g pro.*
***Diabetic Exchanges:** 2 starch, 2 lean meat, 2 vegetable.*

on low for 5-6 hours or until the beans and vegetables are tender. Discard bay leaf.

FREEZE OPTION *Freeze cooled soup in freezer containers. To use, partially thaw in the refrigerator overnight. Heat through in a saucepan, stirring occasionally and adding a little broth or water if necessary.*

(5) INGREDIENTS
Kielbasa Chili

This easy creation combines the flavors of chili dogs in a bowl! I make it when I need a hot, hearty meal in a hurry. It's also great to eat while watching the football game.

—**AUDRA DUVALL** LAS VEGAS, NV

START TO FINISH: 20 MIN.
MAKES: 7 SERVINGS

- 1 **pound smoked kielbasa or Polish sausage, halved and sliced**
- 2 **cans (14½ ounces each) diced tomatoes, undrained**
- 1 **can (15 ounces) chili with beans**
- 1 **can (8¾ ounces) whole kernel corn, drained**
- 1 **can (2¼ ounces) sliced ripe olives, drained**

In a Dutch oven coated with cooking spray, saute kielbasa until browned. Stir in the remaining ingredients. Bring to a boil. Reduce heat; simmer, uncovered, for 4-5 minutes or until heated through.

FREEZE OPTION *Cool chili and transfer to freezer containers. Freeze up to 3 months. To use, thaw in the refrigerator. Place in a saucepan; heat through.*

SLOW COOKER 🍲
Mushroom Barley Soup

Here's a hearty, delicious soup full of vegetables, beans and barley. I like to eat it with warm bread smothered in butter.

—**CONSTANCE SULLIVAN**
OCEANSIDE, CA

PREP: 25 MIN. + SOAKING
COOK: 5 HOURS
MAKES: 12 SERVINGS (3 QUARTS)

- ½ **cup dried great northern beans**
- 1 **pound sliced fresh mushrooms**
- 2 **cups chopped onions**
- 1 **medium leek (white portion only), sliced**
- 2 **tablespoons butter**
- 1 **to 2 garlic cloves, minced**
- 2 **cartons (32 ounces each) chicken broth**
- 3 **celery ribs, thinly sliced**
- 3 **large carrots, chopped**
- ½ **cup medium pearl barley**
- 2 **teaspoons dried parsley flakes**
- 1½ **teaspoons salt**
- 1 **bay leaf**
- ¼ **teaspoon white pepper**

1. Soak beans according to package directions. In a large skillet, cook the mushrooms, onions and leek in butter over medium heat until tender. Add garlic; cook 1 minute longer.
2. Transfer to a 6-quart slow cooker. Drain and rinse beans, discarding liquid. Add beans and remaining ingredients to the slow cooker. Cover and cook

Pepperoni Pizza Chili

Pizza and chili together in one dish—what could be better? Fill folks up at halftime when you dish up bowlfuls of this enticing chili.

—JENNIFER GELORMINO
PITTSBURGH, PA

PREP: 20 MIN. • **COOK:** 30 MIN.
MAKES: 12 SERVINGS (3 QUARTS)

- 2 **pounds ground beef**
- 1 **pound bulk hot Italian sausage**
- 1 **large onion, chopped**
- 1 **large green pepper, chopped**
- 4 **garlic cloves, minced**
- 1 **jar (16 ounces) salsa**
- 1 **can (16 ounces) hot chili beans, undrained**
- 1 **can (16 ounces) kidney beans, rinsed and drained**
- 1 **can (12 ounces) pizza sauce**
- 1 **package (8 ounces) sliced pepperoni, halved**
- 1 **cup water**
- 2 **teaspoons chili powder**
- ½ **teaspoon salt**
- ½ **teaspoon pepper**
- 3 **cups (12 ounces) shredded part-skim mozzarella cheese**

1. In a Dutch oven, cook the beef, sausage, onion, green pepper and garlic over medium heat until the meat is no longer pink; drain.

2. Stir in the salsa, beans, pizza sauce, pepperoni, water, chili powder, salt and pepper. Bring to a boil. Reduce heat; cover and simmer for 20 minutes or until heated through. Sprinkle each serving with cheese.

FREEZE OPTION *Before adding cheese, cool chili. Freeze chili in freezer containers. To use, partially thaw in refrigerator overnight. Heat through in a saucepan, stirring occasionally and adding a little water if necessary. Sprinkle each serving with cheese.*

TOP TIP

I added a pint jar of undrained canned tomatoes from the cellar instead of the plain water. Also added 8 ounces mushrooms and sauteed them with the meat and other veggies. I put the garlic in the pot after I drained the meat...otherwise all of that good flaver drains off. It's a good chili recipe!

—KASSI1 TASTEOFHOME.COM

Chicken and Andouille Gumbo

This dish is my wife's favorite. And who could ask for anything more than that? Hot corn bread or French bread from the bakery makes a great pairing. It's terrific for a cool fall day.

—**BILLY HENSLEY** MOUNT CARMEL, TN

PREP: 40 MIN. • **COOK:** 2 HOURS
MAKES: 9 SERVINGS (3¼ QUARTS)

- 2 tablespoons Cajun seasoning, divided
- 1 teaspoon salt, divided
- ½ teaspoon pepper, divided
- 3 pounds bone-in chicken thighs, skin removed
- ½ cup plus 2 tablespoons canola oil, divided
- ½ cup all-purpose flour
- 1 large onion, finely chopped
- ¾ cup finely chopped green pepper
- ¾ cup finely chopped sweet red pepper
- 2 celery ribs, finely chopped
- 4 garlic cloves, minced
- 4 cups water
- 2 cups chicken stock
- 1½ pounds fully cooked andouille sausage links, sliced
- 2 tablespoons Worcestershire sauce
- 2 bay leaves
  Hot cooked rice
- 3 green onions, chopped

1. In a small bowl, mix 1 tablespoon Cajun seasoning, ½ teaspoon salt and ¼ teaspoon pepper; rub over chicken. In a Dutch oven, brown chicken in 2 tablespoons of oil in batches; remove chicken from pan.

2. Add the remaining oil to the same pan; stir in the flour until blended. Cook and stir mixture over medium-low heat for 30 minutes or until browned (do not burn). Add the onion, peppers and celery; cook and stir for 2-3 minutes or until the vegetables are tender. Add the garlic; cook 1 minute longer.

3. Gradually add water and stock. Stir in the sausage, Worcestershire sauce, bay leaves, chicken and remaining Cajun seasoning, salt and pepper. Bring to a boil. Reduce the heat; cover and simmer for 1 hour or until the chicken is very tender.

4. Remove chicken from pan; cool slightly. Skim fat from gumbo and discard bay leaves. Shred chicken and return to gumbo; heat through. Discard bones. Serve gumbo over rice; top with green onions.

FREEZE OPTION *Place individual portions of cooled gumbo in freezer containers and freeze. To use, partially thaw in refrigerator overnight. Heat through in a saucepan, stirring occasionally and adding a little broth if necessary.*

Hot Italian Sausage Soup

I'm part owner of a small tavern, and on Saturdays we provide soups and deli sandwiches free of charge. Our patrons love soup loaded with zesty sausage and an array of veggies. A hint of brown sugar balances the heat with a little sweetness, making it a real crowd-pleaser.

—**DAN BUTE** OTTAWA, IL

START TO FINISH: 25 MIN.
MAKES: 4 SERVINGS

- 1 **pound bulk hot Italian sausage**
- 1 **can (14½ ounces) Italian stewed tomatoes**
- 1 **can (8 ounces) tomato sauce**
- 1 **cup frozen Italian vegetables**
- ¾ **cup julienned green, sweet red and/or yellow pepper**
- ¼ **cup chopped onion**
- ¼ **cup white wine or chicken broth**
- 1 **teaspoon brown sugar**
- 1 **teaspoon minced fresh parsley**
- ½ **teaspoon Italian seasoning**
- ⅛ **teaspoon salt**
- ⅛ **teaspoon pepper**

1. In a large skillet, cook the sausage over medium heat until no longer pink.

2. Meanwhile, combine the remaining ingredinets in a large saucepan. Bring to a boil. Reduce the heat; cover and simmer for 10 minutes or until vegetables are tender.

3. Drain sausage; add to soup and heat through.

FREEZE OPTION *Cool soup and transfer it to freezer containers. Freeze up to 3 months. To use, thaw in the refrigerator overnight. Transfer soup to a saucepan. Cover and cook over medium heat until heated through.*

Chili Verde

One of my family's favorite recipes, green chili is especially good when peppers are fresh from the garden. But we enjoy it anytime of year.
—**SHERRIE SCETTRINI** SALINAS, CA

PREP: 20 MIN. • **COOK:** 1¾ HOURS
MAKES: 8 SERVINGS

- 4 tablespoons canola oil, divided
- 4 pounds boneless pork, cut into ¾-inch cubes
- ¼ cup all-purpose flour
- 1 can (4 ounces) chopped green chilies
- ½ teaspoon ground cumin
- ¼ teaspoon salt
- ¼ teaspoon pepper
- 3 garlic cloves, minced
- ½ cup minced fresh cilantro
- ½ to 1 cup salsa
- 1 can (14½ ounces) chicken broth
  Flour tortillas, warmed

1. In a Dutch oven, heat 1 tablespoon of oil over medium-high heat. Add 1 pound of pork; cook and stir until lightly browned. Remove and set aside. Repeat with the remaining meat, adding more oil as needed. Return all of the meat to Dutch oven.

2. Sprinkle flour over meat; mix well. Add the chilies, cumin, salt, pepper, garlic, cilantro, salsa and broth. Cover and simmer until pork is tender and chili reaches the desired consistency, about 1½ hours. Serve the chili with warmed tortillas.

PER SERVING *1 serving equals 404 cal., 20 g fat (6 g sat. fat), 133 mg chol., 509 mg sodium, 5 g carb., 1 g fiber, 48 g pro.*

FREEZE IT

Place individual portions of cooled chili in freezer containers and freeze. To use, partially thaw in refrigerator overnight. Heat through in a saucepan, stirring occasionally and adding a little broth if necessary.

Make-Ahead Squash Soup

I make a big batch of this soup when the garden's overflowing with zucchini. In winter when I want to be reminded of summer's goodness, I just heat and serve it. It's also a nice treat to take to a neighbor or sick friend.

—**SUZANNE MCKINLEY** LYONS, GA

PREP: 25 MIN. **COOK:** 20 MIN.
MAKES: 4 BATCHES
(3 SERVINGS EACH)

SOUP BASE

- 3 **pounds zucchini, sliced**
- 2 **cups water**
- 1 **can (14½ ounces) beef broth**
- 1 **cup chopped onion**
- 1½ **teaspoons salt**
- ⅛ **teaspoon garlic powder**

ADDITIONAL INGREDIENTS
(FOR EACH BATCH)

- 1 **cup half and half cream**
  Grated Parmesan cheese
  and crumbled cooked
  bacon, optional

1. In a Dutch oven, combine soup base ingredients ; bring to a boil. Reduce heat; simmer for 20 minutes or until the zucchini is tender. Cool slightly.

2. Puree mixture in batches in a blender or food processor; cool. Place 2 cups into each of 4 freezer containers. May be frozen for up to 3 months.

TO PREPARE SOUP *Thaw soup base in the refrigerator. Transfer to a saucepan. Add cream; cook and stir over medium heat until heated through. Garnish with Parmesan cheese and bacon if desired.*

Easy White Chicken Chili

Eating plenty of chili is one of the best cold-weather strategies. We use chicken and white beans for a twist on the regular bowl of red. It's soothing comfort food.

—**RACHEL LEWIS** DANVILLE, VA

START TO FINISH: 30 MIN.
MAKES: 6 SERVINGS

- 1 **pound lean ground chicken**
- 1 **medium onion, chopped**
- 2 **cans (15 ounces each) cannellini beans, rinsed and drained**
- 1 **can (4 ounces) chopped green chilies**
- 1 **teaspoon ground cumin**
- ½ **teaspoon dried oregano**
- ¼ **teaspoon pepper**
- 1 **can (14½ ounces) reduced-sodium chicken broth**
  Optional toppings: reduced-fat sour cream, shredded cheddar cheese and chopped fresh cilantro

1. In a large saucepan, cook the chicken and the onion over medium-high heat 6-8 minutes or until chicken is no longer pink, breaking up the chicken into crumbles.

2. Place one can of beans in a small bowl, mash slightly. Stir mashed beans, remaining can of beans, chilies, seasonings and broth into the chicken mixture; bring to a boil. Reduce heat; simmer, covered, 12-15 minutes or until the flavors are blended. Serve with toppings as desired.

FREEZE OPTION *Freeze cooled chili in freezer containers. To use, partially thaw chili in the refrigerator overnight. Heat through in a saucepan, stirring occasionally and adding a little broth if necessary.*

PER SERVING *1 cup (calculated without toppings) equals 228 cal., 5 g fat (1 g sat. fat), 54 mg chol., 504 mg sodium, 23 g carb., 6 g fiber, 22 g pro.* **Diabetic Exchanges:** *3 lean meat, 1½ starch.*

and adding a little broth or water if necessary.

PER SERVING *1 cup equals 180 cal., 4 g fat (1 g sat. fat), 4 mg chol., 443 mg sodium, 29 g carb., 7 g fiber, 8 g pro.* **Diabetic Exchanges:** *2 starch, 1 lean meat.*

EAT SMART
Easy Minestrone

This recipe is special because it's one of the few dinners my entire family loves. And I can feel good about serving it because it's full of nutrition and low in fat.

—LAUREN BRENNAN HOOD RIVER, OR

PREP: 25 MIN. • **COOK:** 40 MIN.
MAKES: 11 SERVINGS (2¾ QUARTS)

- 2 **large carrots, diced**
- 2 **celery ribs, chopped**
- 1 **medium onion, chopped**
- 1 **tablespoon olive oil**
- 1 **tablespoon butter**
- 2 **garlic cloves, minced**
- 2 **cans (14½ ounces each) reduced-sodium chicken broth**
- 2 **cans (8 ounces each) no-salt-added tomato sauce**
- 1 **can (16 ounces) kidney beans, rinsed and drained**
- 1 **can (15 ounces) garbanzo beans or chickpeas, rinsed and drained**
- 1 **can (14½ ounces) diced tomatoes, undrained**
- 1½ **cups shredded cabbage**
- 1 **tablespoon dried basil**
- 1½ **teaspoons dried parsley flakes**
- 1 **teaspoon dried oregano**
- ½ **teaspoon pepper**
- 1 **cup uncooked whole wheat elbow macaroni**
- 11 **teaspoons grated Parmesan cheese**

1. In a large saucepan, saute the carrots, celery and onion in oil and butter until tender. Add the garlic; cook 1 minute longer.
2. Stir in the broth, tomato sauce, beans, tomatoes, cabbage, herbs and pepper. Bring to a boil. Reduce heat; cover and simmer for 15 minutes.
3. Add macaroni; cook, uncovered, 6-8 minutes or until macaroni and vegetables are tender. Return soup to a boil. Stir in pasta; heat through. Ladle soup into bowls. Sprinkle with cheese.

FREEZE OPTION *Before adding cheese, freeze cooled soup in freezer containers. To use, partially thaw in refrigerator overnight. Heat through in a saucepan, stirring occasionally*

Freezer Vegetable Soup

When tomatoes and garden vegetables are plentiful, you can easily toss in more or double the recipe. If you want even heartier fare, add cooked ground beef, sausage or meatballs.

—ELIZABETH MOORE FRANKFORT, KY

PREP: 20 MIN. • **COOK:** 35 MIN.
MAKES: 2 BATCHES
(4 SERVINGS EACH)

SOUP BASE
- 4 **cups chopped tomatoes**
- 1 **cup each chopped celery, carrot and onion**
- 2 **teaspoons sugar**
- 1 **teaspoon salt, optional**
- ½ **teaspoon pepper**
- ½ **teaspoon dill weed**

ADDITIONAL INGREDIENTS (FOR EACH BATCH)
- 2 **cups diced potatoes**
- 2 **cups water**

In a Dutch oven, combine the soup base ingredients; bring to a boil over medium heat. Reduce the heat; cover and simmer for 45 minutes. Cool. Place 2 cups into each freezer container; freeze for up to 3 months.
TO PREPARE SOUP *Thaw soup base in refrigerator. Transfer to a Dutch oven. Add potatoes and water; simmer for 30-40 minutes or until tender.*

Tex-Mex Chili

Hearty and spicy, this is a stick-to-your-ribs chili for sure. You can also simmer it up on the stovetop—the longer you cook it, the better!

—ERIC HAYES ANTIOCH, CA

PREP: 20 MIN. • **COOK:** 6 HOURS
MAKES: 12 SERVINGS (1⅓ CUPS EACH)

- **3 pounds beef stew meat**
- **1 tablespoon canola oil**
- **3 garlic cloves, minced**
- **3 cans (16 ounces each) kidney beans, rinsed and drained**
- **3 cans (15 ounces each) tomato sauce**
- **1 can (14½ ounces) diced tomatoes, undrained**
- **1 cup water**
- **1 can (6 ounces) tomato paste**
- **¾ cup salsa verde**
- **1 envelope chili seasoning**
- **2 teaspoons dried minced onion**
- **1 teaspoon chili powder**
- **½ teaspoon crushed red pepper flakes**
- **½ teaspoon ground cumin**
- **½ teaspoon cayenne pepper**
  Shredded cheddar cheese and minced fresh cilantro

1. In a large skillet, brown beef in oil in batches. Add garlic; cook 1 minute longer. Transfer to a 6-qt. slow cooker.

2. Stir in beans, tomato sauce, tomatoes, water, tomato paste, salsa verde and the seasonings. Cover and cook chili on low for 6-8 hours or until meat is tender. Top each serving with cheese and cilantro.

FREEZE OPTION *Before adding toppings, cool chili. Freeze chili in freezer containers. To use, partially thaw in refrigerator overnight. Heat through in a saucepan, stirring occasionally and adding a little broth or water if necessary. Serve with toppings.*

LONE STAR
POT ROAST
PAGE 114

Beef Main Dishes

What makes a meaty, family-pleasing beef dinner even better? Popping one of these gems in the freezer to savor a satisfying meal down the road—with no work!

Hungarian Short Ribs

This is an all-time top meal in our house—as soon as I get ribs, I know which dish my family will ask me to make.

—JOANNE SHEWCHUK ST. BENEDICT, SK

PREP: 15 MIN. • **COOK:** 2½ HOURS
MAKES: 6-8 SERVINGS

- 2 to 3 tablespoons canola oil
- 4 pounds bone-in beef short ribs
- 2 medium onions, sliced
- 1 can (15 ounces) tomato sauce
- 1 cup water
- ¼ cup packed brown sugar
- ¼ cup vinegar
- 1½ teaspoons salt
- 1½ teaspoons ground mustard
- 1½ teaspoons Worcestershire sauce
- ¼ teaspoon paprika
  Cooked wide egg noodles

In a Dutch oven, heat oil over medium-high heat. Brown ribs on all sides. Add onions; cook until tender. Combine all remaining ingredients except noodles; pour over ribs. Reduce heat; cover and simmer for 2-2½ hours or until meat is tender. Thicken gravy if desired. Serve over noodles.

FREEZE OPTION *Freeze cooled rib mixture in freezer containers. To use, partially thaw in refrigerator overnight. Microwave, covered, on high in a microwave-safe dish until heated through, gently stirring and adding a little water if necessary. Serve with noodles.*

Baked Spaghetti

This satisfying pasta bake pleases young and old, company, family and friends! Add a tossed green salad and garlic breadsticks to round out the menu.

—**BETTY RABE** MAHTOMEDI, MN

PREP: 20 MIN.
BAKE: 30 MIN. + STANDING
MAKES: 6-8 SERVINGS

- 8 **ounces uncooked spaghetti, broken into thirds**
- 1 **large egg**
- ½ **cup milk**
- ½ **teaspoon salt**
- ½ **pound ground beef**
- ½ **pound bulk Italian sausage**
- 1 **small onion, chopped**
- ¼ **cup chopped green pepper**
- 1 **jar (14 ounces) meatless spaghetti sauce**
- 1 **can (8 ounces) tomato sauce**
- 1 **to 2 cups (4 to 8 ounces) shredded part-skim mozzarella cheese**

1. Preheat oven to 350°. Cook spaghetti according to package directions.

2. Meanwhile, in a large bowl, beat egg, milk and salt. Drain spaghetti; add to egg mixture and toss to coat. Transfer to a greased 13x9-in. baking dish.

3. In a large skillet, cook beef, sausage, onion and green pepper over medium heat until meat is no longer pink; drain. Stir in spaghetti sauce and tomato sauce. Spoon over the spaghetti mixture.

4. Bake, uncovered, 20 minutes. Sprinkle with the cheese. Bake 10 minutes longer or until cheese is melted. Let stand 10 minutes before cutting.

FREEZE OPTION *Cool spaghetti completely before tossing with egg mixture. Transfer to baking dish; cover and refrigerate. Meanwhile, prepare meat sauce and cool completely before spooning over spaghetti mixture. Cover and freeze unbaked casserole. To use, partially thaw in refrigerator overnight. Remove from refrigerator 30 minutes before baking. Preheat oven to 350°. Bake as directed, increasing time as necessary to heat through and for a thermometer inserted in center to read 165°.*

Lasagna Casserole

Growing up, this was the meal I always wanted on my birthday. My mother made the sauce from scratch, but I use store-bought spaghetti sauce to save time. Replace the ground beef with Italian sausage for more spice.

—**DEB MORRISON** SKIATOOK, OK

PREP: 25 MIN.
BAKE: 1 HOUR + STANDING
MAKES: 6-8 SERVINGS

- 1 **pound ground beef**
- ¼ **cup chopped onion**
- ½ **teaspoon salt**
- ½ **teaspoon pepper, divided**
- 1 **pound medium pasta shells, cooked and drained**
- 4 **cups (16 ounces) shredded part-skim mozzarella cheese, divided**
- 3 **cups (24 ounces) 4% cottage cheese**
- 2 **large eggs, lightly beaten**
- ⅓ **cup grated Parmesan cheese**
- 2 **tablespoons dried parsley flakes**
- 1 **jar (24 ounces) meatless pasta sauce**

1. In a large skillet, cook beef and onion over medium heat until meat is no longer pink; drain. Sprinkle with salt and ¼ teaspoon pepper; set aside.

2. In a large bowl, combine the pasta, 3 cups mozzarella cheese, cottage cheese, eggs, Parmesan cheese, parsley and remaining pepper. Transfer to a greased shallow 3-qt. baking dish. Top with beef mixture and spaghetti sauce (dish will be full).

3. Cover and bake at 350° for 45 minutes. Sprinkle with remaining mozzarella cheese. Bake, uncovered, 15 minutes longer or until bubbly and cheese is melted. Let stand for 10 minutes before serving.

FREEZE OPTION *Sprinkle casserole with remaining mozzarella cheese. Cover and freeze unbaked casserole. To use, partially thaw in refrigerator overnight. Remove from refrigerator 30 minutes before baking. Preheat oven to 350°. Bake casserole as directed, increasing time as necessary to heat through and for a thermometer inserted in center to read 165°.*

DID YOU KNOW?

You can substitute dried minced onion from the spice aisle for chopped onion in casseroles, soups, meat loaves and other cooked recipes. One tablespoon of dried minced onion equals ¼ cup of minced raw onion.

Sirloin in Wine Sauce

This recipe is a family favorite as well as a fabulously easy company dish. Sirloin in a hearty mushroom-wine sauce is fantastic over pasta.

—**BARBARA KAMM** WILMINGTON, DE

START TO FINISH: 30 MIN.
MAKES: 4 SERVINGS

- 2 tablespoons all-purpose flour
- ⅛ teaspoon ground mustard
- 1 pound beef top sirloin steak, thinly sliced
- 2 tablespoons butter
- 1 can (10½ ounces) condensed beef consomme, undiluted
- ½ cup dry red wine or beef broth
- 1 jar (4½ ounces) sliced mushrooms, drained
- ¼ cup chopped green onions
- 1 teaspoon Worcestershire sauce
  Hot cooked linguine

1. In a large resealable plastic bag, combine flour and mustard. Add beef, a few pieces at a time, and shake to coat.

2. In a large skillet, brown beef in butter. Add consomme and wine. Stir in the mushrooms, onions and Worcestershire sauce. Bring to a boil. Reduce heat; simmer, uncovered, for 10-15 minutes or until sauce is thickened. Serve with linguine.

FREEZE OPTION *Cool beef mixture. Freeze in freezer containers. To use, partially thaw in refrigerator overnight. Heat through slowly in a covered skillet, stirring occasionally and adding a little broth or water if necessary. Serve as directed.*

Mini Shepherd's Pies

I like serving these little freezer-friendly pies to company as well as to my husband and three boys.

—**ELLEN OSBORNE** CLARKSVILLE, TN

PREP: 30 MIN. • **BAKE:** 20 MIN.
MAKES: 5 SERVINGS

- 1 pound ground beef
- 3 tablespoons chopped onion
- ½ teaspoon minced garlic
- ⅓ cup chili sauce or ketchup
- 1 tablespoon cider vinegar
- ½ teaspoon salt
- 1¼ cups water
- 3 tablespoons butter
- 1¼ cups mashed potato flakes
- 3 ounces cream cheese, cubed
- 1 tube (12 ounces) refrigerated buttermilk biscuits
- ½ cup crushed potato chips
  Paprika, optional

1. In a large skillet, cook beef and onion over medium heat until meat is no longer pink. Add garlic and cook 1 minute longer; drain. Stir in chili sauce, vinegar and salt; set aside.

2. In a small saucepan, bring water and butter to a boil. Pour into a small bowl. Whisk in potato flakes until blended. Beat in cream cheese until smooth.

3. Press biscuit dough onto the bottoms and up the sides of 10 greased muffin cups. Fill with beef mixture and top with potatoes. Sprinkle with potato chips; press down lightly.

4. Bake at 375° for 20-25 minutes or until golden brown. Sprinkle with paprika if desired. Serve immediately, or cool before placing in a single layer in a freezer container. Cover and freeze for up to 2 months.

TO USE FROZEN PIES *Thaw in the refrigerator for 8 hours. Place on a greased baking sheet. Bake at 375° for 15-18 minutes or until heated through.*

Lone Star Pot Roast

Pot roast becomes especially delicious with the addition of chopped green chilies and taco seasoning.

—HELEN CARPENTER

ALBUQUERQUE, NM

PREP: 20 MIN. • **COOK:** 2 HOURS
MAKES: 6-8 SERVINGS

- 1 **boneless beef chuck roast (3 to 3½ pounds)**
- 2 **tablespoons canola oil**
- 1 **can (14½ ounces) diced tomatoes, undrained**
- 1 **can (4 ounces) chopped green chilies**
- 2 **tablespoons taco seasoning**
- 2 **teaspoons beef bouillon granules**
- 1 **teaspoon sugar**
- ¼ **cup cold water**
- 3 **tablespoons all-purpose flour**

1. In a Dutch oven, brown roast in oil. Combine tomatoes, chilies, taco seasoning, bouillon and sugar; pour over the roast. Cover and simmer 2 to 2½ hours or until meat is tender.
2. Remove roast to a platter and keep warm. For gravy, pour 2 cups pan juices into a saucepan. Combine cold water and flour; stir into pan juices over high heat until thickened and bubbly, about 3 minutes. Serve with roast.
FREEZE OPTION *Place sliced pot roast in freezer containers; top with gravy. Cool and freeze. To use, partially thaw mixture in the refrigerator overnight. Microwave, covered, on high in a microwave-safe dish until heated through, gently stirring and adding a little water if necessary.*

SLOW COOKER

Moroccan Braised Beef

Curry powder is a blend of up to 20 spices, herbs and seeds. Add a pinch of curry to your favorite soups, stews, salads or even rice for an exotic flavor. In this Moroccan stew, begin with 2 teaspoons curry, then add more to your taste.

—TASTE OF HOME TEST KITCHEN

PREP: 20 MIN. • **COOK:** 7 HOURS
MAKES: 6 SERVINGS

- ⅓ **cup all-purpose flour**
- 2 **pounds boneless beef chuck roast, cut into 1-inch cubes**
- 3 **tablespoons olive oil**
- 2 **cans (14½ ounces each) beef broth**
- 2 **cups chopped onions**
- 1 **can (14½ ounces) diced tomatoes, undrained**
- 1 **cup dry red wine**
- 1 **tablespoon curry powder**
- 1 **tablespoon paprika**
- 1 **teaspoon salt**
- 1 **teaspoon ground cumin**
- 1 **teaspoon ground coriander**
- ½ **teaspoon cayenne pepper**
- 1½ **cups golden raisins**
  Hot cooked couscous, optional

1. Place the flour in a large resealable plastic bag; add beef and toss to coat. In a large skillet, brown beef in oil. Transfer to a 5-qt. slow cooker. Stir in the broth, onions, tomatoes, wine and seasonings. Cover and cook on low for 7-8 hours or until the meat is tender.
2. During the last 30 minutes of cooking, stir in the raisins. Serve with couscous if desired.
FREEZE OPTION *Freeze cooled beef mixture in freezer containers. To use, partially thaw in refrigerator overnight. Heat through in a saucepan, stirring occasionally and adding a little broth if necessary. Serve as directed.*

Tasty Burritos

My cousin is of Mexican heritage, and I've watched her make these crunchy burritos for years. The very first time I made them for my own family, they became an instant favorite meal.

—DEBI LANE CHATTANOOGA, TN

START TO FINISH: 30 MIN.
MAKES: 6 SERVINGS

- 1 **pound ground beef**
- 1 **envelope taco seasoning**
- 1 **can (16 ounces) refried beans**
- 6 **flour tortillas (12 inches), warmed**
- 1 **cup (4 ounces) shredded Colby-Monterey Jack cheese**
- 4 **teaspoons canola oil**
  Sour cream and salsa

1. In a large skillet, cook beef over medium heat until no longer pink; drain. Stir in taco seasoning. In a small saucepan, cook refried beans over medium-low heat for 2-3 minutes or until heated through.

2. Spoon about ⅓ cup of beans off-center on each tortilla; top with ¼ cup beef mixture. Sprinkle with cheese. Fold sides and ends of tortillas over filling and roll up.

3. In a large skillet over medium-high heat, brown burritos in oil on all sides. Serve with sour cream and salsa.

FREEZE OPTION *Individually wrap cooled burritos in paper towels and foil; freeze in a resealable plastic freezer bag. To use, remove foil; place paper towel-wrapped burrito on a microwave-safe plate. Microwave on high 3-4 minutes or until heated through, turning once. Let stand 20 seconds.*

Thai Beef Stir-Fry

An easy peanut sauce is the signature complement to tender sirloin and loads of veggies in this Thai restaurant-inspired dish. I like to serve it over spaghetti, but you could also use fried noodles.

—**JANICE FEHR** AUSTIN, MB

PREP: 20 MIN. • **COOK:** 20 MIN.
MAKES: 6 SERVINGS

- ½ **cup packed brown sugar**
- 2 **tablespoons cornstarch**
- 2 **cups beef broth**
- ⅓ **cup reduced-sodium soy sauce**
- 1 **teaspoon onion powder**
- 1 **teaspoon garlic powder**
- 1 **teaspoon ground ginger**
- ¼ **teaspoon hot pepper sauce**
- 2 **pounds boneless beef sirloin steak, cut into thin strips**
- 6 **tablespoons olive oil, divided**
- 2 **cups fresh cauliflowerets**
- 1½ **cups julienned carrots**
- 4 **cups fresh broccoli florets**
- 2 **cups sliced fresh mushrooms**
- ¼ **cup peanut butter**
  Hot cooked spaghetti
- ½ **cup chopped peanuts**

1. In a small bowl, combine the first eight ingredients until smooth; set aside. In a large skillet or wok, stir-fry beef in 3 tablespoons oil until no longer pink. Remove and keep warm.

2. In the same skillet, stir-fry cauliflower and carrots in remaining oil for 5 minutes. Add broccoli; stir-fry for 7 minutes. Add the mushrooms and cook 6-8 minutes longer or until the vegetables are crisp-tender.

3. Stir broth mixture and add to the pan. Bring to a boil; cook and stir for 2 minutes or until thickened. Reduce heat; add beef and peanut butter. Cook and stir over medium heat until peanut butter is blended. Serve with spaghetti. Sprinkle with peanuts.

FREEZE OPTION *Do not cook spaghetti. Freeze cooled beef mixture in freezer containers. To use, partially thaw in refrigerator overnight. Cook spaghetti according to package directions. Place beef mixture in a large skillet; heat through, stirring occasionally and adding a little broth if necessary. Serve with spaghetti and sprinkle with peanuts.*

FREEZE IT

Do not cook spaghetti. Freeze meat sauce in freezer containers. To use, partially thaw in refrigerator overnight. Cook spaghetti according to package directions. Place sauce in a large skillet; heat through, stirring occasionally and adding a little water if necessary. Serve over spaghetti.

SLOW COOKER 🍲

Meat Sauce for Spaghetti

Here's a hearty meat sauce that turns ordinary spaghetti and garlic bread into a feast. When I'm in a hurry, I quickly simmer up this slow cooker recipe in an electric frying pan instead.

—**MARY TALLMAN** ARBOR VITAE, WI

PREP: 30 MIN. • **COOK:** 8 HOURS
MAKES: 9 SERVINGS

- 1 **pound ground beef**
- 1 **pound bulk Italian sausage**
- 1 **can (28 ounces) crushed tomatoes, undrained**
- 1 **medium green pepper, chopped**
- 1 **medium onion, chopped**
- 2 **medium carrots, finely chopped**
- 1 **cup water**
- 1 **can (8 ounces) tomato sauce**
- 1 **can (8 ounces) tomato paste**
- 1 **tablespoon brown sugar**
- 1 **tablespoon Italian seasoning**
- 2 **garlic cloves, minced**
- ½ **teaspoon salt**
- ¼ **teaspoon pepper**
  Hot cooked spaghetti

1. In a large skillet, cook beef and sausage over medium heat until no longer pink; drain.
2. Transfer to a 5-qt. slow cooker. Stir in the tomatoes, green pepper, onion, carrots, water, tomato sauce, tomato paste, brown sugar, Italian seasoning, garlic, salt and pepper. Cover and cook on low for 8-10 hours or until bubbly. Serve with spaghetti.

Sweet-and-Sour Meat Loaf

The sweet-and-sour flavors add a deliciously different twist to this longtime standby. I hardly ever make plain meat loaf anymore. You may not, either, once you've tasted this one.

—**DEBBIE HANEKE** STAFFORD, KS

PREP: 15 MIN. • **BAKE:** 1 HOUR
MAKES: 6 SERVINGS

- 1 **cup dry bread crumbs**
- 1 **teaspoon salt**
- ¼ **teaspoon pepper**
- 2 **large eggs**
- 1½ **pounds ground beef**
- 1 **teaspoon dried minced onion**
- 1 **can (15 ounces) tomato sauce, divided**
- ½ **cup sugar**
- 2 **tablespoons brown sugar**
- 2 **tablespoons cider vinegar**
- 2 **teaspoons prepared mustard**

1. In a large bowl, combine the bread crumbs, salt, pepper and eggs; crumble beef over top and mix well. Add onion and half of the tomato sauce. Press into a 9x5-in. loaf pan.

2. Bake at 350° for 50 minutes. In a saucepan, combine the sugars, vinegar, mustard and remaining tomato sauce; bring to a boil. Pour over meat loaf; bake 10 minutes longer.

FREEZE IT

Securely wrap and freeze cooled meat loaf in plastic wrap and foil. To use, partially thaw in refrigerator overnight. Unwrap meat loaf; reheat on a greased 15x10x1-in. baking pan in a preheated 350° oven until heated through and a thermometer in center reads 165°.

Spicy Bean and Beef Pie

My daughter helped me create this recipe one day when we wanted a one-dish meal. We loved the result.

—**DEBRA DOHY** NEWCOMERSTOWN, OH

PREP: 20 MIN. • **BAKE:** 30 MIN.
MAKES: 8 SERVINGS

- 1 pound ground beef
- 2 to 3 garlic cloves, minced
- 1 can (11½ ounces) condensed bean with bacon soup, undiluted
- 1 jar (16 ounces) thick and chunky picante sauce, divided
- ¼ cup cornstarch
- 1 tablespoon chopped fresh parsley
- 1 teaspoon paprika
- 1 teaspoon salt
- ¼ teaspoon pepper
- 1 can (16 ounces) kidney beans, rinsed and drained
- 1 can (15 ounces) black beans, rinsed and drained
- 2 cups (8 ounces) shredded cheddar cheese, divided
- ¾ cup sliced green onions, divided
    Pastry for double-crust pie (10 inches)
- 1 cup (8 ounces) sour cream
- 1 can (2¼ ounces) sliced ripe olives, drained

1. In a large skillet, cook beef over medium heat until beef is no longer pink. Add garlic; cook 1 minute longer. Drain.

2. In a large bowl, combine the soup, 1 cup of picante sauce, cornstarch, parsley, paprika, salt and pepper. Fold in the beans, 1½ cups of cheese, ½ cup onions and the beef mixture.

3. Line a 9-in. deep-dish pie plate with bottom pastry; fill with bean mixture. Top with remaining pastry; seal and flute edges. Cut slits in top crust.

4. Bake the pie at 425° for 30-35 minutes or until lightly browned. Let stand for 5 minutes before cutting. Garnish each serving with the sour cream, olives and remaining picante sauce, cheese and onions.

FREEZE OPTION *Cover and freeze unbaked pie. To use, remove from the freezer 30 minutes before baking. Cover edges of crust loosely with foil; place on a baking sheet. Bake at 425° for 30 minutes. Reduce heat to 350°; remove foil. Bake pie 55-60 minutes longer or until golden brown. Garnish each serving as directed.*

Pizza Meat Loaf Cups

Leftovers of these little pizza-flavored loaves are convenient to reheat as an after-school snack or quick dinner. We like to drizzle extra pizza sauce on top.

—**SUSAN WOLLIN** MARSHALL, WI

START TO FINISH: 30 MIN.
MAKES: 1 DOZEN

- 1 **large egg, lightly beaten**
- ½ **cup pizza sauce**
- ¼ **cup seasoned bread crumbs**
- ½ **teaspoon Italian seasoning**
- 1½ **pounds ground beef**
- 1½ **cups (6 ounces each) shredded part-skim mozzarella cheese**
  Additional pizza sauce, optional

1. In a large bowl, combine egg, pizza sauce, bread crumbs and Italian seasoning. Crumble beef over mixture and mix well. Divide among 12 greased muffin cups; press onto the bottom and up the sides. Fill centers with cheese.

2. Bake at 375° for 15-18 minutes or until meat is no longer pink. Serve meat loaves immediately with additional pizza sauce if desired. Or cool meat loaves, place in freezer bags and freeze for up to 3 months.

TO USE FROZEN PIZZA CUPS
Thaw in the refrigerator for 24 hours. Heat on a microwave-safe plate on high for 2-3 minutes or until heated through.

Chili Tortilla Bake

A homestyle Tex-Mex casserole is all it takes to gather the whole family around the dinner table. With its popular flavors and bubbly cheese topping, there is never a need to worry about leftovers.

—**CELINE WELDY** CAVE CREEK, AZ

PREP: 20 MIN. • **BAKE:** 25 MIN.
MAKES: 6 SERVINGS

- 1 **pound extra-lean ground beef (95% lean)**
- 2 **cans (8 ounces each) no-salt-added tomato sauce**
- 1 **can (15 ounces) black beans, rinsed and drained**
- 1 **cup frozen corn**
- 1 **can (4 ounces) chopped green chilies**
- 2 **tablespoons dried minced onion**
- 2 **tablespoons chili powder**
- 1 **teaspoon ground cumin**
- ½ **teaspoon garlic powder**
- ½ **teaspoon dried oregano**
- 6 **whole wheat tortillas (8 inches)**
- 1 **cup (4 ounces) shredded reduced-fat cheddar cheese**

1. In a large skillet, cook beef over medium heat until no longer pink. Stir in the tomato sauce, beans, corn, green chilies, onion, chili powder, cumin, garlic powder and oregano; heat through.

2. In an 11x7-in. baking dish coated with cooking spray, layer half of the tortillas, beef mixture and cheese. Repeat layers. Bake, uncovered, at 350° for 25-30 minutes or until bubbly.

FREEZE OPTION *Cool unbaked casserole; cover and freeze. To use, partially thaw in refrigerator overnight. Remove from refrigerator 30 minutes before baking. Preheat oven to 350°. Bake the casserole as directed, increasing time as necessary to heat through and for a thermometer inserted in center to read 165°.*

1. Bring broth and dried mushrooms to a boil in a large saucepan. Remove from heat; let stand 15-20 minutes or until mushrooms are softened. Drain mushrooms, reserving the liquid; finely chop the mushrooms and set aside.

2. Combine flour, salt and pepper in a large resealable plastic bag; set aside 1 tablespoon for sauce. Add beef, a few pieces at a time, to the remaining flour mixture and shake to coat.

3. Brown beef in oil in batches in a Dutch oven. Add portobello mushrooms, carrots and onion; saute until onion is tender. Add garlic, rosemary and rehydrated mushrooms; cook 1 minute. Stir in the reserved flour mixture until blended; gradually add to the mushroom broth.

4. Bring to a boil. Reduce heat; cover and simmer 1½-2 hours or until beef is tender. Combine the cornstarch and cold water until smooth; gradually stir into pan. Bring to a boil; cook and stir for 2 minutes or until thickened. Serve the stew with egg noodles if desired; top each serving with blue cheese.

FREEZE OPTION *Freeze cooled stew in freezer containers up to 6 months. To use, thaw in the refrigerator overnight. Place in a Dutch oven; reheat. Serve with egg noodles if desired; top with blue cheese.*

Mushroom Beef

Top this hearty stew with crumbled blue cheese just before serving to add a burst of flavor. Serve some now and store the rest in the freezer for another meal.

—**NANCY LATULIPPE** SIMCOE, ON

PREP: 35 MIN. • **COOK:** 2 HOURS
MAKES: 9 SERVINGS

- 1 **carton (32 ounces) beef broth**
- 1 **ounce dried mixed mushrooms**
- ¼ **cup all-purpose flour**
- 1 **teaspoon salt**
- 1 **teaspoon pepper**
- 1 **boneless beef chuck roast (2 pounds), cubed**
- 3 **tablespoons canola oil**
- 1 **pound sliced baby portobello mushrooms**
- 5 **medium carrots, chopped**
- 1 **large onion, chopped**
- 3 **garlic cloves, minced**
- 3 **teaspoons minced fresh rosemary or 1 teaspoon dried rosemary, crushed**
- 2 **tablespoons cornstarch**
- 2 **tablespoons cold water**
  Hot cooked egg noodles, optional
- ¼ **cup crumbled blue cheese**

Jamaican-Style Beef Stew

This delicious stew makes a hearty supper with a lighter touch. It's so flavorful, you won't want to stop at just one bowlful!

—JAMES HAYES RIDGECREST, CA

PREP: 25 MIN. • **COOK:** 1¼ HOURS
MAKES: 5 SERVINGS

- 1 tablespoon canola oil
- 1 tablespoon sugar
- 1½ pounds beef top sirloin steak, cut into ¾-inch cubes
- 5 plum tomatoes, finely chopped
- 3 large carrots, cut into ½-inch slices
- 3 celery ribs, cut into ½-inch slices
- 4 green onions, chopped
- ¾ cup reduced-sodium beef broth
- ¼ cup barbecue sauce
- ¼ cup reduced-sodium soy sauce
- 2 tablespoons steak sauce
- 1 tablespoon garlic powder
- 1 teaspoon dried thyme
- ¼ teaspoon ground allspice
- ¼ teaspoon pepper
- ⅛ teaspoon hot pepper sauce
- 1 tablespoon cornstarch
- 2 tablespoons cold water
  Hot cooked rice or mashed potatoes, optional

1. In a Dutch oven, heat oil over medium-high heat. Add sugar; cook and stir for 1 minute or until lightly browned. Add beef and brown on all sides.

2. Stir in the vegetables, broth, barbecue sauce, soy sauce, steak sauce and seasonings. Bring to a boil. Reduce heat; cover and simmer for 1 to 1¼ hours or until meat and vegetables are tender.

3. Combine cornstarch and water until smooth; stir into stew. Bring to a boil; cook and stir for 2 minutes or until thickened. Serve with rice or potatoes if desired.

FREEZE OPTION *Freeze cooled stew in freezer containers. To use, partially thaw in refrigerator overnight. Heat through in a saucepan, stirring occasionally and adding a little water if necessary.*

SLOW COOKER

Machaca Beef Dip Sandwiches

The combination of beef, cumin and chili powder, plus the heat of chipotle peppers, makes these sandwiches great game-day food.

—KAROL EZELL NACOGDOCHES, TX

PREP: 20 MIN. • **COOK:** 8 HOURS
MAKES: 6 SERVINGS

- 1 boneless beef chuck roast (2 to 3 pounds)
- 1 large sweet onion, thinly sliced
- 1 can (14½ ounces) reduced-sodium beef broth
- ½ cup water
- 3 chipotle peppers in adobo sauce, chopped
- 1 tablespoon adobo sauce
- 1 envelope au jus gravy mix
- 1 tablespoon Creole seasoning
- 1 tablespoon chili powder
- 2 teaspoons ground cumin
- 6 French rolls, split
  Guacamole and salsa, optional

1. Place roast in a 3- to 4-qt. slow cooker; top with onion. Combine the broth, water, chipotle peppers, adobo sauce, gravy mix, Creole seasoning, chili powder and cumin; pour over meat. Cover and cook on low for 8-10 hours or until meat is tender.

2. Remove roast; cool slightly. Skim fat from cooking juices. Shred beef with two forks and return to slow cooker; heat through. Using a slotted spoon, place meat on rolls. Serve with guacamole or salsa if desired and the cooking juices.

FREEZE OPTION *Freeze individual portions of cooled meat mixture and juices in freezer containers. To use, partially thaw in refrigerator overnight. Heat through in a saucepan, stirring occasionally. Serve on rolls with guacamole and salsa if desired.*

NOTE *Wear disposable gloves when cutting hot peppers; the oils can burn skin. Avoid touching your face. If desired, you may substitute the following spices for 1 tablespoon of Creole seasoning: ¾ teaspoon each of salt, garlic powder and paprika; and a pinch each of dried thyme, ground cumin and cayenne pepper.*

Potluck Taco Casserole

This is the dish I take most often to potlucks, and the pan comes home empty every time.

—**KIM STOLLER** SMITHVILLE, OH

PREP: 25 MIN. • **BAKE:** 20 MIN.
MAKES: 8 SERVINGS

- 2 **pounds ground beef**
- 2 **envelopes taco seasoning**
- 4 **large eggs**
- ¾ **cup 2% milk**
- 1¼ **cups biscuit/baking mix**
  Dash pepper
- ½ **cup sour cream**
- 2 **to 3 cups chopped lettuce**
- ¾ **cup chopped tomato**
- ¼ **cup chopped green pepper**
- 2 **green onions, chopped**
- 2 **cups (8 ounces) shredded cheddar cheese**

1. Preheat oven to 400°. In a large skillet, cook beef over medium heat 10-12 minutes or until no longer pink, breaking into crumbles; drain. Add taco seasoning and prepare according to package directions. Spoon meat into a greased 13x9-in. baking dish.

2. In a large bowl, beat eggs and milk. Stir in biscuit mix and pepper. Pour over meat. Bake, uncovered, 20-25 minutes or until golden brown. Cool casserole for 5-10 minutes.

3. Spread sour cream over top; sprinkle with the lettuce, tomato, green pepper, onions and cheese.

FREEZE IT

Cool baked casserole; cover and freeze. To use, partially thaw in refrigerator overnight. Remove from refrigerator 30 minutes before baking. Preheat oven to 350°. Unwrap casserole; reheat on a lower oven rack until heated through and a thermometer inserted in center reads 165°. Cool for 5-10 minutes, then top as directed.

Creamy Onion Lasagna

Enjoy a classic dish with a simple and delicious twist! French onion dip adds creamy richness to this surprisingly easy lasagna. Make two and freeze one for later.

—ANN SCHROEDER PEOSTA, IA

PREP: 25 MIN.
BAKE: 55 MIN. + STANDING
MAKES: 12 SERVINGS

- 1 **pound ground beef**
- 1 **jar (24 ounces) roasted garlic Parmesan spaghetti sauce**
- 1 **large egg**
- 1 **cup (8 ounces) 4% cottage cheese**
- 1 **carton (8 ounces) French onion dip**
- 1 **jar (23½ ounces) Italian sausage and garlic spaghetti sauce**
- 12 **no-cook lasagna noodles**
- 3 **cups (12 ounces) shredded part-skim mozzarella cheese**

1. Preheat oven to 375°. In a Dutch oven, cook beef over medium heat until no longer pink; drain. Stir in roasted garlic Parmesan spaghetti sauce. Combine egg, cottage cheese and onion dip.

2. Spread 1 cup Italian sausage and garlic spaghetti sauce in a greased 13x9-in. baking dish. Top with four noodles. Layer with half of cottage cheese mixture, half of beef mixture and 1 cup mozzarella. Repeat layers. Top with remaining noodles, sauce and mozzarella cheese.

3. Cover and bake 50 minutes. Uncover; bake 5-10 minutes or until cheese is melted. Let stand for 15 minutes before cutting.

FREEZE OPTION *Cool unbaked lasagna; cover and freeze. To use, partially thaw in refrigerator overnight. Remove from refrigerator 30 minutes before cooking. Bake as directed, increasing time as necessary to heat through and for a thermometer inserted in center to read 165°.*

Cheeseburger Cups

A terrific recipe for moms with young kids and busy lives, this simple, inexpensive dish is made with handy ingredients and takes just a short time. Best of all, kids will go absolutely crazy for these darling dinner bites!

—JERI MILLHOUSE ASHLAND, OH

START TO FINISH: 30 MIN.
MAKES: 5 SERVINGS

- 1 **pound ground beef**
- ½ **cup ketchup**
- 2 **tablespoons brown sugar**
- 1 **tablespoon prepared mustard**
- 1½ **teaspoons Worcestershire sauce**
- 1 **tube (12 ounces) refrigerated buttermilk biscuits**
- ½ **cup cubed process cheese (Velveeta)**

1. In a large skillet, cook beef over medium heat until no longer pink; drain. Stir in the ketchup, brown sugar, mustard and Worcestershire sauce. Remove from the heat; set aside.

2. Press biscuits onto the bottom and up the sides of 10 greased muffin cups. Spoon beef mixture into cups; top with cheese cubes. Bake at 400° for 14-16 minutes or until golden brown.

FREEZE OPTION *Freeze cooled pastries in a freezer container, separating layers with waxed paper. To use, thaw in the refrigerator for 8 hours. Reheat on a baking sheet in a preheated 375° oven until heated through.*

Beef & Mushroom Braised Stew

Every spring, my family heads to our timber acreage to collect morel mushrooms, and then I cook up this stew with the results. Button mushrooms or baby portobellos will work, too.

—AMY WERTHEIM ATLANTA, IL

PREP: 35 MIN. • **BAKE:** 1½ HOURS
MAKES: 6 SERVINGS

- 1 **boneless beef chuck roast (2 to 3 pounds), cut into 1-inch cubes**
- ¼ **teaspoon salt**
- ¼ **teaspoon pepper**
- 3 **tablespoons olive oil**
- 1 **pound sliced fresh mushrooms**
- 2 **medium onions, sliced**
- 2 **garlic cloves, minced**
- 1 **carton (32 ounces) beef broth**
- 1 **cup dry red wine**
- ½ **cup brandy**
- 1 **tablespoon tomato paste**
- ¼ **teaspoon each dried parsley flakes, rosemary, sage leaves, tarragon and thyme**
- 3 **tablespoons all-purpose flour**
- 3 **tablespoons water**
  Hot mashed potatoes

1. Preheat oven to 325°. Sprinkle beef with salt and pepper. In an ovenproof Dutch oven, heat oil over medium heat; brown beef in batches. Remove from pan.

2. Add mushrooms and onions to pan; cook and stir until tender. Add garlic; cook 1 minute longer. Stir in broth, wine, brandy, tomato paste and herbs. Return beef to pan. Bring to a boil.

3. Bake, covered, 1 hour. In a small bowl, mix flour and water until smooth; gradually stir into stew. Bake, covered, 30 minutes longer or until stew is thickened and beef is tender. Skim fat. Serve stew with potatoes.

FREEZE OPTION *Freeze cooled stew in freezer containers. To use, partially thaw in refrigerator overnight. Heat through in a saucepan, stirring occasionally and adding a little broth or water if necessary.*

Stroganoff Sandwiches

This recipe is ideal for a game day, either at a tailgate party or at home. I often make the meat mixture ahead of time and add the sour cream just before serving.

—**SUSAN GRAHAM** CHEROKEE, IA

PREP: 10 MIN. • **COOK:** 30 MIN.
MAKES: 8 SERVINGS

- 1½ **pounds ground beef**
- 1 **medium onion, chopped**
- ½ **cup sliced fresh mushrooms**
- 6 **to 8 bacon strips, cooked and crumbled**
- 2 **garlic cloves, minced**
- 2 **tablespoons all-purpose flour**
- ½ **teaspoon salt**
- ½ **teaspoon paprika**
- ⅛ **teaspoon ground nutmeg**
- 1 **can (10¾ ounces) condensed cream of mushroom soup, undiluted**
- 1 **cup (8 ounces) sour cream**
- 8 **hamburger buns, split**

1. In a large skillet, cook beef, onion and mushrooms over medium heat until meat is no longer pink; drain. Add bacon and garlic. Combine the flour, salt, paprika and nutmeg; gradually stir into beef mixture until blended.

2. Stir in soup (mixture will be thick) and heat through. Add sour cream. Cook 3-4 minutes longer or until heated through, stirring occasionally (do not boil). Serve on buns.

FREEZE IT

Freeze cooled meat mixture in freezer containers. To use, partially thaw in refrigerator overnight. Heat through in a saucepan, stirring occasionally and adding a little water if necessary. Serve on buns.

Italian Stuffed Shells

A friend brought me this casserole when I was recovering from an accident. Now I share it with friends and take it to parties. The cheesy stuffed shells are such a nice change of pace from the usual lasagna or spaghetti dish.

—**BEVERLY AUSTIN** FULTON, MO

PREP: 50 MIN. • **BAKE:** 35 MIN.
MAKES: 6-8 SERVINGS

- 1 **pound ground beef**
- 1 **cup chopped onion**
- 1 **garlic clove, minced**
- 2 **cups hot water**
- 1 **can (12 ounces) tomato paste**
- 1 **tablespoon beef bouillon granules**
- 1½ **teaspoons dried oregano**
- 1 **large egg, lightly beaten**
- 2 **cups (16 ounces) 4% cottage cheese**
- 2 **cups (8 ounces) shredded part-skim mozzarella cheese, divided**
- ½ **cup grated Parmesan cheese**
- 24 **jumbo shell noodles, cooked and drained**

1. In a large skillet, cook beef, onion and garlic over medium heat until meat is no longer pink; drain. Stir in the water, tomato paste, bouillon and oregano; simmer, uncovered, for 30 minutes.

2. Meanwhile, in a large bowl, combine the egg, cottage cheese, 1 cup mozzarella and Parmesan cheese. Stuff shells with cheese mixture.

3. Arrange in a greased 3-qt. baking dish. Pour meat sauce over shells. Cover and bake at 350° for 30 minutes. Uncover; sprinkle with the remaining mozzarella cheese. Bake 5 minutes longer or until cheese is melted.

FREEZE OPTION *After assembling, sprinkle casserole with remaining mozzarella cheese. Cover and freeze unbaked casserole. To use, partially thaw in refrigerator overnight. Remove from refrigerator 30 minutes before baking. Preheat oven to 350°. Bake casserole as directed, increasing time as necessary to heat through and for a thermometer inserted in center to read 165°.*

Southwestern Spaghetti Casserole

A close friend made this Mexican-Italian bake for me almost 20 years ago, and I've prepared it regularly ever since. It comes together in a snap with items I keep on hand.

—ROSE TURNER MINNICK
CHRISTIANSBURG, VA

PREP: 15 MIN. • **BAKE:** 25 MIN.
MAKES: 8 SERVINGS

- 12 **ounces uncooked spaghetti**
- 1½ **pounds ground beef**
- 1 **small onion, chopped**
- 1 **envelope taco seasoning**
- 1 **jar (26 ounces) spaghetti sauce**
- 1 **jar (4½ ounces) sliced mushrooms, drained**
- 1 **can (2¼ ounces) sliced ripe olives, drained**
- 2 **cups (8 ounces) shredded cheddar cheese**
  Shredded lettuce, diced tomatoes, sour cream, salsa and picante sauce

1. Cook spaghetti according to package directions. Meanwhile, in a large skillet, cook beef and onion over medium heat until meat is no longer pink; drain.
2. Stir in the taco seasoning, spaghetti sauce, mushrooms and olives. Drain spaghetti; stir into the beef mixture. Transfer to a greased shallow 3-qt. baking dish; sprinkle with cheese.
3. Bake, uncovered, at 350° for 25-30 minutes or until heated through. Serve with lettuce, tomatoes, sour cream, salsa and picante sauce.
FREEZE OPTION *Cool unbaked casserole; cover and freeze. To use, partially thaw in the refrigerator overnight. Remove from refrigerator 30 minutes before baking. Bake casserole as directed, increasing time as necessary to heat through and for a thermometer inserted in center to read 165°. Serve with lettuce, tomatoes, sour cream, salsa and picante sauce.*

⑤INGREDIENTS
Taco Puffs

I got this recipe from a friend years ago and still make these cheesy sandwiches regularly. I serve them for dinner along with a steaming bowl of soup or fresh green salad. Any leftovers taste even better the next day for lunch.

—JAN SCHMID HIBBING, MN

START TO FINISH: 30 MIN.
MAKES: 8 SERVINGS

- 1 **pound ground beef**
- ½ **cup chopped onion**
- 1 **envelope taco seasoning**
- 2 **tubes (16.3 ounces each) large refrigerated flaky biscuits**
- 2 **cups (8 ounces) shredded cheddar cheese**

1. In a large skillet, cook beef and onion over medium heat until meat is no longer pink; drain. Add the taco seasoning and prepare according to package directions. Cool slightly.
2. Flatten half of the biscuits into 4-in. circles; place in greased 15x10x1-in. baking pans. Spoon ¼ cup meat mixture onto each; sprinkle with ¼ cup shredded cheese. Flatten the remaining biscuits; place on top and pinch edges to seal tightly. Bake at 400° for 15 minutes or until golden brown.
FREEZE OPTION *Freeze cooled pastries in a resealable plastic freezer bag. To use, microwave pastry on high on a microwave-safe plate until heated through.*

West Coast Snappy Joes

Meet my California-inspired sloppy joe. Load it up with whatever taco toppings you like. The meat filing is also incredible served over mac and cheese.

—**DEVON DELANEY** WESTPORT, CT

START TO FINISH: 30 MIN.
MAKES: 6 SERVINGS

- 1 **pound lean ground beef (90% lean)**
- 1 **medium onion, chopped**
- 1 **garlic clove, minced**
- 1 **can (8 ounces) tomato sauce**
- ⅓ **cup soft sun-dried tomato halves (not packed in oil), chopped**
- ⅓ **cup chopped roasted sweet red peppers**
- 2 **tablespoons chopped pickled jalapeno peppers**
- 2 **tablespoons tomato paste**
- 1 **tablespoon brown sugar**
- 1 **tablespoon balsamic vinegar**
- ½ **teaspoon Montreal steak seasoning**
- ½ **teaspoon pepper**
- 6 **hamburger buns, split**
  Optional toppings: chopped avocado, sour cream, shredded cheddar cheese and chopped green onions

1. In a large skillet, cook beef, onion and garlic over medium heat 6-8 minutes or until beef is no longer pink, breaking up beef into crumbles; drain.

2. Stir in tomato sauce, sun-dried tomatoes, roasted peppers, jalapenos, tomato paste, brown sugar, vinegar, steak seasoning and pepper. Bring to a boil. Reduce heat; simmer, uncovered, 4-6 minutes or until thickened, stirring occasionally. Serve on buns with toppings as desired.

FREEZE OPTION *Freeze cooled meat mixture in freezer containers. To use, partially thaw in refrigerator overnight. Heat through in a saucepan, stirring occasionally and adding a little water if necessary.*

NOTE *This recipe was tested with sun-dried tomatoes that are ready to use without soaking. When using other sun-dried tomatoes that are not oil-packed cover with boiling water and let stand until soft. Drain before using.*

PER SERVING *1 sandwich (calculated without optional toppings) equals 288 cal., 8 g fat (3 g sat. fat), 47 mg chol., 575 mg sodium, 32 g carb., 3 g fiber, 20 g pro.* **Diabetic Exchanges:** *3 starch, 3 lean meat.*

Zucchini Pizza Casserole

My husband has a hearty appetite, our two kids never tire of pizza, and I grow lots of zucchini. So this tasty casserole is absolutely tops with us. Once you've tried the recipe, you may even decide to grow more zucchini!

—LYNN BERNSTETTER

WHITE BEAR LAKE, MN

PREP: 20 MIN. • **BAKE:** 40 MIN.
MAKES: 6-8 SERVINGS

- 4 **cups shredded unpeeled zucchini**
- ½ **teaspoon salt**
- 2 **large eggs**
- ½ **cup grated Parmesan cheese**
- 2 **cups (8 ounces) shredded part-skim mozzarella cheese, divided**
- 1 **cup (4 ounces) shredded cheddar cheese, divided**
- 1 **pound ground beef**
- ½ **cup chopped onion**
- 1 **can (15 ounces) Italian tomato sauce**
- 1 **medium green pepper, chopped**

1. Place zucchini in strainer; toss with salt. Let stand 10 minutes. Squeeze out moisture.

2. Combine zucchini with the eggs, Parmesan and half of the mozzarella and cheddar cheeses. Press into a greased 13x9-in. baking dish.

3. Bake, uncovered, at 400° for 20 minutes. Meanwhile, cook beef and onion over medium heat until meat is no longer pink; drain. Add tomato sauce; spoon over zucchini mixture.

4. Sprinkle with remaining cheeses; add green pepper. Bake 20 minutes longer or until heated through.

FREEZE OPTION *Cool baked casserole; cover and freeze. To use, partially thaw in refrigerator overnight. Remove from refrigerator 30 minutes before baking. Preheat oven to 350°. Unwrap casserole; reheat on a lower oven rack until heated through and a thermometer inserted in center reads 165°.*

FREEZE IT

Cool unbaked casserole; cover and freeze for up to 3 months. Thaw in the refrigerator overnight. Remove from refrigerator 30 minutes before baking. Bake according to directions.

Pepperoni Mac 'n' Cheese

This cheesy, meaty meal is easy to make and can be prepared ahead of time. I decreased the recipe size so we can enjoy it more often.

—**BARBARA WALKER** BROOKVILLE, KS

PREP: 20 MIN. • **BAKE:** 20 MIN.
MAKES: 4 SERVINGS

- 1 **cup uncooked elbow macaroni**
- ½ **pound lean ground beef (90% lean)**
- 6 **small fresh mushrooms, halved**
- ⅓ **cup chopped onion**
- 1 **can (8 ounces) tomato sauce**
- 1 **package (3½ ounces) sliced pepperoni**
- 2 **tablespoons sliced ripe olives**
- 1 **teaspoon sugar**
- ¾ **teaspoon Italian seasoning**
- ¼ **teaspoon pepper**
- ¼ **cup shredded cheddar cheese**
- ¼ **cup shredded part-skim mozzarella cheese**

1. Cook macaroni according to package directions. Meanwhile, in a large skillet, cook the beef, mushrooms and onion over medium heat until meat is no longer pink; drain. Stir in tomato sauce, pepperoni, olives, sugar, Italian seasoning and pepper.
2. Drain macaroni; add to meat mixture. Transfer to a 1½-qt. baking dish coated with cooking spray. Sprinkle with cheeses.
3. Bake casserole, uncovered, at 350° for 20-25 minutes or until heated through.

Bavarian Pot Roast

Since all of my grandparents were German, it's no wonder that so many Bavarian recipes have been handed down to me over the years. The Midwest has a large German population, so I feel this recipe represents the area well.

—**SUSAN ROBERTSON**

HAMILTON, OH

PREP: 15 MIN. • **COOK:** 2¾ HOURS
MAKES: 8-10 SERVINGS

- 1 **boneless beef chuck pot roast (about 3 pounds)**
- 2 **tablespoons canola oil**
- 1¼ **cups water**
- ¾ **cup beer or beef broth**
- 1 **can (8 ounces) tomato sauce**
- ½ **cup chopped onion**
- 2 **tablespoons sugar**
- 1 **tablespoon vinegar**
- 2 **teaspoons salt**
- 1 **teaspoon ground cinnamon**
- 1 **bay leaf**
- ½ **teaspoon pepper**
- ½ **teaspoon ground ginger**
  Cornstarch and water, optional

1. In a Dutch oven, brown roast in hot oil. Combine water, beer, tomato sauce, onion, sugar, vinegar, salt, cinnamon, bay leaf, pepper and ginger. Pour over meat and bring to a boil. Reduce heat; cover and simmer until the meat is tender, about 2½-3 hours.

2. Remove meat. Discard bay leaf. If desired, thicken juices with cornstarch and water.

FREEZE IT

Place sliced pot roast in freezer containers; top with cooking juices. Cool and freeze. To use, partially thaw in refrigerator overnight. Microwave, covered, on high in a microwave-safe dish until heated through, gently stirring and adding a little broth to pot roast if necessary.

Mozzarella-Stuffed Meatballs

It's fun to watch my friends eat these for the first time. They're delighted to find melted cheese in the centers!

—MICHAELA ROSENTHAL INDIO, CA

PREP: 20 MIN. • **COOK:** 15 MIN.
MAKES: 6 SERVINGS

- 1 **large egg, lightly beaten**
- ¼ **cup Italian salad dressing**
- 1½ **cups cubed bread**
- 2 **tablespoons minced fresh parsley**
- 2 **garlic cloves, minced**
- ½ **teaspoon dried oregano**
- ½ **teaspoon pepper**
- ¼ **teaspoon salt**
- ½ **pound ground pork**
- ½ **pound ground sirloin**
- 3 **ounces fresh mozzarella cheese**
- 2 **tablespoons canola oil**
- 1 **jar (26 ounces) marinara sauce**

1. In a large bowl, combine the first eight ingredients. Crumble pork and beef over mixture; mix well. Cut mozzarella into eighteen ½-in. cubes. Divide meat mixture into 18 portions; shape around cheese cubes.

2. In a large skillet, cook meatballs in oil in batches until no longer pink; drain. In a large saucepan, heat marinara sauce; add meatballs and heat through.

FREEZE OPTION *Freeze cooled meatball mixture in freezer containers. To use, partially thaw in refrigerator overnight. Heat through in a covered saucepan, gently stirring and adding a little water if necessary.*

Meaty Manicotti

This sausage and beef manicotti has been popular at potlucks. You can assemble it ahead of time.

—LORI THOMPSON NEW LONDON, TX

PREP: 20 MIN.+ COOLING
BAKE: 45 MIN.
MAKES: 7 SERVINGS

- 14 **uncooked manicotti shells**
- 1 **pound ground beef**
- ¾ **pound bulk Italian sausage**
- 2 **garlic cloves, minced**
- 2 **cups (8 ounces) shredded part-skim mozzarella cheese**
- 1 **package (3 ounces) cream cheese, cubed**
- ¼ **teaspoon salt**
- 4 **cups meatless spaghetti sauce, divided**
- ¼ **cup grated Parmesan cheese**

1. Cook manicotti shells according to package directions. Meanwhile, in a large skillet, cook the beef and sausage over medium heat until meat is no longer pink. Add garlic; cook 1 minute longer. Drain. Remove from heat. Cool for 10 minutes.

2. Drain shells and rinse in cold water. Stir the mozzarella cheese, cream cheese and salt into meat mixture. Spread 2 cups spaghetti sauce in a greased 13x9-in. baking dish.

3. Stuff each shell with about ¼ cup meat mixture; arrange over sauce. Pour remaining sauce over top. Sprinkle with Parmesan cheese.

4. Cover and bake at 350° for 40 minutes. Uncover; bake for 5-10 minutes longer or until bubbly and heated through.

FREEZE OPTION *Cover and freeze unbaked casserole. To use, partially thaw in refrigerator overnight. Remove from refrigerator 30 minutes before baking. Bake casserole as directed, increasing time as necessary to heat through and for a thermometer inserted in center to read 165°.*

Pizza Noodle Bake

Here's a family-pleasing casserole that comes together in a snap. It's perfect for a weeknight meal. I like to double the recipe and freeze one.
—**BERNICE KNUTSON** SOLDIER, IA

PREP: 25 MIN. • **BAKE:** 15 MIN.
MAKES: 6 SERVINGS

- 10 ounces uncooked egg noodles
- 1½ pounds ground beef
- ½ cup finely chopped onion
- ¼ cup chopped green pepper
- 1 jar (14 ounces) pizza sauce
- 1 can (4 ounces) mushroom stems and pieces, drained
- 1 cup (4 ounces) shredded cheddar cheese
- 1 cup (4 ounces) shredded part-skim mozzarella cheese
- 1 package (3½ ounces) sliced pepperoni

1. Cook noodles according to package directions. Meanwhile, in a large skillet, cook beef, onion and green pepper over medium heat until meat is no longer pink; drain. Add pizza sauce and mushrooms; heat through.

2. Drain noodles. In a greased 13x9-in. baking dish, layer half of the noodles, beef mixture, cheeses and pepperoni. Repeat layers. Cover and bake at 350° for 15-20 minutes or until heated through.

FREEZE OPTION *Cover and freeze unbaked casserole for up to 3 months. Remove from freezer 30 minutes before baking (do not thaw). Cover and bake at 350° for 45-50 minutes. Uncover; bake 15-20 minutes longer or until heated through.*

Skillet Shepherd's Pie

This is the best shepherd's pie I've ever tasted. It's quick to make, and I usually have most of the ingredients on hand.
—**TIRZAH SANDT** SAN DIEGO, CA

START TO FINISH: 30 MIN.
MAKES: 6 SERVINGS

- 1 pound ground beef
- 1 cup chopped onion
- 2 cups frozen corn, thawed
- 2 cups frozen peas, thawed
- 2 tablespoons ketchup
- 1 tablespoon Worcestershire sauce
- 2 teaspoons minced garlic
- 1 tablespoon cornstarch
- 1 teaspoon beef bouillon granules
- ½ cup cold water
- ½ cup sour cream
- 3½ cups mashed potatoes (prepared with milk and butter)
- ¾ cup shredded cheddar cheese

1. In a large skillet, cook beef and onion over medium heat until meat is no longer pink; drain. Stir in the corn, peas, ketchup, Worcestershire sauce and garlic. Reduce heat; cover and cook for 5 minutes.

2. Combine the cornstarch, bouillon and water until well blended; stir into beef mixture. Bring to a boil; cook and stir for 2 minutes or until thickened. Stir in sour cream and heat through (do not boil).

3. Spread mashed potatoes over the top; sprinkle with cheese. Cover and cook until potatoes are heated through and cheese is melted.

FREEZE OPTION *Prepare beef mixture as directed but do not add sour cream. Freeze cooled meat mixture in a freezer container. To use, partially thaw in refrigerator overnight. Heat through in a large skillet, stirring occasionally and adding a little water if necessary. Stir in sour cream and proceed as directed.*

Taco Stuffed Pasta Shells

Here's a kid-friendly dish so flavorful and fun, no one will guess that it uses low-fat ingredients. This makes an ideal weeknight supper.

—ANNE THOMSEN WESTCHESTER, OH

PREP: 25 MIN. • **BAKE:** 25 MIN.
MAKES: 6 SERVINGS

- 18 uncooked jumbo pasta shells
- 1½ pounds lean ground beef (90% lean)
- 1 bottle (16 ounces) taco sauce, divided
- 3 ounces fat-free cream cheese, cubed
- 2 teaspoons chili powder
- ¾ cup shredded reduced-fat Mexican cheese blend, divided
- 20 baked tortilla chip scoops, coarsely crushed

1. Cook pasta according to package directions. Meanwhile, in a large nonstick skillet over medium heat, cook beef until no longer pink; drain. Add ½ cup taco sauce, cream cheese and chili powder; cook and stir until blended. Stir in ¼ cup cheese blend.

2. Drain pasta and rinse in cold water; stuff each shell with about 2 tablespoons beef mixture. Arrange in an 11x7-in. baking dish coated with cooking spray. Spoon remaining taco sauce over the top.

3. Cover and bake at 350° for 20 minutes. Sprinkle with remaining cheese blend. Bake, uncovered, 5-10 minutes or until heated through and cheese is melted. Sprinkle with chips.

FREEZE IT

Sprinkle casserole with remaining cheese blend. Cover and freeze unbaked casserole. To use, partially thaw in refrigerator overnight. Remove from refrigerator 30 minutes before baking. Preheat oven to 350°. Bake casserole as directed, increasing time as necessary to heat through and for a thermometer inserted in center to read 165°. Sprinkle with chips.

Moist & Savory Meat Loaf

Stop searching for a go-to meat loaf recipe. This is it! Your family will be delighted with this mixture of beef, pork and sauteed onion with a sweet- and-tangy sauce baked on top. Cheesy crackers are the secret ingredient in this one.

—TASTE OF HOME TEST KITCHEN

PREP: 20 MIN.
BAKE: 1¼ HOURS + STANDING
MAKES: 8 SERVINGS

- 1 **medium onion, chopped**
- 2 **teaspoons canola oil**
- 2 **large eggs, lightly beaten**
- ⅓ **cup 2% milk**
- 2 **teaspoons Worcestershire sauce**
- 2 **teaspoons Dijon mustard**
- ⅔ **cup finely crushed Cheez-It crackers**
- 1 **teaspoon salt**
- ½ **teaspoon pepper**
- ½ **teaspoon dried thyme**
- 1½ **pounds ground beef**
- ½ **pound ground pork**
- ¾ **cup ketchup**
- ¼ **cup packed brown sugar**

1. Saute onion in oil in a small skillet until tender. Cool to room temperature.
2. Combine the eggs, milk, Worcestershire sauce, mustard, crackers, salt, pepper, thyme and onion in a large bowl. Crumble beef and pork over mixture and mix well. Shape into a loaf; place in a greased 11x7-in. baking dish.
3. Bake, uncovered, at 350° for 1 hour. Combine ketchup and brown sugar; spread half of sauce over meat loaf. Bake 15-20 minutes longer or until no pink remains and a thermometer reads 160°. Let stand for 10 minutes before slicing. Serve meat loaf with remaining sauce.

FREEZE OPTION *Bake meat loaf without sauce. Securely wrap and freeze cooled meat loaf in plastic wrap and foil. To use, partially thaw in refrigerator overnight. Unwrap meat loaf and place in a greased shallow baking pan. Prepare sauce as directed; spread half of the sauce over the meat loaf. Reheat meat loaf in a 350° oven until heated through and a thermometer inserted in center reads 165°. Serve with remaining sauce.*

STUFFED CHICKEN ROLLS
PAGE 160

Poultry Favorites

There's no need to order takeout when you have this much tasty goodness on ice. Here, you can whip up handy favorites like pizza, potpie, chimichangas and pasta.

2 cans (10 ounces each) enchilada sauce
Minced fresh cilantro
¾ cup reduced-fat plain Greek yogurt

1. Preheat oven to 375°. In a large nonstick skillet, cook turkey, onion and seasonings over medium heat until turkey is no longer pink. Stir in cream cheese and ½ cup Mexican cheese blend until melted. Stir in beans, corn, tomatoes, chilies and salsa.

2. Place ½ cup turkey mixture off center on each tortilla. Roll up and place in two 13x9-in. baking dishes coated with cooking spray, seam side down. Top with enchilada sauce and remaining cheese.

3. Bake enchiladas, uncovered, for 15-20 minutes or until heated through. Sprinkle with cilantro; serve with yogurt.

FREEZE OPTION *Cool unbaked casseroles; cover and freeze. To use, partially thaw in refrigerator overnight. Remove from refrigerator 30 minutes before baking. Bake casseroles as directed, increasing time to 20-25 minutes or until heated through and a thermometer inserted in center reads 165°.*

PER SERVING *1 enchilada equals 343 cal., 13 g fat (5 g sat. fat), 51 mg chol., 795 mg sodium, 37 g carb., 5 g fiber, 19 g pro. Diabetic Exchanges: 3 lean meat, 2½ starch.*

EAT SMART

Black Bean Turkey Enchiladas

My best friend and I created this recipe because we wanted a meal that's easy to prepare, affordable and nutritious. We both have hectic schedules, so when we're feeling crunched for time, it's a relief to have these wholesome enchiladas waiting in the freezer.

—**HOLLY BABER** SEATTLE, WA

PREP: 35 MIN. • **BAKE:** 15 MIN.
MAKES: 14 SERVINGS

1¼ pounds lean ground turkey
1 small onion, chopped
1 teaspoon reduced-sodium taco seasoning
½ teaspoon ground cumin
¼ teaspoon pepper
1 package (8 ounces) reduced-fat cream cheese, cubed
1 cup (4 ounces) shredded Mexican cheese blend, divided
1 can (15 ounces) black beans, rinsed and drained
1½ cups frozen corn, thawed
1 can (14½ ounces) fire-roasted diced tomatoes, drained
2 cans (4 ounces each) chopped green chilies
¼ cup salsa
14 whole wheat tortillas (8 inches), warmed

Sesame Orange Chicken

Put this flavor-packed dish together in the morning, then go out and live your life. An enticing aroma will greet you when you get home. Use a rice cooker, too, and dinner will practically make itself!

—DARLENE BRENDEN SALEM, OR

PREP: 20 MIN. • **COOK:** 4 HOURS
MAKES: 0 SERVINGS

- ½ cup all-purpose flour
- 4 pounds boneless skinless chicken thighs
- ⅔ cup honey barbecue sauce
- ⅔ cup orange marmalade
- ½ cup orange juice
- ¼ cup reduced-sodium soy sauce
- 1 tablespoon minced fresh gingerroot
- ½ teaspoon crushed red pepper flakes
- 2 tablespoons sesame seeds, toasted
  Hot cooked rice

1. Place the flour in a large resealable plastic bag. Add the chicken, a few pieces at a time, and shake to coat. Transfer to a 4- or 5-qt. slow cooker.

2. Combine barbecue sauce, marmalade, orange juice, soy sauce, ginger and pepper flakes; pour over chicken. Cover and cook on low 4-6 hours or until chicken is tender. Sprinkle with sesame seeds. Serve with rice.

FREEZE OPTION *Before sprinkling with sesame seeds, cool chicken mixture. Freeze in freezer containers. To use, partially thaw in refrigerator overnight. Microwave, covered, on high in a microwave-safe dish until heated through, gently stirring and adding a little broth or water if necessary. Serve chicken as directed.*

DID YOU KNOW?

Boneless skinless chicken thighs work well in the slow cooker. It's easy to keep the meat moist because it has a higher fat content than white meat.

(5) INGREDIENTS

Broccoli Chicken Casserole

All ages really seem to go for this scrumptious meal in one. It takes just a handful of ingredients and minutes to put together. When I have them, I add dried cranberries to the stuffing mix for a festive boost in flavor and color!

—JENNIFER SCHLACHTER
BIG ROCK, IL

PREP: 15 MIN. • **BAKE:** 30 MIN.
MAKES: 6 SERVINGS

- 1 **package (6 ounces) chicken stuffing mix**
- 2 **cups cubed cooked chicken**
- 1 **cup frozen broccoli florets, thawed**
- 1 **can (10¾ ounces) condensed broccoli cheese soup, undiluted**
- 1 **cup (4 ounces) shredded cheddar cheese**

1. Preheat oven to 350°. Prepare stuffing mix according to package directions, using 1½ cups water.

2. In large bowl, combine chicken, broccoli and soup; transfer to a greased 11x7-in. baking dish. Top with stuffing; sprinkle with cheese. Bake, covered, 20 minutes. Uncover; bake 10-15 minutes longer or until heated through.

FREEZE IT

Transfer individual portions of cooled casserole to freezer containers; freeze. To use, partially thaw in refrigerator overnight. Transfer to a microwave-safe dish and microwave, covered, on high until a thermometer inserted in center reads 165°, stirring occasionally and adding a little broth if necessary.

Favorite Chicken Potpie

This chilly-day favorite makes two golden pies, so you can serve one at dinner and save the other for a busy night.

—**KAREN JOHNSON** BAKERSFIELD, CA

PREP: 40 MIN.
BAKE: 35 MIN. + STANDING
MAKES: 2 POTPIES
(8 SERVINGS EACH)

- 2 **cups diced peeled potatoes**
- 1¾ **cups sliced carrots**
- 1 **cup butter, cubed**
- ⅔ **cup chopped onion**
- 1 **cup all-purpose flour**
- 1¾ **teaspoons salt**
- 1 **teaspoon dried thyme**
- ¾ **teaspoon pepper**
- 3 **cups chicken broth**
- 1½ **cups milk**
- 4 **cups cubed cooked chicken**
- 1 **cup frozen peas**
- 1 **cup frozen corn**
- 2 **packages (14.1 ounces each) refrigerated pie pastry**

1. Preheat oven to 425°. Place potatoes and carrots in a large saucepan; add water to cover. Bring to a boil. Reduce the heat; cook, covered, 8-10 minutes or until crisp-tender; drain.

2. In a large skillet, heat butter over medium-high heat. Add onion; cook and stir until tender. Stir in flour and seasonings until blended. Gradually stir in broth and milk. Bring to a boil, stirring constantly; cook and stir for 2 minutes or until thickened. Stir in chicken, peas, corn and potato mixture; remove from the heat.

3. Unroll a pastry sheet into each of two 9-in. pie plates; trim even with rims. Add chicken mixture. Unroll remaining pastry; place over filling. Trim, seal and flute edges. Cut slits in tops of pies.

4. Bake 35-40 minutes or until crust is lightly browned. Let stand 15 minutes before cutting.

FREEZE OPTION *Cover and freeze unbaked pies. To use, remove from freezer 30 minutes before baking (do not thaw). Preheat oven to 425°. Place the pies on baking sheets; cover edges loosely with foil. Bake for 30 minutes. Reduce oven setting to 350°; bake 70-80 minutes longer or until crust is golden brown and a thermometer inserted in center reads 165°.*

Three-Cheese Turkey Manicotti

This is my husband's favorite dish. He always requests it, even on holidays! You'll love the variety of cheeses and spices that jazz it up. It's restaurant-quality, but at a quarter of the price.

—LUANNE WALLACE BENNETT
POWDER SPRINGS, GA

PREP: 30 MIN. • **BAKE:** 35 MIN.
MAKES: 6 SERVINGS

- 12 **uncooked manicotti shells**
- 1 **pound ground turkey**
- 1 **large sweet onion, chopped**
- 1 **jar (24 ounces) three-cheese spaghetti sauce**
- 2 **teaspoons sugar**
- 2 **teaspoons Italian seasoning**
- 1 **teaspoon onion powder**
- 1 **teaspoon garlic powder**
- 2 **cups (8 ounces) shredded cheddar-Monterey Jack cheese**
- 1 **carton (15 ounces) ricotta cheese**
- ½ **cup grated Parmesan cheese, divided**
- 1 **large egg, beaten**

1. Cook manicotti according to package directions. Meanwhile, in a large skillet, cook turkey and onion over medium heat until meat is no longer pink; drain. Stir in the spaghetti sauce, sugar, Italian seasoning, onion powder and garlic powder. Place 1 cup meat sauce in a greased 13x9-in. baking dish.

2. Drain manicotti. In a large bowl, combine the cheddar-Monterey Jack cheese, ricotta cheese, ¼ cup Parmesan cheese and egg. Stuff into manicotti shells. Place shells over meat sauce. Top with remaining sauce. Sprinkle with the remaining Parmesan cheese.

3. Cover and bake at 350° for 35-40 minutes or until bubbly.

FREEZE OPTION *Cover and freeze unbaked manicotti casserole for up to 1 month. To use, thaw in the refrigerator overnight. Let stand at room temperature for 30 minutes before baking. Bake as directed.*

Chicken Tortilla Bake

My mother frequently made this heartwarming casserole when I was growing up. Chicken, cheese and zippy green chilies are a classic, comforting mix.

—JERRI MOROR RIO RANCHO, NM

PREP: 20 MIN. • **BAKE:** 30 MIN.
MAKES: 6-8 SERVINGS

- 3 **cups shredded cooked chicken**
- 2 **cans (4 ounces each) chopped green chilies**
- 1 **cup chicken broth**
- 1 **can (10¾ ounces) condensed cream of mushroom soup, undiluted**
- 1 **can (10¾ ounces) condensed cream of chicken soup, undiluted**
- 1 **small onion, finely chopped**
- 12 **corn tortillas, warmed**
- 2 **cups (8 ounces) shredded cheddar cheese**

1. In a large bowl, combine the chicken, chilies, broth, soups and onion; set aside. Layer half of the tortillas in a greased 13x9-in. baking dish, cutting to fit pan if desired. Top with half of the chicken mixture and half of the cheese. Repeat layers.

2. Bake casserole, uncovered, at 350° for 30 minutes or until heated through.

FREEZE OPTION *Cover and freeze unbaked casserole. To use, partially thaw in refrigerator overnight. Remove from the refrigerator 30 minutes before baking. Bake casserole as directed, increasing time as necessary to heat through and for a thermometer to read 165°.*

EAT SMART

Asian Chicken Thighs

A sweet-tangy sauce coats juicy chicken thighs in this simple skillet dish. I like to serve it with rice or ramen noodle slaw.

—**DAVE FARRINGTON** MIDWEST CITY, OK

PREP: 15 MIN. • **COOK:** 50 MIN.
MAKES: 5 SERVINGS

- 5 teaspoons olive oil
- 5 bone-in chicken thighs (about 1¾ pounds), skin removed
- ⅓ cup water
- ¼ cup packed brown sugar
- 2 tablespoons orange juice
- 2 tablespoons reduced-sodium soy sauce
- 2 tablespoons ketchup
- 1 tablespoon white vinegar
- 4 garlic cloves, minced
- ½ teaspoon crushed red pepper flakes
- ¼ teaspoon Chinese five-spice powder
- 2 teaspoons cornstarch
- 2 tablespoons cold water
  Sliced green onions
  Hot cooked rice, optional

1. In a large skillet, heat oil over medium heat. Add chicken; cook 8-10 minutes on each side or until golden brown. In a small bowl, whisk water, brown sugar, orange juice, soy sauce, ketchup, vinegar, garlic, pepper flakes and five-spice powder. Pour over chicken. Bring to a boil. Reduce heat; simmer, uncovered, for 30-35 minutes or until chicken is tender, turning occasionally.
2. In a small bowl, mix the cornstarch and cold water until smooth; stir into pan. Bring to a boil; cook and stir 1 minute or until the sauce is thickened. Sprinkle with green onions. If desired, serve with rice.

FREEZE OPTION *Cool chicken. Freeze in freezer containers. To use, partially thaw in the refrigerator overnight. Heat slowly in a covered skillet until a thermometer inserted in chicken reads 165°, stirring occasionally and adding a little water if necessary.*

PER SERVING *1 chicken thigh (calculated without rice) equals 292 cal., 14 g fat (3 g sat. fat), 87 mg chol., 396 mg sodium, 15 g carb., trace fiber, 25 g pro.* ***Diabetic Exchanges:*** *3 lean meat, 1 starch, 1 fat.*

Italian Turkey Sandwiches

I hope you enjoy these tasty turkey sandwiches as much as our family does. The recipe makes plenty, so it's great for potlucks. Leftovers are just as good reheated the next day.

—CAROL RILEY OSSIAN, IN

PREP: 10 MIN. • **COOK:** 5 HOURS
MAKES: 12 SERVINGS

- 1 **bone-in turkey breast (6 pounds), skin removed**
- 1 **medium onion, chopped**
- 1 **small green pepper, chopped**
- ¼ **cup chili sauce**
- 3 **tablespoons white vinegar**
- 2 **tablespoons dried oregano or Italian seasoning**
- 4 **teaspoons beef bouillon granules**
- 12 **kaiser or hard rolls, split**

1. Place turkey breast in a greased 5-qt. slow cooker. Add onion and green pepper.

2. Combine chili sauce, vinegar, oregano and bouillon; pour over turkey and vegetables. Cover and cook on low for 5-6 hours or until turkey is tender.

3. Shred turkey with two forks and return to the slow cooker; heat through. Spoon ½ cup onto each roll.

PER SERVING *1 sandwich equals 374 cal., 4 g fat (1 g sat. fat), 118 mg chol., 724 mg sodium, 34 g carb., 2 g fiber, 49 g pro.* ***Diabetic Exchanges:*** *6 lean meat, 2 starch.*

FREEZE IT

Place cooled meat and juice mixture in freezer containers. To use, partially thaw in refrigerator overnight. Microwave, covered, on high in a microwave-safe dish until heated through, gently stirring and adding a little water if necessary.

FREEZE OPTION *Freeze cooled baked calzones in resealable plastic freezer bags. To use, place the calzones on greased baking sheets. Cover with foil and reheat in a preheated 350° oven for 25 minutes. Uncover; bake for 5-10 minutes longer or until heated through.*

⑤INGREDIENTS **SLOW COOKER** 🍲

Maple Mustard Chicken

This recipe is one of my husband's favorites. It only calls for four ingredients, and we try to have them on hand all the time for a delicious and cozy dinner anytime!
—**JENNIFER SEIDEL** MIDLAND, MI

PREP: 5 MIN. • **COOK:** 3 HOURS
MAKES: 6 SERVINGS

- 6 **boneless skinless chicken breast halves (6 ounces each)**
- ½ **cup maple syrup**
- ⅓ **cup stone-ground mustard**
- 2 **tablespoons quick-cooking tapioca**
  Hot cooked brown rice

Place chicken in a 3-qt. slow cooker. In a small bowl, combine the syrup, mustard and tapioca; pour over chicken. Cover and cook on low for 3-4 hours or until tender. Serve with rice.
FREEZE OPTION *Cool the chicken in the sauce. Freeze in freezer containers. To use, partially thaw in refrigerator overnight. Heat through slowly in a covered skillet until a thermometer inserted in chicken reads 165°, stirring occasionally and adding a little broth or water if necessary.*

Loaded Chicken & Gouda Calzones

When I had my daughter, I had lots of meals in the freezer to make those first few weeks easier. These calzones were a favorite! We loved being able to pull them out and have dinner in minutes. Dip 'em in spaghetti sauce, pesto—even ranch dressing.
—**ELISABETH LARSEN**
PLEASANT GROVE, UT

PREP: 40 MIN. • **BAKE:** 15 MIN.
MAKES: 8 SERVINGS

- 1 **tablespoon olive oil**
- ½ **pound sliced fresh mushrooms**
- 1 **small onion, finely chopped**
- 2 **garlic cloves, minced**
- 1 **package (10 ounces) frozen chopped spinach, thawed and squeezed dry**
- 2 **cups shredded cooked chicken breast**
- 1 **cup chopped roasted sweet red peppers, drained**
- 6 **bacon strips, cooked and crumbled**
- ½ **teaspoon salt**
- ¼ **teaspoon pepper**
- 2 **loaves (1 pound each) frozen whole wheat bread dough, thawed**
- 2 **cups (8 ounces) shredded Gouda cheese**
- 1 **large egg white, lightly beaten**

1. Preheat oven to 400°. In a large skillet, heat oil over medium-high heat. Add the mushrooms and onion; cook and stir 3-5 minutes or until tender. Add garlic; cook 1 minute longer. Remove from heat. Stir in the spinach, chicken, red peppers, bacon, salt and pepper.
2. On a lightly floured surface, divide each loaf of dough into four portions; press or roll each into an 8-in. circle. Place ½ cup filling over half of each circle to within ½ in. of edge. Top each with ¼ cup cheese. Fold dough over filling; pinch edge to seal.
3. Place on greased baking sheets. Brush tops with egg white. Bake 14-17 minutes or until golden brown and heated through. Serve warm.

Three-Cheese Chicken Bake

Whenever I bring this pasta bake to a party, I come home with an empty dish. I think it's the bright colors plus the combination of pimientos, mushrooms and cheese.

—VICKI RAATZ WATERLOO, WI

PREP: 15 MIN. • **BAKE:** 55 MIN.
MAKES: 12-15 SERVINGS

- ½ **cup chopped onion**
- ½ **cup chopped green pepper**
- 3 **tablespoons butter**
- 1 **can (10¾ ounces) condensed cream of chicken soup, undiluted**
- 1 **jar (8 ounces) sliced mushrooms, drained**
- 1 **jar (2 ounces) diced pimientos, drained**
- ½ **teaspoon dried basil**
- 1 **package (8 ounces) noodles, cooked and drained**
- 3 **cups diced cooked chicken**
- 2 **cups ricotta cheese**
- 2 **cups (8 ounces) shredded cheddar cheese**
- ½ **cup grated Parmesan cheese**
- ¼ **cup buttered bread crumbs**

1. In a large skillet, saute onion and green pepper in butter until tender. Remove from the heat. Stir in the soup, mushrooms, pimientos and basil; set aside.

2. In a large bowl, combine the noodles, chicken and cheeses; add mushroom sauce and mix well. Transfer to a greased 13x9-in. baking dish.

3. Bake, uncovered, at 350° for 40-45 minutes or until bubbly. Sprinkle with crumbs. Bake for 15 minutes longer or until top is browned.

4. Freeze option *Cool the unbaked casserole; cover and freeze. To use, partially thaw in refrigerator overnight. Remove from refrigerator 30 minutes before baking. Bake casserole as directed, increasing time as necessary to heat through and for a thermometer to read 165°.*

TOP TIP

I used fresh mushrooms and doubled the recipe. Left out the pimientos and used roasted red peppers instead. Everyone loved it, even my very picky grandson. No leftovers. Great dish.

—NANCYE49 TASTEOFHOME.COM

Chicken Noodle Casserole

Everyone who tries my casserole asks for the recipe. It's so simple to make that sometimes I feel like I'm cheating.

—**KAY PEDERSON** YELLVILLE, AR

PREP: 25 MIN. • **BAKE:** 40 MIN.
MAKES: 6 SERVINGS

- 1 **can (10¾ ounces) condensed cream of chicken soup, undiluted**
- ½ **cup mayonnaise**
- 2 **tablespoons lemon juice**
- 2 **cups cubed cooked chicken**
- 1 **small onion, chopped**
- ¼ **cup chopped green pepper**
- ¼ **cup chopped sweet red pepper**
- 1 **cup (4 ounces) shredded Monterey Jack cheese, divided**
- 1 **cup (4 ounces) shredded sharp cheddar cheese, divided**
- 12 **ounces egg noodles, cooked and drained**

1. In a large bowl, combine the soup, mayonnaise and lemon juice. Stir in the chicken, onion, peppers, ½ cup Monterey Jack cheese and ½ cup cheddar cheese. Add egg noodles and toss to coat.

2. Transfer to a greased 2-qt. baking dish. Bake, uncovered, at 350° for 30-35 minutes. Sprinkle with remaining cheeses. Bake 10 minutes longer or until the vegetables are tender and cheese is melted.

FREEZE IT

Sprinkle remaining cheeses over unbaked casserole. Cover and freeze. To use, partially thaw in refrigerator overnight. Remove from refrigerator 30 minutes before baking. Preheat oven to 350°. Bake casserole as directed, increasing time as necessary to heat through and for a thermometer inserted in center to read 165°.

Saucy Garlic Chicken

Roasted garlic lends a rich flavor to this appealing entree, and it complements the spinach nicely. Ideal for entertaining, the recipe can be assembled in advance and popped in the oven when dinner guests arrive.

—JOANNA JOHNSON
FLOWER MOUND, TX

PREP: 40 MIN. + COOLING
BAKE: 35 MIN.
MAKES: 6 SERVINGS

- 4 **whole garlic bulbs**
- 2 **tablespoons olive oil, divided**
- 1 **package (9 ounces) fresh baby spinach**
- ¾ **teaspoon salt, divided**
- ½ **teaspoon coarsely ground pepper, divided**
- 6 **boneless skinless chicken breast halves (6 ounces each)**
- 6 **tablespoons butter, cubed**
- 6 **tablespoons all-purpose flour**
- 3 **cups 2% milk**
- 2½ **cups grated Parmesan cheese, divided**
- ⅛ **teaspoon nutmeg**
  Hot cooked pasta
  Chopped tomato and minced fresh parsley, optional

1. Remove papery outer skin from garlic (do not peel or separate cloves). Cut tops off of garlic bulbs; brush bulbs with 1 tablespoon oil. Wrap each bulb in heavy-duty foil. Bake at 425° for 30-35 minutes or until softened. Cool for 10-15 minutes.

2. Meanwhile, place spinach in a greased 13x9-in. baking dish; sprinkle with ¼ teaspoon each of salt and pepper. In a large skillet, brown chicken in remaining oil on both sides; place over spinach.

3. In a large saucepan, melt butter. Stir in flour until smooth; gradually add milk. Bring to a boil; cook and stir 1-2 minutes or until thickened. Stir in 2 cups cheese, nutmeg and remaining salt and pepper.

4. Transfer to a blender; squeeze softened garlic into blender. Cover and process until smooth. Pour mixture over chicken.

5. Cover and bake at 425° for 30-35 minutes or until a thermometer reads 170° and sauce is bubbly. Uncover; sprinkle with remaining cheese. Bake 5 minutes longer. Serve with pasta. Sprinkle with tomato and parsley if desired.

FREEZE OPTION *Substitute 5 ounces frozen chopped spinach that has been thawed and squeezed dry for fresh spinach. Cool unbaked casserole and sprinkle with the remaining cheese; cover and freeze. To use, partially thaw in refrigerator overnight. Remove from the refrigerator 30 minutes before baking. Preheat oven to 425°. Bake casserole as directed, increasing time as necessary to heat through and for a thermometer inserted in chicken to read 170°.*

Tart Cranberry Chicken

My husband loves chicken when it's nice and moist, like it is in this autumn recipe. I serve it over hot fluffy rice with a salad and warm rolls on the side. The ruby-red sauce has a tart and cinnamony flavor.

—**DOROTHY BATEMAN** CARVER, MA

PREP: 20 MIN. • **COOK:** 20 MIN.
MAKES: 6 SERVINGS

- ½ cup all-purpose flour
- ½ teaspoon salt
- ¼ teaspoon pepper
- 6 boneless skinless chicken breast halves (4 ounces each)
- 3 tablespoons butter
- 1 cup water
- 1 cup fresh or frozen cranberries
- ½ cup packed brown sugar
  Dash ground nutmeg
- 1 tablespoon red wine vinegar, optional
  Hot cooked rice

1. In a shallow dish, combine flour, salt and pepper; dredge chicken. In a skillet, melt butter over medium heat. Brown the chicken on both sides. Remove and keep warm.

2. Add water, cranberries, brown sugar, nutmeg and, if desired, vinegar to the pan; cook and stir until the berries burst, about 5 minutes. Return chicken to skillet. Cover and simmer for 20-30 minutes or until chicken is tender, basting occasionally with the sauce. Serve with rice.

FREEZE OPTION *Place chicken in freezer containers; top with sauce. If desired, place rice in separate freezer containers. Cool and freeze. To use, partially thaw in the refrigerator overnight. Microwave, covered, on high in a microwave-safe dish until heated through, gently stirring and adding a little water to chicken if necessary.*

Fiesta Chicken

Chili powder and picante sauce kick up the heat to just right in this hearty main dish. It's a snap to put together on busy nights, since it uses convenience foods.

—**TERESA PETERSON** KASSON, MN

PREP: 15 MIN. • **BAKE:** 40 MIN.
MAKES: 6-8 SERVINGS

- 1 can (10¾ ounces) condensed cream of chicken soup, undiluted
- 1 can (10¾ ounces) condensed cream of mushroom soup, undiluted
- 2 small tomatoes, chopped
- ⅓ cup picante sauce
- 1 medium green pepper, chopped
- 1 small onion, chopped
- 2 to 3 teaspoons chili powder
- 12 corn tortillas (6 inches), cut into 1-inch strips
- 3 cups cubed cooked chicken
- 1 cup (4 ounces) shredded Colby cheese

1. In a large bowl, combine soups, tomatoes, picante sauce, green pepper, onion and chili powder. In a greased 13x9-in. baking dish, layer half of the tortilla strips, chicken, soup mixture and cheese. Repeat the layers.

2. Cover and bake at 350° for 40-50 minutes or until bubbly.

FREEZE OPTION *Cover and freeze unbaked casserole. To use, partially thaw in refrigerator overnight. Remove from the refrigerator 30 minutes before baking. Bake casserole as directed, increasing time as necessary to heat through and for a thermometer to read 165°.*

FREEZE IT

To use frozen turkey mixture, thaw in the refrigerator; place in a saucepan and heat through. Spoon ⅔ cup turkey mixture onto each bun.

EAT SMART

Potluck Sloppy Joes

For a change of pace, consider swapping out the green pepper in these tasty sloppy joes for an Anaheim, if available. These long light green peppers have just a bit of bite.

—**RICK BOLTE** MONTCLAIR, CA

PREP: 30 MIN. • **COOK:** 15 MIN.
MAKES: 12 SERVINGS

- 3 **pounds lean ground turkey**
- 3 **celery ribs, chopped**
- 2 **medium onions, chopped**
- 1 **large green pepper, chopped**
- 1¾ **cups ketchup**
- 1 **can (8 ounces) no-salt-added tomato sauce**
- 3 **tablespoons all-purpose flour**
- 3 **tablespoons sugar**
- 3 **tablespoons cider vinegar**
- 1 **tablespoon prepared mustard**
- 12 **whole wheat hamburger buns, split and toasted**

1. In a large nonstick skillet, cook turkey, celery, onions and pepper over medium heat until meat is no longer pink; drain.
2. Stir in the ketchup, tomato sauce, flour, sugar, vinegar and mustard. Bring to a boil. Reduce the heat; cover and simmer for 10-15 minutes or until heated through. Spoon ⅔ cup turkey mixture onto each bun.
3. Or, cool turkey mixture and freeze in freezer containers for up to 3 months.
PER SERVING *1 sandwich equals 360 cal., 11 g fat (3 g sat. fat), 90 mg chol., 785 mg sodium, 41 g carb., 4 g fiber, 24 g pro.* **Diabetic Exchanges:** *3 lean meat, 2½ starch.*

Chicken Thighs with Shallots & Spinach

What could be better than an entree that comes with its own creamy vegetable side? It makes a nice presentation, comes together in no time flat and is healthy, too.

—GENNA JOHANNES

WRIGHTSTOWN, WI

START TO FINISH: 30 MIN.
MAKES: 6 SERVINGS

- 6 **boneless skinless chicken thighs (about 1½ pounds)**
- ½ **teaspoon seasoned salt**
- ½ **teaspoon pepper**
- 1½ **teaspoons olive oil**
- 4 **shallots, thinly sliced**
- ⅓ **cup white wine or reduced-sodium chicken broth**
- 1 **package (10 ounces) fresh spinach, trimmed**
- ¼ **teaspoon salt**
- ¼ **cup fat-free sour cream**

1. Sprinkle the chicken with seasoned salt and pepper. In a large nonstick skillet coated with cooking spray, heat olive oil over medium heat. Add chicken; cook for 6 minutes on each side or until a thermometer reads 170°. Remove from pan; keep warm.

2. In same pan, cook and stir shallots until tender. Add wine; bring to a boil. Cook until wine is reduced by half. Add spinach and salt; cook and stir just until spinach is wilted. Stir in sour cream; serve with chicken.

FREEZE OPTION *Before adding sour cream, cool chicken and spinach mixture. Freeze in freezer containers. To use, partially thaw in refrigerator overnight. Heat through slowly in a covered skillet until a thermometer inserted in chicken reads 165°, stirring occasionally. Stir in sour cream.*

PER SERVING *1 chicken thigh with ¼ cup spinach mixture equals 225 cal., 10 g fat (2 g sat. fat), 77 mg chol., 338 mg sodium, 8 g carb., 1 g fiber, 24 g pro.* **Diabetic Exchanges:** *3 lean meat, 1½ fat, 1 vegetable.*

Honey Mustard Chicken

Try different styles of mustard, such as Dijon, sweet hot mustard or even Chinese—each will give your dish a different taste. For spicier chicken, substitute cayenne pepper for some or all of the chili powder.

—RICHARD GALLOP PUEBLO, CO

PREP: 15 MIN. • **BAKE:** 45 MIN.
MAKES: 6 SERVINGS

- ½ **cup honey**
- ¼ **cup prepared mustard**
- 1 **envelope ranch salad dressing mix**
- 1 **tablespoon dried parsley flakes**
- 1½ **teaspoons Italian seasoning**
- ½ **teaspoon dried basil**
- ½ **teaspoon chili powder**
- ¼ **teaspoon garlic powder**
- ¼ **teaspoon pepper**
- 6 **chicken drumsticks**
- 6 **bone-in chicken thighs**

1. For the sauce, combine the first nine ingredients. Set aside ½ cup for serving. Place the chicken in a greased 15x10x1-in. baking pan; drizzle with the remaining sauce.

2. Bake, uncovered, at 350° for 45-50 minutes or until a thermometer reads 180°, basting occasionally with pan juices. Warm reserved sauce; serve with chicken.

FREEZE OPTION *Cool chicken; freeze with reserved sauce in freezer containers. To use, partially thaw in refrigerator overnight. Heat through slowly in a covered skillet until a thermometer reads 165°, stirring occasionally and adding a little broth or water if necessary.*

Buffalo Chicken Pizza

If your family likes spicy chicken wings, they'll love this rendition that turns it into pizza. Serve it up with blue cheese dressing and crisp celery, just like the tasty original.

—**SHARI DIGIROLAMO** NEWTON, PA

PREP: 20 MIN. • **BAKE:** 20 MIN.
MAKES: 8 SERVINGS

- 1 tube (13.8 ounces) refrigerated pizza crust
- 1 cup Buffalo wing sauce, divided
- 1½ cups (6 ounces) shredded cheddar cheese
- 1½ cups (6 ounces) part-skim shredded mozzarella cheese
- 2 pounds boneless skinless chicken breasts, cubed
- ½ teaspoon each garlic salt, pepper and chili powder
- 2 tablespoons butter
- ½ teaspoon dried oregano
  Celery sticks and blue cheese salad dressing

1. Unroll pizza crust into a lightly greased 15x10x1-in. baking pan; flatten dough and build up edges slightly. Bake at 400° for 7 minutes. Brush dough with 3 tablespoons Buffalo wing sauce. Combine cheddar and mozzarella cheeses; sprinkle a third over the crust. Set aside.

2. In a large skillet, cook the cubed chicken, garlic salt, pepper and chili powder in butter until chicken is no longer pink. Add the remaining Buffalo wing sauce; cook and stir over medium heat 5 minutes longer.

3. Spoon over pizza. Sprinkle with the oregano and remaining cheese mixture.

4. Bake for 18-20 minutes or until crust is golden brown and cheese is melted. Serve with celery and blue cheese dressing.

FREEZE OPTION *Bake pizza crust as directed; cool. Top with all the ingredients as directed and securely wrap and freeze unbaked pizza. To use, unwrap the pizza; bake as directed, increasing time as necessary.*

NOTE *This recipe was tested with Frank's Red Hot Buffalo Wing Sauce.*

Baked Chicken Chimichangas

I developed this quick and easy recipe through trial and error. My friends all love it when I cook these, and they're much healthier than deep-fried chimichangas.

—**RICKEY MADDEN** CLINTON, SC

PREP: 20 MIN. • **BAKE:** 20 MIN.
MAKES: 6 SERVINGS

- 1½ cups cubed cooked chicken breast
- 1½ cups picante sauce, divided
- ½ cup shredded reduced-fat cheddar cheese
- ⅔ cup chopped green onions, divided
- 1 teaspoon ground cumin
- 1 teaspoon dried oregano
- 6 flour tortillas (8 inches), warmed
- 1 tablespoon butter, melted

1. Preheat oven to 375°. In a small bowl, combine chicken, ¾ cup picante sauce, cheese, ¼ cup onions, cumin and oregano. Spoon ½ cup mixture down the center of each tortilla. Fold sides and ends over filling and roll up. Place seam side down in a 15x10x1-in. baking pan coated with cooking spray. Brush with butter.

2. Bake, uncovered, for 20-25 minutes or until heated through. Top with remaining picante sauce and onions.

PER SERVING *1 chimichanga equals 269 cal., 8 g fat (3 g sat. fat), 39 mg chol., 613 mg sodium, 31 g carb., 1 g fiber, 17 g pro.* **Diabetic Exchanges:** *2 lean meat, 1½ starch, 1 vegetable, ½ fat.*

FREEZE IT

Cover and freeze unbaked casserole up to 3 months. To use, thaw in the refrigerator overnight. Remove from the refrigerator 30 minutes before baking. Bake according to directions.

Greek Goddess Pasta Bake

I've brought this Mediterranean-inspired dish to many potlucks, and it always gets rave reviews. There's never a crumb left. Plus it's simple, healthy, hearty and made from ingredients that are easy to find.

—ANNE TAGLIENTI
KENNETT SQUARE, PA

PREP: 20 MIN. • **BAKE:** 25 MIN.
MAKES: 8 SERVINGS

- 1 package (13¼ ounces) whole wheat penne pasta
- 4 cups cubed cooked chicken breast
- 1 can (29 ounces) tomato sauce
- 1 can (14½ ounces) diced tomatoes, drained
- 1 package (10 ounces) frozen chopped spinach, thawed and squeezed dry
- 2 cans (2¼ ounces each) sliced ripe olives, drained
- ¼ cup chopped red onion
- 2 tablespoons chopped green pepper
- 1 teaspoon dried basil
- 1 teaspoon dried oregano
- ½ cup shredded part-skim mozzarella cheese
- ½ cup crumbled feta cheese

1. Cook pasta according to package directions; drain. In a large bowl, combine the penne pasta, chicken, tomato sauce, tomatoes, spinach, olives, onion, green pepper, basil and oregano.

2. Transfer to a 13x9-in. baking dish coated with cooking spray. Sprinkle with cheeses. Bake, uncovered, at 400° for 25-30 minutes or until heated through and cheese is melted.

FREEZE OPTION *Cool the unbaked casserole; cover and freeze. To use, partially thaw in the refrigerator overnight. Remove from refrigerator 30 minutes before baking. Preheat oven to 400°. Bake the casserole as directed, increasing time as necessary to heat through and for a thermometer inserted in center to read 165°.*

Chicken Aloha

This chicken is a welcome way to cook a quick, delicious meal.

—BETH CORBIN SARASOTA, FL

PREP: 10 MIN. • **BAKE:** 25 MIN.
MAKES: 6 SERVINGS

- **6 boneless skinless chicken breast halves (4 ounces each)**
- **1 bottle (14 ounces) ketchup**
- **1 can (10¾ ounces) condensed tomato soup, undiluted**
- **1 medium green pepper, coarsely chopped**
- **⅓ cup cider vinegar**
- **¼ cup packed brown sugar**
- **1 teaspoon ground mustard**
- **1 can (8 ounces) pineapple chunks, undrained**
  Hot cooked rice

1. Place chicken in a greased 13x9-in. baking dish. Combine ketchup, soup, pepper, vinegar, brown sugar and mustard; stir in pineapple. Pour over chicken.
2. Bake, uncovered, at 375° for 25-35 minutes or until a thermometer reads 165°. Serve with rice.

FREEZE OPTION *Cool chicken mixture. Freeze in freezer containers. To use, partially thaw in refrigerator overnight. Heat through slowly in a covered skillet until a thermometer inserted in chicken reads 165°, stirring occasionally.*

SLOW COOKER 🍲
Stuffed Chicken Rolls

Just thinking about this dish sparks my appetite. The ham and cheese rolled inside make a tasty surprise. These rolls are especially nice served over rice or pasta.

—JEAN SHERWOOD KENNETH CITY, FL

PREP: 25 MIN. + CHILLING
COOK: 4 HOURS • **MAKES:** 6 SERVINGS

- **6 boneless skinless chicken breast halves (8 ounces each)**
- **6 slices fully cooked ham**
- **6 slices Swiss cheese**
- **¼ cup all-purpose flour**
- **¼ cup grated Parmesan cheese**
- **½ teaspoon rubbed sage**
- **¼ teaspoon paprika**
- **¼ teaspoon pepper**
- **¼ cup canola oil**
- **1 can (10¾ ounces) condensed cream of chicken soup, undiluted**
- **½ cup chicken broth**
  Chopped fresh parsley, optional

1. Flatten chicken to ¼-in. thickness; top with ham and cheese. Roll up and tuck in ends; secure with toothpicks.
2. In a shallow bowl, combine the flour, cheese, sage, paprika and pepper; coat chicken rolls on all sides. In a large skillet, brown the chicken in oil over medium-high heat.
3. Transfer to a 5-qt. slow cooker. Combine soup and broth; pour over chicken. Cover and cook on low for 4-5 hours or until chicken is tender. Remove toothpicks. Garnish with parsley if desired.

FREEZE OPTION *Cool the chicken mixture. Freeze in freezer containers. To use, partially thaw in refrigerator overnight. Heat through slowly in a covered skillet, stirring occasionally, until a thermometer inserted in chicken reads 165°.*

TOP TIP

To keep parsley fresh for up to a month, trim the ends of the stems and place the bunch in a tumbler with an inch of water. Be sure no loose leaves are in the water. Tie a produce bag around the tumbler to trap humidity; store in the refrigerator.

Chicken-Cheddar Tortilla Bake

Enjoy the taste of Mexican enchiladas without all the work in this easy, freezes-like-a-dream casserole. To increase the nutrition, use whole wheat tortillas and cook the chicken with a couple of chopped bell or poblano peppers.

—*TASTE OF HOME* TEST KITCHEN

PREP: 25 MIN. • **BAKE:** 25 MIN.
MAKES: 6 SERVINGS

- 1 **pound boneless skinless chicken breasts, cubed**
- ½ **teaspoon ground cumin**
- ¼ **teaspoon salt**
- 1 **tablespoon plus 1 teaspoon olive oil, divided**
- 1 **can (16 ounces) refried beans**
- 1 **can (14½ ounces) diced tomatoes with mild green chilies, drained**
- 8 **flour tortillas (8 inches), cut into 1-inch strips**
- 1 **can (11 ounces) Mexicorn, drained**
- 2 **cups (8 ounces) shredded cheddar cheese**

1. In a large skillet, saute the chicken, cumin and salt in 1 tablespoon oil until chicken is no longer pink.

2. Combine the refried beans and tomatoes; spread 1 cup into a greased 11x7-in. baking dish. Top with 24 tortilla strips; layer with half of the corn, bean mixture, chicken and cheddar cheese. Repeat layers.

3. Using remaining tortilla strips, make a lattice crust over filling; brush with remaining oil. Bake, uncovered, at 350° for 25-30 minutes or until heated through and cheese is melted.

4. Serve immediately or, before baking, cover and freeze casserole for up to 3 months.

TO USE FROZEN CASSEROLE
Thaw frozen casserole in the refrigerator overnight. Remove from the refrigerator 30 minutes before baking. Bake according to directions.

EAT SMART

Pesto Chicken Pizza

This is the only pizza I make. Keeping the spices simple helps the flavors shine. The pizza tastes amazing, and it's good for you, too.

—HEATHER THOMPSON

WOODLAND HILLS, CA

PREP: 35 MIN. + RISING • **BAKE:** 20 MIN.
MAKES: 8 SLICES

- 2 teaspoons active dry yeast
- 1 cup warm water (110° to 115°)
- 2¾ cups bread flour
- 1 tablespoon plus 2 teaspoons olive oil, divided
- 1 tablespoon sugar
- 1½ teaspoons salt, divided
- ½ pound boneless skinless chicken breasts, cut into ½-inch pieces
- 1 small onion, halved and thinly sliced
- ½ each small green, red and yellow peppers, julienned
- ½ cup sliced fresh mushrooms
- 3 tablespoons prepared pesto
- 1½ cups (6 ounces) shredded part-skim mozzarella cheese
- ¼ teaspoon pepper

1. In a large bowl, dissolve yeast in warm water. Beat in 1 cup bread flour, 1 tablespoon oil, sugar and 1 teaspoon salt. Beat in remaining flour until combined.

2. Turn onto a lightly floured surface; knead until smooth and elastic, about 6-8 minutes. Place in a bowl coated with cooking spray, turning once to coat the top. Cover dough and let rise in a warm place until doubled, about 1 hour.

3. In a large nonstick skillet over medium heat, cook the chicken, onion, peppers and mushrooms in remaining oil until chicken is no longer pink and vegetables are tender. Remove from heat; set aside.

4. Punch dough down; roll into a 15-in. circle. Transfer to a 14-in. pizza pan. Build up edges slightly. Spread with pesto. Top with the chicken mixture and cheese. Sprinkle with pepper and remaining salt.

5. Bake at 400° for 18-20 minutes or until crust and cheese are lightly browned.

FREEZE OPTION *Securely wrap and freeze unbaked pizza. To use, unwrap pizza; bake as directed, increasing time as necessary.*

PER SERVING *1 slice equals 293 cal., 10 g fat (3 g sat. fat), 30 mg chol., 601 mg sodium, 35 g carb., 2 g fiber, 18 g pro.* **Diabetic Exchanges:** *2 starch, 1 lean meat, 1 fat.*

SAUSAGE SUPREME PIZZA
Substitute Italian sausage for the chicken and ½ cup pizza sauce for the pesto. If desired, substitute a prebaked 12-inch pizza crust.

PEPPERONI PIZZA *Omit vegetables. Substitute ½ cup pizza sauce for the pesto; layer with 25 slices pepperoni. Increase cheese to 2 cups. If desired, use prebaked 12-inch pizza crust.*

Broccoli Chicken Skillet

Thanks to this recipe, you're just 25 minutes from a cheesy chicken dish the whole family will love!

—TASTE OF HOME TEST KITCHEN

START TO FINISH: 25 MIN.
MAKES: 4 SERVINGS

- 1½ **pounds boneless skinless chicken breasts, cubed**
- 2 **cups frozen broccoli florets**
- 1 **cup julienned carrots**
- ½ **cup chopped onion**
- 1 **tablespoon olive oil**
- 1 **can (10¾ ounces) condensed cream of broccoli soup, undiluted**
- 1 **cup stuffing mix**
- 1 **cup milk**
- ¼ **cup raisins**
- ⅛ **teaspoon pepper**
- 1 **cup (4 ounces) shredded Colby cheese**

1. In a large skillet, saute the chicken, broccoli, carrots and onion in oil for 5-6 minutes or until chicken is no longer pink.

2. Stir in the soup, stuffing mix, milk, raisins and pepper. Cook, uncovered, over medium heat for 8-10 minutes or until heated through. Sprinkle with cheese. Remove from the heat; cover and let stand until cheese is melted.

FREEZE OPTION *Before adding cheese, cool casserole; cover and freeze. To use, partially thaw in refrigerator overnight. Remove from refrigerator 30 minutes before reheating. Preheat oven to 350°. Cover casserole with foil; bake 20-30 minutes or until heated through and a thermometer inserted in center reads 165°. Sprinkle with cheese.*

Chicken Broccoli Shells

This cheesy entree can be made ahead of time and popped in the oven when company arrives. I round out the meal with a tossed salad and warm bread.

—**KAREN JAGGER** COLUMBIA CITY, IN

PREP: 15 MIN. • **BAKE:** 30 MIN.
MAKES: 7 SERVINGS

- 1 jar (16 ounces) Alfredo sauce
- 2 cups frozen chopped broccoli, thawed
- 2 cups diced cooked chicken
- 1 cup (4 ounces) shredded cheddar cheese
- ¼ cup shredded Parmesan cheese
- 21 jumbo pasta shells, cooked and drained

1. In a large bowl, combine the Alfredo sauce, broccoli, chicken and cheeses. Spoon into pasta shells. Place in a greased 13x9-in. baking dish.

2. Cover and bake at 350° for 30-35 minutes or until casserole is heated through.

FREEZE OPTION *Cover and freeze unbaked casserole. To use, partially thaw in refrigerator overnight. Remove from refrigerator 30 minutes before baking. Preheat oven to 350°. Bake casserole as directed, increasing time as necessary to heat through and for a thermometer inserted in center to read 165°.*

Corn Bread Chicken Bake

To make the most of leftover corn bread, try this hearty main-dish casserole. It's moist, delicious and good on any occasion.

—**MADGE BRITTON** AFTON, TN

PREP: 20 MIN. • **BAKE:** 45 MIN.
MAKES: 8-10 SERVINGS

- 1¼ **pounds boneless skinless chicken breasts**
- 6 **cups cubed corn bread**
- 8 **bread slices, cubed**
- 1 **medium onion, chopped**
- 2 **cans (10¾ ounces each) condensed cream of chicken soup, undiluted**
- 1 **cup chicken broth**
- 2 **tablespoons butter, melted**
- 1½ **to 2 teaspoons rubbed sage**
- 1 **teaspoon salt**
- ½ **to 1 teaspoon pepper**

1. Place chicken in a large skillet and cover with water; bring to a boil. Reduce heat; cover and simmer for 12-14 minutes or until a thermometer reads 170°. Drain and cut into cubes.

2. In a large bowl, combine the remaining ingredients. Add chicken. Transfer to a greased 13x9-in. baking dish.

3. Bake, uncovered, at 350° for 45 minutes or until casserole is heated through.

FREEZE OPTION *Cover and freeze unbaked casserole. To use, partially thaw in refrigerator overnight. Remove from refrigerator 30 minutes before baking. Bake casserole as directed, increasing time as necessary to heat through and for a thermometer inserted in center to read 165°.*

Lemon-Herb Roasted Turkey

Lemon and thyme are the standout flavors in this golden, tender and moist turkey. It's so easy to make, you just can't go wrong.

—**FELECIA SMITH** GEORGETOWN, TX

PREP: 30 MIN.
BAKE: 2¼ HOURS + STANDING
MAKES: 14-16 SERVINGS

- ½ **cup butter, melted**
- 3 **tablespoons lemon juice**
- 2 **teaspoons grated lemon peel**
- 1 **teaspoon minced fresh thyme or ¼ teaspoon dried thyme**
- 1 **turkey (14 to 16 pounds)**
- 2 **teaspoons salt**
- 2 **teaspoons pepper**
- 1 **medium lemon, halved**
- 1 **medium onion, quartered**
- 14 **garlic cloves, peeled**
- 24 **fresh thyme sprigs**
- 1 **tablespoon all-purpose flour**
- 1 **turkey-size oven roasting bag**

1. In a small bowl, combine the butter, lemon juice, lemon peel and minced thyme. Pat the turkey dry. Sprinkle salt and pepper over skin of turkey and inside cavity; brush with butter mixture. Place the lemon, onion, garlic and thyme sprigs inside cavity. Tuck wings under turkey; tie drumsticks together.

2. Place the flour in the oven bag and shake to coat. Place bag in a roasting pan; add turkey to bag, breast side up. Cut six ½-in. slits in the top of the bag; close the bag with the tie provided.

3. Bake at 350° for 2¼-2¾ hours or until a thermometer reads 180°. Remove turkey to a serving platter and keep warm. Let stand for 15 minutes before carving. If desired, thicken pan drippings for gravy.

FREEZE OPTION *Freeze cooled turkey and gravy in freezer containers. To use, partially thaw in refrigerator overnight. Heat through in a covered skillet, gently stirring and adding a little broth or water if necessary.*

SLOW COOKER 🍲
Honey Pineapple Chicken

I adapted a dinnertime favorite for my slow cooker because it's so much easier to do the preparation in advance, then let the chicken cook on its own while I take care of other things. Your family will love this combination of sweet and savory flavors.

—CAROL GILLESPIE
CHAMBERSBURG, PA

PREP: 15 MIN. • **COOK:** 3 HOURS
MAKES: 8 SERVINGS

- 3 pounds boneless skinless chicken breast halves
- 2 tablespoons canola oil
- 1 can (8 ounces) unsweetened crushed pineapple, undrained
- 1 cup packed brown sugar
- ½ cup honey
- ⅓ cup lemon juice
- ¼ cup butter, melted
- 2 tablespoons prepared mustard
- 2 teaspoons reduced-sodium soy sauce

1. In a large skillet, brown chicken in oil in batches on both sides; transfer to a 5-qt. slow cooker. In a small bowl, combine the remaining ingredients; pour over chicken.

2. Cover and cook on low for 3-4 hours or until meat is tender. Strain cooking liquid, reserving pineapple. Serve pineapple with the chicken.

FREEZE OPTION *Cool chicken mixture. Freeze in freezer containers. To use, partially thaw in refrigerator overnight. Heat through slowly in a covered skillet until a thermometer inserted in chicken reads 165°, stirring occasionally and adding a little water if necessary.*

EAT SMART
BBQ Chicken Sandwiches

These are great sandwiches and are a cinch to make. For a spicier taste, eliminate the ketchup and increase the amount of salsa to 1 cup.

—LETICIA LEWIS KENNEWICK, WA

PREP: 20 MIN. • **COOK:** 15 MIN.
MAKES: 6 SERVINGS

- ½ cup chopped onion
- ½ cup diced celery
- 1 garlic clove, minced
- 1 tablespoon butter
- ½ cup salsa
- ½ cup ketchup
- 2 tablespoons brown sugar
- 2 tablespoons cider vinegar
- 1 tablespoon Worcestershire sauce
- ½ teaspoon chili powder
- ¼ teaspoon salt
- ⅛ teaspoon pepper
- 2 cups shredded cooked chicken
- 6 hamburger buns, split and toasted

1. In a large saucepan, saute the onion, celery and garlic in butter until tender. Stir in the salsa, ketchup, brown sugar, vinegar, Worcestershire sauce, chili powder, salt and pepper.

2. Stir in chicken. Bring to a boil. Reduce heat; cover and simmer for 15 minutes. Serve about ⅓ cup of chicken mixture on each bun.

PER SERVING *1 sandwich equals 284 cal., 8 g fat (3 g sat. fat), 47 mg chol., 770 mg sodium, 35 g carb., 3 g fiber, 18 g pro.* **Diabetic Exchanges:** *2 starch, 2 lean meat.*

FREEZE IT

Freeze cooled meat mixture in freezer containers. To use, partially thaw in refrigerator overnight. Heat through in a saucepan, stirring occasionally and adding a little water if necessary. Serve in hamburger buns.

SLOW COOKER

Zesty Chicken Marinara

A friend served this delicious Italian-style chicken before a church social, and I fell in love with it. My husband says it tastes like a dish you'd get at a restaurant.

—LINDA BAUMANN RICHFIELD, WI

PREP: 15 MIN. • **COOK:** 4 HOURS
MAKES: 4 SERVINGS

- 4 bone-in chicken breast halves (12 to 14 ounces each), skin removed
- 2 cups marinara sauce
- 1 medium tomato, chopped
- ½ cup Italian salad dressing
- 1½ teaspoons Italian seasoning
- 1 garlic clove, minced
- ½ pound uncooked angel hair pasta
- ½ cup shredded part-skim mozzarella cheese

1. Place chicken in a 4-qt. slow cooker. In a small bowl, combine the marinara sauce, tomato, salad dressing, Italian seasoning and garlic; pour over chicken. Cover and cook on low 4-5 hours or until chicken is tender.
2. Cook pasta according to the package directions; drain. Serve chicken and sauce with pasta; sprinkle with cheese.

FREEZE IT

Do not cook pasta. Freeze cooled chicken mixture in freezer containers. To use, partially thaw in refrigerator overnight. Cook pasta according to package directions. Place chicken mixture in a large skillet; heat until a thermometer inserted in chicken reads 165°, stirring occasionally and adding a little water if necessary. Serve with pasta and cheese as directed.

Louisiana Red Beans and Rice

Smoked turkey sausage and red pepper flakes add zip to this slow-cooked New Orleans classic.

—JULIA BUSHREE COMMERCE CITY, CO

PREP: 20 MIN. • **COOK:** 8 HOURS
MAKES: 8 SERVINGS

- 4 cans (16 ounces each) kidney beans, rinsed and drained
- 1 can (14½ ounces) diced tomatoes, undrained
- 1 package (14 ounces) smoked turkey sausage, sliced
- 3 celery ribs, chopped
- 1 large onion, chopped
- 1 cup chicken broth
- 1 medium green pepper, chopped
- 1 small sweet red pepper, chopped
- 6 garlic cloves, minced
- 1 bay leaf
- ½ teaspoon crushed red pepper flakes
- 2 green onions, chopped
  Hot cooked rice

1. In a 4- or 5-qt. slow cooker, combine the first 11 ingredients. Cook, covered, on low 8-10 hours or until vegetables are tender.

2. Stir before serving. Remove bay leaf. Serve with green onions and rice.

FREEZE OPTION *Discard bay leaf. Freeze cooled bean mixture in freezer containers. To use, partially thaw in refrigerator overnight. Heat through in a saucepan, stirring occasionally and adding a little broth or water if necessary. Serve as directed.*

EAT SMART

Turkey Mole Tacos

Unlike traditional tacos, these taste complete as they are, without any need for garnishes and sauces. I also make them using bite-sized pieces of chicken thighs—just increase the cooking time accordingly.

—HELEN GLAZIER SEATTLE, WA

PREP: 25 MIN. • **COOK:** 20 MIN.
MAKES: 6 SERVINGS

- 1¼ pounds lean ground turkey
- 1 celery rib, chopped
- 4 green onions, chopped
- 2 garlic cloves, minced
- 1 can (14½ ounces) diced tomatoes, undrained
- 1 jar (7 ounces) roasted sweet red peppers, drained and chopped
- 2 ounces 53% cacao dark baking chocolate, chopped
- 4 teaspoons chili powder
- 1 teaspoon ground cumin
- ½ teaspoon salt
- ¼ teaspoon ground cinnamon
- ¼ cup lightly salted mixed nuts, coarsely chopped
- 12 corn tortillas (6 inches), warmed

1. In a large nonstick skillet coated with cooking spray, cook the turkey, celery, green onions and garlic over medium heat until meat is no longer pink and vegetables are tender; drain.

2. Stir in the tomatoes, red peppers, chocolate, chili powder, cumin, salt and cinnamon. Bring to a boil. Reduce heat; cover and simmer for 10 minutes, stirring occasionally.

3. Remove from the heat; stir in nuts. Place about ⅓ cup filling on each tortilla.

FREEZE OPTION *Freeze cooled meat mixture in freezer containers. To use, partially thaw in refrigerator overnight. Heat through in a saucepan, stirring occasionally and adding a little water if necessary.*

PER SERVING *2 tacos equals 369 cal., 15 g fat (5 g sat. fat), 75 mg chol., 612 mg sodium, 37 g carb., 6 g fiber, 22 g pro.*
Diabetic Exchanges: 3 lean meat, 2 starch, 1 vegetable, 1 fat.

GRILLED PORK TENDERLOINS
PAGE 191

Pork Specialties

Set aside a little time to prep these savory meals using pork, ham or sausage, and you'll reap the benefits with irresistible dinners that are ready when you are.

Bacon Tortellini Bake

I stirred up an easy pasta and figured that if my family liked it, others might, too. Broccoli and bacon add fabulous crunch.

—**AMY LENTS** GRAND FORKS, ND

PREP: 25 MIN. • **BAKE:** 15 MIN.
MAKES: 6 SERVINGS

- 1 package (20 ounces) refrigerated cheese tortellini
- 3 cups small fresh broccoli florets
- ½ pound bacon strips, cut into 1-inch pieces
- 2 garlic cloves, minced
- 1 tablespoon all-purpose flour
- 1 teaspoon dried basil
- ½ teaspoon salt
- ⅛ teaspoon coarsely ground pepper
- 2 cups 2% milk
- ¾ cup shredded part-skim mozzarella cheese, divided
- ¾ cup grated Parmesan cheese, divided
- 2 teaspoons lemon juice

1. Preheat oven to 350°. Cook tortellini according to package directions, adding broccoli during the last 2 minutes; drain.

2. Meanwhile, in a large skillet, cook the bacon over medium heat until crisp, stirring occasionally. Remove with a slotted spoon; drain on paper towels. Discard drippings, reserving 1 tablespoon in pan.

3. Reduce heat to medium-low. Add garlic to drippings in pan; cook and stir 1 minute. Stir in flour, basil, salt and pepper until blended; gradually whisk in milk. Bring to a boil, stirring constantly; cook and stir for 3-5 minutes or until slightly thickened. Remove from heat.

4. Stir in ½ cup mozzarella cheese, ½ cup Parmesan cheese and lemon juice. Add tortellini mixture and bacon; toss to combine. Transfer to a greased 13x9-in. baking dish; sprinkle with remaining cheeses. Bake, uncovered, 15-20 minutes or until heated through and broccoli is tender.

FREEZE OPTION *Sprinkle remaining cheeses over the unbaked casserole. Cover and freeze. To use, partially thaw in refrigerator overnight. Remove from refrigerator 30 minutes before baking. Preheat oven to 350°. Bake casserole as directed, increasing time as necessary to heat through and for a thermometer inserted in the center to read 165°.*

FREEZE IT

Place cooled meat mixture in freezer containers. To use, partially thaw in refrigerator overnight. Microwave, covered, on high in a microwave-safe dish until heated through, gently stirring and adding a little water if necessary.

BBQ Country Ribs

I created this sauce for ribs many years ago when I adapted a recipe I saw in a magazine. I often triple the sauce and keep some in my freezer to use on chicken, beef or pork.

—**BARBARA GERRIETS** TOPEKA, KS

PREP: 25 MIN. • **BAKE:** 2 HOURS
MAKES: 8 SERVINGS

- 2½ **pounds boneless country-style pork ribs**
- 2 **teaspoons liquid smoke, optional**
- ½ **teaspoon salt**
- 1 **cup water**

BARBECUE SAUCE
- ⅔ **cup chopped onion**
- 1 **tablespoon canola oil**
- ¾ **cup each water and ketchup**
- ⅓ **cup lemon juice**
- 3 **tablespoons sugar**
- 3 **tablespoons Worcestershire sauce**
- 2 **tablespoons prepared mustard**
- ½ **teaspoon salt**
- ½ **teaspoon pepper**
- ¼ **teaspoon liquid smoke, optional**

1. Place ribs in an 11x7-in. baking dish coated with cooking spray. Sprinkle with liquid smoke if desired and salt. Add water to pan. Cover and bake at 350° for 1 hour.
2. Meanwhile, in a saucepan, saute onion in oil until tender. Add remaining ingredients; bring to a boil. Reduce heat; simmer, uncovered, for 15 minutes or until slightly thickened.
3. Drain ribs; top with half of the sauce. Cover and bake 1 hour longer or until tender, basting every 20 minutes. Serve with the remaining sauce.

Individual Pork & Cranberry Potpies

My neighbor gave me this recipe years ago, and I love how these pies are different from the usual chicken potpie. Freezing them allows my family to enjoy them any time of year. They are especially good for an easy dinner during the cold winter months.

—**MARY SHENK** DEKALB, IL

PREP: 45 MIN. • **BAKE:** 15 MIN.
MAKES: 8 SERVINGS

- 2 **cups fresh or frozen cranberries, thawed**
- 4 **celery ribs, sliced**
- 1 **medium onion, chopped**
- 2½ **cups apple cider or juice**
- 3 **tablespoons brown sugar**
- 4 **garlic cloves, minced**
- 4 **teaspoons grated orange peel**
- 1 **tablespoon beef or chicken bouillon granules**
- 1 **teaspoon dried rosemary, crushed or dried thyme**
- 6 **tablespoons all-purpose flour**
- ¾ **cup water**
- 5 **cups chopped cooked pork**
- 1 **package (14.1 ounces) refrigerated pie pastry**

1. Preheat oven to 450°. In a large saucepan, combine the first nine ingredients; bring to a boil. Reduce heat; simmer, uncovered, until berries pop, about 10 minutes.

2. In a small bowl, mix flour and water until smooth; stir into cranberry mixture. Return to a boil, stirring constantly; cook and stir 1-2 minutes or until thickened. Stir in pork; remove from heat.

3. On a work surface, unroll pastry sheets. Roll each to a 12-in. circle. Using a 5-in. disposable foil potpie pan as a guide (top side down), cut out eight 5½-in. pastry circles, rerolling scraps as needed.

4. Divide pork mixture among eight 5-in. disposable foil pans. Place pastry circles over tops of pies; flute the edges. Cut slits in pastry.

5. Place potpies on baking sheets. Bake 15-20 minutes or until crust is golden brown and filling is bubbly.

FREEZE OPTION *Cover and freeze unbaked potpies. To use, bake frozen pies on baking sheets in a preheated 400° oven 40-50 minutes or until golden brown and a thermometer inserted in center reads 165°.*

Parmesan Pork Roast

A wonderful sweet and savory flavor comes from just a few pantry staples in this easy roast.

—**KAREN WARNER** LOUISVILLE, OH

PREP: 15 MIN. • **COOK:** 5½ HOURS
MAKES: 10 SERVINGS

- 1 **boneless pork loin roast (4 pounds)**
- ⅔ **cup grated Parmesan cheese**
- ½ **cup honey**
- 3 **tablespoons soy sauce**
- 2 **tablespoons dried basil**
- 2 **tablespoons minced garlic**
- 2 **tablespoons olive oil**
- ½ **teaspoon salt**
- 2 **tablespoons cornstarch**
- ¼ **cup cold water**

1. Cut roast in half. Place in a 3-qt. slow cooker. In a small bowl, combine the cheese, honey, soy sauce, basil, garlic, oil and salt; pour over pork. Cover and cook on low for 5½-6 hours or until a thermometer reads 160°.

2. Remove meat to a serving platter; keep warm. Skim fat from cooking juices; transfer to a small saucepan. Bring liquid to a boil. Combine cornstarch and water until smooth. Gradually stir into pan. Bring to a boil; cook and stir for 2 minutes or until thickened. Serve with pork.

FREEZE OPTION *Cool pork and gravy. Freeze sliced pork and gravy in freezer containers. To use, partially thaw in refrigerator overnight. Heat through slowly in a covered skillet, stirring occasionally and adding a little broth or water if necessary.*

Muffin Tin Pizzas

Soon after I baked these mini pizzas, my kids were already eagerly asking for more. No-cook sauce and refrigerated pizza dough make this meal a snap.

—MELISSA HAINES VALPARAISO, IN

PREP: 25 MIN. • **BAKE:** 10 MIN.
MAKES: 8 SERVINGS

- 1 **can (15 ounces) tomato sauce**
- 1 **can (6 ounces) tomato paste**
- 1 **teaspoon dried basil**
- ½ **teaspoon garlic salt**
- ¼ **teaspoon onion powder**
- ¼ **teaspoon sugar**
- 1 **tube (11 ounces) refrigerated thin pizza crust**
- 1½ **cups (6 ounces) shredded part-skim mozzarella cheese**
- ½ **cup finely chopped fresh mushrooms**
- ½ **cup finely chopped fresh broccoli**
- 16 **slices pepperoni, halved**

1. Preheat oven to 425°. In a small bowl, mix the first six ingredients.

2. Unroll pizza crust; cut into 16 squares. Press squares onto bottoms and up sides of 16 ungreased muffin cups, allowing corners to hang over the edges.

3. Spoon 1 tablespoon sauce mixture into each cup. Top with cheese, mushrooms, broccoli and the pepperoni. Bake for 10-12 minutes or until crusts are golden brown. Serve the remaining sauce mixture, warmed if desired, with pizzas.

FREEZE IT

Freeze cooled baked pizzas in a resealable plastic freezer bag. To use, reheat on a baking sheet in a preheated 425° oven until heated through.

Slow-Cooked Pork Burritos

I've been making this recipe for more than 20 years, changing it here and there until I arrived at this delicious version. It's a favorite for company and family alike.

—SHARON BELMONT LINCOLN, NE

PREP: 20 MIN. • **COOK:** 8 HOURS
MAKES: 14 SERVINGS

- 1 **boneless pork sirloin roast (3 pounds)**
- ¼ **cup reduced-sodium chicken broth**
- 1 **envelope reduced-sodium taco seasoning**
- 1 **tablespoon dried parsley flakes**
- 2 **garlic cloves, minced**
- ½ **teaspoon pepper**
- ¼ **teaspoon salt**
- 1 **can (16 ounces) refried beans**
- 1 **can (4 ounces) chopped green chilies**
- 14 **flour tortillas (8 inches), warmed**
  Optional toppings: shredded lettuce, chopped tomatoes, chopped green pepper, guacamole, reduced-fat sour cream and shredded reduced-fat cheddar cheese

1. Cut roast in half; place in a 4- or 5-qt. slow cooker. In a small bowl, mix broth, taco seasoning, parsley, garlic, pepper and salt; pour over roast. Cook, covered, on low 8-10 hours or until meat is very tender.

2. Remove pork from slow cooker; cool slightly. Shred meat with two forks. Skim fat from cooking juices. Return cooking juices and pork to slow cooker. Stir in beans and chilies; heat through.

3. Spoon ½ cup pork mixture across center of each tortilla; add toppings as desired. Fold bottom and sides of tortilla over filling and roll up.

TO FREEZE BURRITOS *Roll up burritos without toppings. Wrap individually in paper towels, then foil. Transfer to a resealable plastic bag. May be frozen for up to 2 months. To use frozen burritos, remove foil. Place paper towel-wrapped burritos on a microwave-safe plate. Microwave on high 3-4 minutes or until heated through. Serve with toppings as desired.*

PER SERVING *1 burrito (calculated without optional toppings) equals 320 cal., 9 g fat (3 g sat. fat), 61 mg chol., 606 mg sodium, 33 g carb., 2 g fiber, 26 g pro.* **Diabetic Exchanges:** *2 starch, 2 lean meat, 1 fat.*

Italian Spiral Meat Loaf

Take a classic comfort food to fantastic new heights with this impressive recipe. Sausage, pizza sauce and mozzarella give meat loaf an Italian accent.

—**MEGAN KRUMM** SCHERERVILLE, IN

PREP: 40 MIN. • **BAKE:** 1¼ HOURS
MAKES: 12 SERVINGS

- 2 **large eggs, lightly beaten**
- 1 **cup pizza sauce, divided**
- 1 **cup seasoned bread crumbs**
- 1 **medium onion, chopped**
- 1 **medium green pepper, chopped**
- 1 **teaspoon dried oregano**
- 1 **garlic clove, minced**
- ½ **teaspoon salt**
- ¼ **teaspoon pepper**
- 2 **pounds lean ground beef (90% lean)**
- 1 **pound bulk Italian sausage**
- ½ **pound sliced deli ham**
- 2 **cups (8 ounces) shredded part-skim mozzarella cheese, divided**
- 1 **jar (6 ounces) sliced mushrooms, drained**

1. Preheat oven to 375°. In a large bowl, combine the eggs, ¾ cup pizza sauce, bread crumbs, onion, green pepper, oregano, garlic, salt and pepper. Crumble beef and sausage over mixture and mix well.

2. On a piece of parchment paper, pat beef mixture into a 12x10-in. rectangle. Layer the ham, 1½ cups cheese and mushrooms over beef mixture to within 1 in. of edges. Roll up jelly-roll style, starting with a short side and peeling parchment paper away as you roll. Seal seam and ends. Place seam side down in a greased 13x9-in. baking dish; brush with remaining pizza sauce.

3. Bake, uncovered, 1 hour. Sprinkle with remaining cheese. Bake 15-20 minutes longer or until no pink remains and a thermometer reads 160°. Using two large spatulas, carefully transfer meat loaf to a serving platter.

FREEZE OPTION *Securely wrap and freeze cooled meat loaf in plastic wrap and foil. To use, partially thaw in refrigerator overnight. Unwrap meat loaf; reheat on a greased shallow baking pan in a preheated 350° oven until heated through and a thermometer reads 165°.*

⑤ INGREDIENTS

Apricot-Glazed Ham

Glazing a bone-in ham with apricot jam gives it an attractive look and delicious flavor.

—**GALELAH DOWELL** FAIRLAND, OK

PREP: 15 MIN. • **BAKE:** 1¼ HOURS
MAKES: 18-20 SERVINGS

- ½ **fully cooked bone-in ham (6 to 8 pounds)**
- ½ **cup packed brown sugar**
- 2 **to 3 tablespoons ground mustard**
  Whole cloves
- ½ **cup apricot preserves**

1. Place ham on a rack in a shallow roasting pan. Score the surface of the ham, making diamond shapes ½ in. deep. Combine brown sugar and mustard; rub over surface of ham. Insert a clove in the center of each diamond.

2. Place ham on a rack in a shallow roasting pan. Bake, uncovered, at 325° for 1 hour. Spoon preserves over ham. Bake 15-30 minutes longer or until a thermometer reads 140° and ham is heated through.

FREEZE OPTION *Freeze cooled sliced ham in freezer containers. To use, partially thaw in the refrigerator overnight. Microwave, covered, on high in a microwave-safe dish until heated through.*

Deluxe Pizza Loaf

Because this savory stromboli is made with frozen bread dough, it comes together in no time. I often add thinly sliced ham to the filling of cheese, pepperoni, mushrooms, peppers and olives. It's tasty served with pizza sauce for dipping.

—JENNY BROWN WEST LAFAYETTE, IN

PREP: 20 MIN. • **BAKE:** 35 MIN.
MAKES: 10-12 SLICES

- 1 loaf (1 pound) frozen bread dough, thawed
- 2 large eggs, separated
- 1 tablespoon grated Parmesan cheese
- 1 tablespoon olive oil
- 1 teaspoon minced fresh parsley
- 1 teaspoon dried oregano
- ½ teaspoon garlic powder
- ¼ teaspoon pepper
- 8 ounces sliced pepperoni
- 2 cups (8 ounces) shredded part-skim mozzarella cheese
- 1 can (4 ounces) mushroom stems and pieces, drained
- ¼ to ½ cup pickled pepper rings
- 1 medium green pepper, diced
- 1 can (2¼ ounces) sliced ripe olives
- 1 can (15 ounces) pizza sauce

1. Preheat oven to 350°. On a greased baking sheet, roll out dough into a 15x10-in. rectangle. In a small bowl, combine the egg yolks, Parmesan cheese, oil, parsley, oregano, garlic powder and pepper. Brush over dough.

2. Sprinkle with the pepperoni, mozzarella cheese, mushrooms, pepper rings, green pepper and olives. Roll up, jelly-roll style, starting with a long side; pinch seam to seal and tuck ends of loaf under.

3. Place seam side down; brush with egg whites. Do not let rise. Bake 35-40 minutes or until golden brown. Warm the pizza sauce; serve with sliced loaf.

FREEZE OPTION *Freeze cooled unsliced pizza loaf in heavy-duty foil. To use, remove from freezer 30 minutes before reheating. Remove from foil and reheat loaf on a greased baking sheet in a preheated 325° oven until heated through. Serve as directed.*

Pizza-Style Manicotti

Ham, pepperoni and string cheese make little bundles that are stuffed into manicotti shells. It's a fun hands-on recipe that the kids can help prepare.

— JUDY ARMSTRONG PRAIRIEVILLE, LA

PREP: 20 MIN. • **BAKE:** 25 MIN.
MAKES: 4 SERVINGS

- 8 **uncooked manicotti shells**
- 1 **jar (24 ounces) spaghetti sauce**
- 8 **slices deli ham (about 6 ounces)**
- 8 **fresh basil leaves**
- 8 **pieces string cheese**
- 24 **slices pepperoni**
- 1 **can (2¼ ounces) sliced ripe olives, drained**
- 1 **cup shredded Parmesan cheese**

1. Cook manicotti according to package directions for al dente; drain. Preheat oven to 350°.

2. Pour 1 cup sauce into an 11x7-in. baking dish. On a short side of each ham slice, layer one basil leaf, one piece string cheese and three slices pepperoni; roll up. Insert in manicotti shells; arrange in a single layer in the baking dish.

3. Pour remaining sauce over the top. Sprinkle with olives and Parmesan cheese. Bake, uncovered, 25-30 minutes or until heated through.

FREEZE OPTION *Cover unbaked casserole and freeze for up to 3 months. Thaw in refrigerator overnight. Remove from the refrigerator 30 minutes before baking. Cover and bake at 375° for 25-30 minutes or until pasta is tender. Let stand 10 minutes before serving.*

Asian Pork Tenderloins

This mouthwatering tenderloin is a summer favorite at our house, and it's so easy to make. The Asian-inspired marinade is a real treat. It's handy to prep extra for the freezer, to make future meals a breeze .

—JOAN HALLFORD
NORTH RICHLAND HILLS, TX

PREP: 10 MIN. + MARINATING
GRILL: 20 MIN. + STANDING
MAKES: 8 SERVINGS

- ¼ **cup olive oil**
- ⅓ **cup lime juice**
- 2 **tablespoons minced garlic**
- 2 **tablespoons minced fresh gingerroot**
- 2 **tablespoons soy sauce**
- 2 **teaspoons Dijon mustard Dash cayenne pepper**
- 4 **pork tenderloins (¾ pound each)**

1. For marinade, combine the first seven ingredients in a blender; cover and process until blended. Divide marinade between two large resealable plastic bags; add two tenderloins to each bag. Seal bags and turn to coat; refrigerate for at least 4 hours or overnight.

2. Prepare grill for indirect heat. Drain pork, discarding marinade in bags. Moisten a paper towel with cooking oil; using long-handled tongs, lightly coat the grill rack.

3. Grill pork, covered, over indirect medium heat for 20-30 minutes or until a thermometer reads 145°. Let stand 10 minutes before slicing.

FREEZE IT

Freeze uncooked pork in bag with marinade. To use, completely thaw in refrigerator. Grill as directed.

Southwest Pork Chops

I love to cook but hate to grocery shop, and one day I found myself with nothing but some pork chops, canned black beans and delicious tomatoes. This is the dish I came up with.

—**VICKI BLAINE** PLYMOUTH, MI

START TO FINISH: 30 MIN.
MAKES: 4 SERVINGS

- 1 medium onion, chopped
- 2 tablespoons olive oil, divided
- 1½ teaspoons minced garlic
- 2 cans (14½ ounces each) diced tomatoes, drained
- 1 can (15 ounces) black beans, rinsed and drained
- ¾ cup chicken broth
- 1½ teaspoons chili powder
- ½ teaspoon dried oregano
- ½ teaspoon ground cumin
- ⅛ teaspoon crushed red pepper flakes
- 4 bone-in pork loin chops (½ inch thick and 6 ounces each)
- ¼ teaspoon salt
- ¼ teaspoon pepper
  Hot cooked rice
- 2 tablespoons minced fresh cilantro, optional

1. In a large skillet, saute onion in 1 tablespoon oil for 3-4 minutes or until tender. Add garlic; cook 1 minute longer. Stir in the tomatoes, beans, broth, chili powder, oregano, cumin and pepper flakes. Bring to a boil. Reduce heat; simmer, uncovered, for 4-5 minutes or until heated through.
2. Meanwhile, in another skillet, brown pork chops on both sides in remaining oil over medium-high heat. Sprinkle with salt and pepper. Pour tomato mixture over chops. Cover and simmer for 10-15 minutes or until a thermometer reads 160°. Using a slotted spoon, serve over rice. Sprinkle with cilantro if desired.
FREEZE OPTION *Cool pork chop mixture. Freeze in freezer containers. To use, partially thaw in refrigerator overnight. Heat through slowly in a covered skillet until a thermometer inserted in pork reads 165°, stirring occasionally and adding a little broth or water if necessary. Serve as directed.*

Hearty Red Beans & Rice

My husband loves this quick and satisfying entree. The entire family will gobble it up!

—**SHERRI MILLER** GREENCASTLE, IN

START TO FINISH: 30 MIN.
MAKES: 6 SERVINGS

- 1 pound bulk Italian sausage
- 1 medium green pepper, chopped
- 1 small onion, chopped
- 1 garlic clove, minced
- 1 can (16 ounces) kidney beans, rinsed and drained
- 1 can (15 ounces) pinto beans, rinsed and drained
- 1 can (10¾ ounces) condensed tomato soup, undiluted
- 1 cup salsa
- 1 teaspoon Italian seasoning
  Hot cooked rice

In a Dutch oven, cook sausage, green pepper, onion and garlic over medium heat until meat is no longer pink; drain. Add beans, soup, salsa and Italian seasoning; heat through. Serve with rice.
FREEZE OPTION *Cool and place in a freezer container; freeze up to 3 months. To use, thaw in refrigerator. Transfer to a large saucepan; heat through. Serve with rice.*

Pepperoni Pizzazz

True comfort food in my book, this pasta covers all the bases: cheese, pepperoni and veggies tossed with a spicy red sauce.

—MARGE UNGER LA PORTE, IN

PREP: 10 MIN. • **BAKE:** 45 MIN.
MAKES: 9 SERVINGS

- 8 ounces uncooked penne pasta
- 3½ cups spaghetti sauce, divided
- 1 package (8 ounces) sliced pepperoni
- 1 jar (4½ ounces) sliced mushrooms, drained
- ½ cup chopped green pepper
- ½ cup chopped onion
- ½ cup grated Parmesan cheese
- ½ teaspoon garlic powder
- ½ teaspoon salt
- ⅛ teaspoon pepper
- ⅛ teaspoon crushed red pepper flakes
- 1 can (8 ounces) tomato sauce
- 2 cups (8 ounces) shredded part-skim mozzarella cheese

1. Cook pasta according to package directions. Meanwhile, combine 2½ cups spaghetti sauce, pepperoni, mushrooms, green pepper, onion, Parmesan cheese, garlic powder, salt, pepper and red pepper flakes in a bowl. Drain pasta; add to sauce mixture and mix well.

2. Transfer to a greased 3-qt. baking dish. Combine tomato sauce and remaining spaghetti sauce; pour over top.

3. Cover and bake at 350° for 40-45 minutes or until bubbly. Sprinkle with mozzarella cheese. Bake, uncovered, 5-10 minutes longer or until the cheese is melted. Let stand for 5 minutes before serving.

FREEZE OPTION *Cool unbaked casserole; cover and freeze. To use, partially thaw in the refrigerator overnight. Remove from refrigerator 30 minutes before baking. Preheat oven to 350°. Bake casserole as directed, increasing time as necessary to heat through and for a thermometer inserted in center to read 165°.*

Pork and Green Chili Casserole

I work at a local hospital and also part time for some area doctors, so I'm always on the lookout for good, quick recipes to fix for my family. Some of my co-workers and I often exchange recipes. This zippy casserole is one that was brought to a picnic at my house. People raved over it.

—DIANNE ESPOSITE

NEW MIDDLETOWN, OH

PREP: 20 MIN. • **BAKE:** 30 MIN.
MAKES: 6 SERVINGS

- 1½ **pounds boneless pork, cut into ½-inch cubes**
- 1 **tablespoon canola oil**
- 1 **can (15 ounces) black beans, rinsed and drained**
- 1 **can (10¾ ounces) condensed cream of chicken soup, undiluted**
- 1 **can (14½ ounces) diced tomatoes, undrained**
- 2 **cans (4 ounces each) chopped green chilies**
- 1 **cup quick-cooking brown rice**
- ¼ **cup water**
- 2 **to 3 tablespoons salsa**
- 1 **teaspoon ground cumin**
- ½ **cup shredded cheddar cheese**

1. Preheat oven to 350°. In a large skillet, brown pork in oil; drain. Stir in the beans, soup, tomatoes, chilies, rice, water, salsa and cumin.

2. Pour into an ungreased 2-qt. baking dish. Bake, uncovered, 30 minutes or until bubbly. Sprinkle with cheese; let stand 5 minutes before serving.

FREEZE IT

Sprinkle cheese over cooled unbaked casserole. Cover and freeze. To use, partially thaw in refrigerator overnight. Remove from refrigerator 30 minutes before baking. Preheat oven to 350°. Bake casserole as directed, increasing time as necessary to heat through and for a thermometer inserted in center to read 165°.

Mini Pork Pies

I discovered my love of pork pies as a child when I used to help my father deliver oil on Saturdays and we would stop at a local pork pie place for lunch. Now, as an adult, I host Christmas Eve for my very large French Canadian family, and everyone expects to find my little pork pies—it just wouldn't be Christmas Eve without them.
—**RENEE MURBY** JOHNSTON, RI

PREP: 1 HOUR • **BAKE:** 15 MIN.
MAKES: 10 SERVINGS

- 1 **tablespoon cornstarch**
- 1¼ **cups reduced-sodium chicken broth**
- 2 **pounds ground pork**
- 3 **garlic cloves, minced**
- 1½ **teaspoons salt**
- ¼ **teaspoon pepper**
- ⅛ **to ¼ teaspoon ground cloves**
- ⅛ **to ¼ teaspoon ground nutmeg**
- ⅛ **teaspoon cayenne pepper**
- 2 **packages (14.1 ounces each) refrigerated pie pastry**
- 1 **large egg**
- 2 **teaspoons 2% milk**

1. Preheat the oven to 425°. In a small saucepan, mix the cornstarch and broth until blended; bring to a boil, stirring constantly. Cook and stir for 1-2 minutes or until thickened. Remove from heat.
2. In a large skillet, cook pork, garlic and seasonings over medium heat 6-8 minutes or until pork is no longer pink, breaking up pork into crumbles; drain. Add broth mixture; cook and stir 1-2 minutes or until thickened. Cool slightly.
3. Unroll each pastry sheet. On a work surface, roll each into a 12-in. circle. Using floured round cookie cutters, cut twenty 4-in. circles and twenty 2¾-in. circles, rerolling the scraps as needed. Place the large pastry circles in ungreased muffin cups, pressing onto bottoms and up the sides.
4. Fill each with 3 tablespoons pork mixture. Place small circles over filling; press edges with a fork to seal. In a small bowl, whisk egg and milk; brush over tops. Cuts slits in pastry.
5. Bake 15-20 minutes or until golden brown. Carefully remove pies to wire racks. Serve warm.
FREEZE OPTION *Freeze cooled pies in freezer containers. To use, partially thaw pies in the refrigerator overnight. Reheat on ungreased baking sheets in a preheated 350° oven for 14-17 minutes or until heated through.*

Pork Chops Ole

This recipe is a fun and simple way to give pork chops a south-of-the-border flair. The flavorful seasoning, rice and melted cheddar cheese make the dish a crowd-pleaser.

—**LAURA TURNER** CHANNELVIEW, TX

PREP: 15 MIN. • **BAKE:** 1 HOUR
MAKES: 4-6 SERVINGS

- **6 pork loin chops (½ inch thick)**
- **2 tablespoons canola oil Seasoned salt and pepper to taste**
- **1½ cups water**
- **1 can (8 ounces) tomato sauce**
- **¾ cup uncooked long grain rice**
- **2 tablespoons taco seasoning**
- **1 medium green pepper, chopped**
- **½ cup shredded cheddar cheese**

1. In a large skillet, brown pork chops in oil; sprinkle with seasoned salt and pepper.
2. Meanwhile, in a greased 13x9-in. baking dish, combine the water, tomato sauce, rice and taco seasoning.
3. Arrange chops over rice; top with green pepper. Cover and bake at 350° for 1 hour or until the rice and meat are tender. Uncover; sprinkle with cheese.
FREEZE OPTION *Omit the water and substitute 1 package (8.8 ounces) ready-to-serve long grain rice for the uncooked rice. Assemble casserole as directed. Cool unbaked casserole; cover and freeze. To use, partially thaw in refrigerator overnight. Remove from the refrigerator 30 minutes before baking. Bake casserole as directed, increasing time as necessary.*

Sweet-and-Sour Pork

I stir up a homemade sweet-and-sour sauce for this colorful combination of tender pork, crunchy vegetables and tangy pineapple. Serve it over hot rice, chow mein noodles or both.

—**ELEANOR DUNBAR** PEORIA, IL

PREP: 15 MIN. + MARINATING
COOK: 20 MIN. • **MAKES:** 4 SERVINGS

- **⅔ cup packed brown sugar**
- **⅔ cup cider vinegar**
- **⅔ cup ketchup**
- **2 teaspoons reduced-sodium soy sauce**
- **1 pound boneless pork loin, cut into 1-inch cubes**
- **1 tablespoon canola oil**
- **1 medium onion, cut into chunks**
- **2 medium carrots, sliced**
- **1 medium green pepper, cut into 1-inch pieces**
- **½ teaspoon minced garlic**
- **¼ teaspoon ground ginger**
- **1 can (8 ounces) pineapple chunks, drained Hot cooked rice, optional**

1. In a small bowl, combine the brown sugar, vinegar, ketchup and soy sauce. Pour half into a large resealable plastic bag; add pork. Seal bag and turn to coat; refrigerate for 30 minutes. Set remaining marinade aside.
2. Drain and discard marinade from pork. In a large skillet, cook pork in oil for 3 minutes. Add the onion, carrots, green pepper, garlic and ginger; saute until pork is tender. Add reserved marinade. Bring to a boil; cook for 1 minute. Stir in pineapple. Serve with rice if desired.

FREEZE IT

Cool pork mixture. Freeze in freezer containers. To use, partially thaw in refrigerator overnight. Heat through slowly in a covered skillet, stirring occasionally and adding a little broth or water if necessary. Serve over rice.

Mexican Pork & Pinto Beans

We've lived in Arizona for decades, and to us, Arizona-style cooking means Mexican-style cooking—and vice versa. Nothing tastes better than chili-spiced pork with tortillas.

—**ANNE FATOUT** PHOENIX, AZ

PREP: 30 MIN. • **COOK:** 4 HOURS
MAKES: 16 SERVINGS (4 QUARTS)

- 1 bone-in pork loin roast (3 pounds), trimmed
- 1 package (16 ounces) dried pinto beans, soaked overnight
- 4 to 5 cloves garlic, minced
- 2 tablespoons chili powder
- 1 to 1½ teaspoons ground cumin
- 1 teaspoon dried oregano
- 2 cans (4 ounces each) chopped green chilies
  Pepper to taste
- 5 medium carrots, sliced
- 4 celery ribs, sliced
- 1 can (14½ ounces) diced tomatoes, undrained
- 3 small zucchini, sliced
  Flour tortillas, warmed

1. In a stockpot, combine the first eight ingredients; cover with water. Bring to a boil. Reduce heat; simmer, covered, 3 to 4 hours or until meat and beans are tender.

2. Remove pork; cool slightly. Stir carrots, celery and tomatoes into bean mixture; return to a boil. Reduce heat; simmer, covered, until vegetables are crisp-tender. Add zucchini; cook 8-10 minutes longer or until crisp-tender.

3. Meanwhile, remove pork from bone; discard bone. Cut pork into bite-size pieces; return to pot and heat through. Serve with tortillas.

FREEZE IT

Freeze cooled pork mixture in freezer containers. To use, partially thaw in refrigerator overnight. Microwave, covered, on high in a microwave-safe dish until heated through, gently stirring and adding a little broth or water if necessary. Serve with tortillas.

Hawaiian Pork Roast

Preparing a pork roast with bananas, liquid smoke and soy sauce produces a wonderfully tender meat with flavor that recalls the specialty I've so enjoyed at Hawaiian luaus.

—**MARY GAYLORD** BALSAM LAKE, WI

PREP: 10 MIN. + MARINATING
BAKE: 4½ HOURS
MAKES: 8-10 SERVINGS

- 1 **boneless pork shoulder butt roast (3 to 4 pounds)**
- 4 **teaspoons liquid smoke**
- 4 **teaspoons soy sauce**
- 2 **unpeeled ripe bananas**
- ½ **cup water**

1. Place the roast on a 22x18-in. piece of heavy-duty foil; sprinkle with liquid smoke and soy sauce. Wash bananas and place at the base of each side of roast. Pull sides of foil up round meat; add water. Seal foil tightly; wrap again with another large piece of foil. Place in a shallow baking pan; refrigerate overnight, turning several times.

2. Place foil-wrapped meat in a roasting pan. Bake at 400° for 1 hour. Reduce heat to 325°; continue baking for 3½ hours. Drain; discard bananas and liquid. Shred meat with a fork.

FREEZE OPTION *Freeze cooled meat with some of the juices in freezer containers. To use, partially thaw in refrigerator overnight. Heat through in a saucepan, stirring occasionally and adding a little water if necessary.*

Southwestern Pork & Pasta

This dish is packed with family-pleasing flavor. Boneless skinless chicken breasts may be used instead of the pork if you like.

—**NICOLE FILIZETTI** STEVENS POINT, WI

PREP: 25 MIN. • **COOK:** 20 MIN.
MAKES: 10 SERVINGS

- 1 **package (16 ounces) penne pasta**
- 2 **pounds pork tenderloin, cut into 1-inch cubes**
- 2 **tablespoons olive oil**
- 8 **green onions, chopped**
- 4 **garlic cloves, minced**
- 3 **cans (14½ ounces each) diced tomatoes with mild green chilies, undrained**
- 2 **cans (15 ounces each) black beans, rinsed and drained**
- 1 **package (16 ounces) frozen corn, thawed**
- 1 **jar (16 ounces) salsa**
- 1 **tablespoon chili powder**
- 1 **teaspoon salt**
- 1 **teaspoon ground cumin**
- 1 **teaspoon paprika or smoked paprika**
- ½ **teaspoon pepper**
- ¼ **teaspoon cayenne pepper**
- 1 **tablespoon cornstarch**
- 2 **tablespoons cold water**
  Sour cream

1. Cook pasta according to package directions. Meanwhile, in a Dutch oven, cook pork in oil in batches over medium heat until no longer pink; return all to the pan. Add onions and garlic; cook 1 minute longer. Stir in the tomatoes, beans, corn, salsa and spices. Bring to a boil. Reduce the heat; simmer, uncovered, for 5 minutes.

2. Combine the cornstarch and water until smooth. Gradually stir into pan. Bring to a boil; cook and stir for 2 minutes or until slightly thickened. Drain pasta; add to pork mixture and toss to coat.

3. Serve desired amount of pasta with sour cream. Cool remaining pasta; transfer to freezer containers. Cover and freeze for up to 3 months.

TO USE FROZEN PASTA *Thaw in the refrigerator. Place in an ungreased shallow microwave-safe dish. Cover and microwave on high until heated through. Serve with sour cream.*

Grilled Pork Tenderloins

We do a lot of grilling during the summer, and this recipe is one my family asks for again and again.

—BETSY CARRINGTON
LAWRENCEBURG, TN

PREP: 10 MIN. + MARINATING
GRILL: 20 MIN.
MAKES: 8-10 SERVINGS

- ⅓ **cup honey**
- ⅓ **cup soy sauce**
- ⅓ **cup teriyaki sauce**
- 3 **tablespoons brown sugar**
- 1 **tablespoon minced fresh gingerroot**
- 3 **garlic cloves, minced**
- 4 **teaspoons ketchup**
- ½ **teaspoon onion powder**
- ½ **teaspoon ground cinnamon**
- ¼ **teaspoon cayenne pepper**
- 2 **pork tenderloins (about 1 pound each)**

1. Combine first 10 ingredients. Pour half of marinade into a large resealable plastic bag; add pork. Seal bag and turn to coat; refrigerate 8 hours, turning occasionally. Refrigerate remaining marinade.

2. Drain pork, discarding the marinade. Grill pork, covered, over indirect medium-hot heat for 20-35 minutes or until a thermometer reads 145°, turning and basting occasionally with reserved marinade. Let stand 5 minutes before slicing.

FREEZE OPTION *Freeze uncooked pork in bag with marinade. Transfer reserved marinade to a freezer container; freeze. To use, completely thaw tenderloins and marinade in refrigerator. Grill as directed.*

⑤ INGREDIENTS
Ham & Swiss Stromboli

It's easy to change up this recipe with your favorite cheeses or meats. The dish makes a welcome dinner to take to someone in need.

—TRICIA BIBB HARTSELLE, AL

START TO FINISH: 30 MIN.
MAKES: 6 SERVINGS

- 1 **tube (11 ounces) refrigerated crusty French loaf**
- 6 **ounces sliced deli ham**
- ¼ **cup finely chopped onion**
- 8 **bacon strips, cooked and crumbled**
- 6 **ounces sliced Swiss cheese**
  Honey mustard, optional

1. Preheat oven to 375°. Unroll dough on a baking sheet. Place ham down center third of dough to within 1 in. of ends; top with onion, bacon and cheese. Fold long sides of dough over filling, pinching seam and ends to seal; tuck ends under. Cut several slits in top.

2. Bake 20-25 minutes or until golden brown. Cut into slices. If desired, serve with mustard.

FREEZE OPTION *Securely wrap and freeze cooled unsliced stromboli in heavy-duty foil. To use, reheat stromboli on an ungreased baking sheet in a preheated 375° oven until heated through and a thermometer inserted in center reads 165°.*

Herbed Pork Roast with Gravy

An easy rub made with pantry ingredients packs on surprising flavor. This irresistible pork roast is my husband's favorite dish.

—JEAN HARRIS CENTRAL POINT, OR

PREP: 10 MIN. • **BAKE:** 2 HOURS
MAKES: 6-8 SERVINGS

- ¼ **cup packed brown sugar**
- 1 **tablespoon dried thyme**
- 1 **teaspoon each garlic salt, pepper, rubbed sage and dried rosemary, crushed**
- 1 **boneless pork loin roast (3 to 4 pounds)**
- ¼ **cup all-purpose flour**

1. Combine brown sugar and seasonings; rub over roast. Place roast, fat side up, on a rack in a roasting pan. Bake, uncovered, at 325° for 2 hours or until a thermometer reads 160°.

2. Remove roast from pan. Pour pan drippings into a large measuring cup; add water to measure 2 cups. Place flour in a small saucepan; stir in pan drippings until blended. Bring to a boil over medium heat. Cook and stir for 2 minutes or until thickened. Slice roast and serve with gravy.

FREEZE OPTION *Place sliced roast in freezer containers; top with gravy. Cool and freeze. To use, partially thaw pork in the refrigerator overnight. Microwave, covered, on high in a microwave-safe dish until heated through, gently stirring and adding a little water if necessary.*

Pork, Bean & Rice Burritos

A combination of spices is key to this slow-cooked pork—my family's favorite burrito filling. The aroma that fills the air as the pork slowly simmers will remind you of a Mexican restaurant. It's a perfect recipe for tailgate parties.

—**VALONDA SEWARD** COARSEGOLD, CA

PREP: 25 MIN. • **COOK:** 6 HOURS
MAKES: 10 SERVINGS

SPICE RUB

- 2½ teaspoons garlic powder
- 2 teaspoons onion powder
- 1¼ teaspoons salt
- 1 teaspoon white pepper
- 1 teaspoon pepper
- ½ teaspoon ground cumin
- ½ teaspoon dried oregano
- ½ teaspoon cayenne pepper

BURRITOS

- 1 boneless pork shoulder butt roast (3 pounds)
- 1 cup water
- 2 tablespoons beef bouillon granules
- 10 flour tortillas (10 inches)
- 3 cups canned pinto beans, rinsed and drained
- 3 cups hot cooked Spanish rice
  Optional toppings: salsa, chopped tomato, shredded lettuce, sour cream and guacamole

1. Mix spice rub ingredients; rub over pork. Transfer to a 6-qt. slow cooker. In a small bowl, mix water and beef granules; pour around roast. Cook, covered, on low for 6-8 hours or until meat is tender.

2. Remove roast; cool slightly. Reserve ½ cup cooking juices; discard remaining juices. Shred pork with two forks. Return pork and reserved juices to slow cooker; heat through.

3. Spoon a scant ⅓ cup shredded pork across center of each tortilla; top with a scant ⅓ cup each beans and rice. Fold bottom and sides of tortilla over filling and roll up. Serve with toppings as desired.

FREEZE OPTION *Cool filling ingredients before making burritos. Individually wrap burritos in paper towels and foil; freeze in a resealable plastic freezer bag. To use, remove foil; place paper towel-wrapped burrito on a microwave-safe plate. Microwave on high for 3-4 minutes or until heated through, turning once. Let stand 20 seconds. Serve with toppings of your choice.*

TOP TIP

For the Spanish rice in this recipe, use Uncle Ben's brand microwaveable ready-to-serve Spanish rice or Near East brand Spanish rice pilaf mix, prepared according to the package directions.

GREEK PASTA BAKE
PAGE 199

Other Entrees

Family dinners are easy with these from-the-freezer classics: bubbly mac 'n' cheese, crispy fish nuggets, crowd-pleasing lasagna and much, much more.

heat. Add shallots and garlic; cook and stir until tender. Transfer to a food processor. Add sweet potatoes, ricotta cheese, liqueur, nutmeg and the remaining salt and pepper; process until blended.

3. Place 1 tablespoon filling in the center of a wonton wrapper. (Cover remaining wrappers with a damp paper towel until ready to use.) Moisten wrapper edges with water. Fold one corner diagonally over filling to form a triangle; press edges to seal. Bring opposite corners up over filling; moisten with water and press to attach. Repeat.

4. In a Dutch oven, bring water to a boil. Reduce heat to a gentle boil. Cook tortellini in batches for 30-60 seconds or until they float. Remove with a slotted spoon; keep warm.

5. In a small heavy saucepan, melt butter over medium heat. Add sage; heat 5-7 minutes or until butter is golden brown, stirring constantly. Remove from heat; stir in cherries and hazelnuts. Serve with tortellini. Top with cheese.

FREEZE OPTION *Freeze the uncooked tortellini on waxed paper-lined baking sheets until firm. Transfer to resealable plastic freezer bags; return to freezer. To use, cook tortellini as directed, increasing time to 1 1/2 - 2 minutes or until they float. Serve as directed.*

TO MAKE AHEAD *The sweet potato puree can be made and refrigerated the day before the wontons are filled.*

NOTE *Look for herbes de Provence in the spice aisle.*

Sweet Potato Tortellini with Hazelnut Sauce

Using wonton wrappers instead of fresh pasta dough makes homemade tortellini easier to prepare. For your more formal dinners, tortellini "hats" are an impressive vegetarian entree.

—CHARLENE CHAMBERS
ORMOND BEACH, FL

PREP: 1 HOUR
COOK: 10 MIN./BATCH
MAKES: 8 SERVINGS

- 3 **large sweet potatoes, peeled and cubed**
- 1/4 **cup olive oil, divided**
- 1 1/2 **teaspoons herbes de Provence**
- 3/4 **teaspoon salt, divided**
- 1/2 **teaspoon pepper, divided**
- 2 **shallots, chopped**
- 2 **garlic cloves, minced**
- 1 **cup whole-milk ricotta cheese**
- 1 **tablespoon hazelnut liqueur**
- 1/4 **teaspoon ground nutmeg**
- 72 **wonton wrappers**
- 3 **quarts water**
- 3/4 **cup unsalted butter, cubed**
- 3 **tablespoons minced fresh sage**
- 1/2 **cup dried cherries, chopped**
- 1/4 **cup chopped hazelnuts, toasted**
- 1 **cup shaved Asiago cheese**

1. Preheat oven to 400°. Place the sweet potatoes in a greased 15x10x1-in. baking pan; toss with 2 tablespoons oil, herbes de Provence, 1/2 teaspoon salt and 1/4 teaspoon pepper. Roast for 25-30 minutes or until tender, stirring once. Cool slightly.

2. In a small skillet, heat the remaining oil over medium-high

Pumpkin Lasagna

Skeptical friends are always amazed by this delectable lasagna. No-cook noodles and canned pumpkin make it a cinch to prepare.

—TAMARA HURON NEW MARKET, AL

PREP: 25 MIN.
BAKE: 55 MIN. + STANDING
MAKES: 6 SERVINGS

- ½ **pound sliced fresh mushrooms**
- 1 **small onion, chopped**
- ½ **teaspoon salt, divided**
- 2 **teaspoons olive oil**
- 1 **can (15 ounces) solid-pack pumpkin**
- ½ **cup half-and-half cream**
- 1 **teaspoon dried sage leaves**
  Dash pepper
- 9 **no-cook lasagna noodles**
- 1 **cup reduced-fat ricotta cheese**
- 1 **cup (4 ounces) shredded part-skim mozzarella cheese**
- ¾ **cup shredded Parmesan cheese**

1. In a small skillet, saute the mushrooms, onion and ¼ teaspoon salt in oil until tender; set aside.

2. In a small bowl, combine the pumpkin, cream, sage, pepper and remaining salt.

3. Spread ½ cup pumpkin sauce in an 11x7-in. baking dish coated with cooking spray. Top the sauce with three noodles (noodles will overlap slightly). Spread ½ cup of pumpkin sauce to the edges of the noodles. Top with half of the mushroom mixture, ½ cup ricotta, ½ cup mozzarella and ¼ cup Parmesan cheese. Repeat the layers. Top with remaining noodles and sauce.

4. Cover and bake at 375° for 45 minutes. Uncover; sprinkle with the remaining Parmesan cheese. Bake 10-15 minutes longer or until cheese is melted. Let stand for 10 minutes before cutting.

FREEZE OPTION *Cover and freeze unbaked lasagna. To use, partially thaw in refrigerator overnight. Remove from the refrigerator 30 minutes before baking. Preheat oven to 375°. Bake as directed, increasing time as necessary to heat through and for a thermometer inserted in center to read 165°.*

PER SERVING *1 piece equals 310 cal., 12 g fat (6 g sat. fat), 36 mg chol., 497 mg sodium, 32 g carb., 5 g fiber, 17 g pro.* **Diabetic Exchanges:** *2 starch, 2 fat, 1 lean meat.*

Classic Crab Cakes

Maryland is known for good seafood, and crab cakes are a traditional favorite. I learned to make them from a chef in a restaurant where they were a best seller. The crab's sweet and mild flavor is sparked by the blend of other ingredients.

—**DEBBIE TERENZINI** LUSBY, MD

START TO FINISH: 20 MIN.
MAKES: 8 SERVINGS

- 1 **pound fresh or canned crabmeat, drained, flaked and cartilage removed**
- 2 **to 2½ cups soft bread crumbs**
- 1 **large egg, beaten**
- ¾ **cup mayonnaise**
- ⅓ **cup each chopped celery, green pepper and onion**
- 1 **tablespoon seafood seasoning**
- 1 **tablespoon minced fresh parsley**
- 2 **teaspoons lemon juice**
- 1 **teaspoon Worcestershire sauce**
- 1 **teaspoon prepared mustard**
- ¼ **teaspoon pepper**
- ⅛ **teaspoon hot pepper sauce**
- 2 **to 4 tablespoons canola oil, optional**
  Lemon slices, optional

Combine crab, bread crumbs, egg, mayonnaise, vegetables and seasonings. Shape into eight patties. Broil or cook in a skillet in oil for 4 minutes on each side or until golden brown. Serve with lemon if desired.

FREEZE OPTION *Freeze cooled crab cakes in freezer containers, separating layers with waxed paper. To use, reheat crab cakes on a baking sheet in a preheated 325° oven until heated through.*

Greek Pasta Bake

Lemon and herbs complement the subtle sweetness of cinnamon in this savory Mediterranean pasta dish.

—CAROL STEVENS BASYE, VA

PREP: 40 MIN. • **BAKE:** 1 HOUR
MAKES: 6 SERVINGS

- ½ pound ground beef
- ½ pound ground lamb
- 1 large onion, chopped
- 4 garlic cloves, minced
- 3 teaspoons dried oregano
- 1 teaspoon dried basil
- ½ teaspoon salt
- ¼ teaspoon pepper
- ¼ teaspoon dried thyme
- 1 can (15 ounces) tomato sauce
- 1 can (14½ ounces) diced tomatoes, undrained
- 1 tablespoon lemon juice
- 1 teaspoon sugar
- ¼ teaspoon ground cinnamon
- 2 cups uncooked rigatoni or large tube pasta
- 4 ounces feta cheese, crumbled

1. In a large skillet, cook beef and lamb over medium heat until no longer pink; drain. Stir in the onion, garlic, oregano, basil, salt, pepper and thyme. Add the tomato sauce, tomatoes and lemon juice. Bring to a boil. Reduce heat; simmer mixture, uncovered, for 20 minutes; stirring occasionally.

2. Stir in sugar and cinnamon. Simmer mixture, uncovered, for 15 minutes longer.

3. Meanwhile, cook the pasta according to package directions; drain. Stir into meat mixture.

4. Transfer to a greased 2-qt. baking dish. Sprinkle with feta cheese. Cover and bake at 325° for 45 minutes. Uncover; bake for 15 minutes longer or until heated through.

FREEZE OPTION *Cool unbaked casserole; cover and freeze. To use, partially thaw casserole in refrigerator overnight. Remove from the refrigerator 30 minutes before baking. Preheat oven to 325°. Bake casserole as directed, increasing time as necessary to heat through and for a thermometer inserted in c enter to read 165°.*

Five-Cheese Jumbo Shells

Using five cheeses in one dish doesn't usually translate to something that's considered as light and as flavorful as these meatless shells!

—**LISA RENSHAW** KANSAS CITY, MO

PREP: 45 MIN.
BAKE: 50 MIN. + STANDING
MAKES: 8 SERVINGS

- 24 **uncooked jumbo pasta shells**
- 1 **tablespoon olive oil**
- 1 **medium zucchini, shredded and squeezed dry**
- ½ **pound baby portobello mushrooms, chopped**
- 1 **medium onion, finely chopped**
- 2 **cups reduced-fat ricotta cheese**
- ½ **cup shredded part-skim mozzarella cheese**
- ½ **cup shredded provolone cheese**
- ½ **cup grated Romano cheese**
- 1 **large egg, lightly beaten**
- 1 **teaspoon Italian seasoning**
- ½ **teaspoon crushed red pepper flakes**
- 1 **jar (24 ounces) meatless spaghetti sauce**
- ¼ **cup grated Parmesan cheese**

1. Preheat oven to 350°. Cook shells according to the package directions for al dente; drain and rinse in cold water.

2. In a large skillet, heat the oil over medium-high heat. Add the vegetables; cook and stir until tender. Remove from heat. In a bowl, combine the ricotta, mozzarella, provolone and Romano cheeses; stir in egg, seasonings and vegetables.

3. Spread 1 cup of sauce into a 13x9-in. baking dish coated with cooking spray. Fill the pasta shells with the cheese mixture; place in baking dish. Top shells with the remaining sauce and sprinkle with Parmesan cheese.

4. Bake, covered, 40 minutes. Bake, uncovered, 10 minutes longer or until the cheese is melted. Let stand 10 minutes before serving.

FREEZE OPTION *Cool unbaked casserole; cover and freeze. To use, partially thaw in refrigerator overnight. Remove from refrigerator 30 minutes before baking. Preheat oven to 350°. Cover casserole with foil; bake 50 minutes. Uncover and bake 15-20 minutes longer or until heated through and a thermometer inserted in center reads 165°.*

PER SERVING *3 stuffed shells equals 298 cal., 9 g fat (5 g sat. fat), 55 mg chol., 642 mg sodium, 36 g carb., 3 g fiber, 18 g pro.* ***Diabetic Exchanges:*** *2 starch, 2 lean meat, ½ fat.*

Groundnut Stew

My Aunt Linda, a missionary in Africa for more than 40 years, gave me the recipe for this thick, interesting dish with chunks of lamb, pork, eggplant and okra and a hint of peanut butter.

—**HEATHER EWALD** BOTHELL, WA

START TO FINISH: 30 MIN.
MAKES: 7 SERVINGS

- 6 **ounces lamb stew meat, cut into ½-inch pieces**
- 6 **ounces pork stew meat, cut into ½-inch pieces**
- 2 **tablespoons peanut oil**
- 1 **large onion, cut into wedges**
- 1 **large green pepper, cut into wedges**
- 1 **cup chopped tomatoes**
- 4 **cups cubed eggplant**
- 2 **cups water**
- ½ **cup fresh or frozen sliced okra**
- ⅓ **cup creamy peanut butter**
- 1 **teaspoon salt**
- ½ **teaspoon pepper**
   Hot cooked rice

1. In a large skillet, brown meat in the oil; set aside. In a food processor, combine the onion, green pepper and tomatoes; cover and process until blended.
2. In a large saucepan, combine the eggplant, water, okra and onion mixture. Bring to a boil. Reduce heat; cook, uncovered, for 7-9 minutes or until the vegetables are tender.
3. Stir in peanut butter, salt, pepper and browned meat. Cook, uncovered, for 10 minutes or until heated through. Serve with rice.

Red Clam Sauce

Luscious clam sauce tastes like you have worked on it all day. Instead, it cooks hands-free while you do other things. What a great way to jazz up pasta.

—JOANN BROWN LATROBE, PA

PREP: 25 MIN. • **COOK:** 3 HOURS
MAKES: 4 SERVINGS

- 1 **medium onion, chopped**
- 1 **tablespoon canola oil**
- 2 **garlic cloves, minced**
- 2 **cans (6½ ounces each) chopped clams, undrained**
- 1 **can (14½ ounces) diced tomatoes, undrained**
- 1 **can (6 ounces) tomato paste**
- ¼ **cup minced fresh parsley**
- 1 **bay leaf**
- 1 **teaspoon sugar**
- 1 **teaspoon dried basil**
- ½ **teaspoon dried thyme**
- 6 **ounces linguine, cooked and drained**

1. In a small skillet, saute onion in oil until tender. Add the garlic; cook 1 minute longer.
2. Transfer to a 1½- or 2-qt. slow cooker. Stir in the clams, tomatoes, tomato paste, parsley, bay leaf, sugar, basil and thyme.
3. Cover and cook sauce on low for 3-4 hours or until heated through. Discard the bay leaf. Serve with linguine.
FREEZE OPTION *Cool; place in a freezer container. Cover and freeze for up to 3 months. To use, thaw in refrigerator overnight. Place in a saucepan; heat sauce through, stirring occasionally. Serve with linguine.*

Oven-Fried Fish Nuggets

My husband and I love fried fish, but we're trying to cut back on dietary fat. This recipe is a hit with us both. He likes it as much as deep-fried, and that's saying a lot!

—LADONNA REED PONCA CITY, OK

START TO FINISH: 25 MIN.
MAKES: 4 SERVINGS

- ⅓ **cup seasoned bread crumbs**
- ⅓ **cup crushed cornflakes**
- 3 **tablespoons grated Parmesan cheese**
- ½ **teaspoon salt**
- ¼ **teaspoon pepper**
- 1½ **pounds cod fillets, cut into 1-inch cubes**
  Butter-flavored cooking spray

1. In a shallow bowl, combine the bread crumbs, cornflakes, Parmesan cheese, salt and pepper. Coat fish with butter-flavored spray, then roll in crumb mixture.
2. Place fish on a baking sheet coated with cooking spray. Bake at 375° for 15-20 minutes or until fish flakes easily with a fork.
PER SERVING *1 serving equals 171 cal., 2 g fat (1 g sat. fat), 66 mg chol., 415 mg sodium, 7 g carb., trace fiber, 29 g pro.*
***Diabetic Exchanges:** 5 lean meat, ½ starch.*
OVEN-FRIED CHICKEN NUGGETS *Substitute cubed boneless skinless chicken breasts for the cod. Bake as directed until chicken is no longer pink.*

FREEZE IT

Cover and freeze unbaked fish nuggets on a waxed paper-lined baking sheet until firm. Transfer to a resealable plastic freezer bag; return to freezer. To use, preheat oven to 375°. Bake nuggets on a rack on a greased baking sheet 15-20 minutes or until fish flakes easily with a fork.

1. For the sauce, in a large saucepan, combine the first six ingredients and bring to a boil. Reduce heat; simmer, uncovered, for 4-5 minutes or until sauce thickened, stirring occasionally. Spoon 2 tablespoons sauce over each tortilla.

2. In a large bowl, combine the Monterey Jack, 2 cups cheddar cheese, onions, sour cream, parsley, salt and pepper. Place about ⅓ cup down the center of each tortilla. Roll up and place seam side down in two greased 13x9-in. baking dishes. Pour the remaining sauce over top.

3. Bake, uncovered, at 350° for 20 minutes. Sprinkle with the remaining cheddar cheese. Bake for 4-5 minutes longer or until cheese is melted. Garnish with lettuce, olives and sour cream if desired.

FREEZE OPTION *Cover and freeze unbaked enchiladas. To use, partially thaw in the refrigerator overnight. Remove from refrigerator 30 minutes before baking. Preheat oven to 350°. Bake as directed, increasing time as necessary to heat through and for a thermometer inserted in the center to read 165°.*

Cheese Enchiladas

You won't go home with any leftovers when you bring these easy enchiladas to a potluck. With a homemade tomato sauce and cheesy filling, they always go fast. You can substitute any type of cheese you wish.
—**ASHLEY SCHACKOW** DEFIANCE, OH

PREP: 25 MIN. • **BAKE:** 25 MIN.
MAKES: 8 SERVINGS

- 2 cans (15 ounces each) tomato sauce
- 1⅓ cups water
- 2 tablespoons chili powder
- 2 garlic cloves, minced
- 1 teaspoon dried oregano
- ½ teaspoon ground cumin
- 16 flour tortillas (8 inches), warmed
- 4 cups (16 ounces) shredded Monterey Jack cheese
- 2½ cups (10 ounces) shredded cheddar cheese, divided
- 2 medium onions, finely chopped
- 1 cup (8 ounces) sour cream
- ¼ cup minced fresh parsley
- ½ teaspoon salt
- ½ teaspoon pepper
  Shredded lettuce, sliced ripe olives and additional sour cream, optional

DID YOU KNOW?

Oregano comes in two types. The sweet Mediterranean one is often simply labeled oregano. It belongs to the mint family. Mexican oregano, a member of the verbena family, has a more intense flavor and citrusy notes.

Lamb & Stout Stew

My grandmother used to make this stew as a special Sunday meal. It's a memorable treat from Ireland. If you like your stew thick and rich, you've got to try it.

—VICKIE DESOURDY WASHINGTON, NC

PREP: 40 MIN. • **BAKE:** 1½ HOURS
MAKES: 8 SERVINGS (2½ QUARTS)

- 2 **pounds lamb stew meat, cut into 1-inch cubes**
- 1 **tablespoon butter**
- 1 **tablespoon olive oil**
- 1 **pound carrots, sliced**
- 2 **medium onions, thinly sliced**
- 2 **garlic cloves, minced**
- 1½ **cups reduced-sodium chicken broth**
- 1 **bottle (12 ounces) Guinness stout or additional reduced-sodium chicken broth**
- 6 **medium red potatoes, peeled and cut into 1-inch cubes**
- 4 **bay leaves**
- 2 **fresh thyme sprigs**
- 2 **fresh rosemary sprigs**
- 2 **teaspoons salt**
- 1½ **teaspoons pepper**
- ¼ **cup heavy whipping cream**

1. Preheat oven to 325°. In an ovenproof Dutch oven, brown lamb in butter and oil in batches. Remove and keep warm. In the same pan, saute carrots and onions in the drippings until crisp-tender. Add garlic; cook 1 minute. Gradually add broth and beer. Stir in lamb, potatoes, bay leaves, thyme, rosemary, salt and pepper.

2. Cover and bake 1½-2 hours or until the meat and vegetables are tender, stirring every 30 minutes. Discard the bay leaves, thyme and rosemary. Stir in cream; heat through.

FREEZE OPTION *Place individual portions of stew in freezer containers and freeze up to 3 months. To use, partially thaw in refrigerator overnight. Heat through in a saucepan, stirring occasionally and adding a little water if necessary.*

PER SERVING *1¼ cups equals 311 cal., 12 g fat (5 g sat. fat), 88 mg chol., 829 mg sodium, 23 g carb., 4 g fiber, 26 g pro.* ***Diabetic Exchanges:** 3 lean meat, 2 vegetable, 1 starch, 1 fat.*

EAT SMART

Lemony Chickpeas

These saucy chickpeas add just a little heat to meatless Mondays. They're especially good over fluffy brown rice.

—APRIL STREVELL RED BANK, NJ

START TO FINISH: 30 MIN.
MAKES: 4 SERVINGS

- 2 cups uncooked instant brown rice
- 1 tablespoon olive oil
- 1 medium onion, chopped
- 2 cans (15 ounces each) chickpeas or garbanzo beans, rinsed and drained
- 1 can (14 ounces) diced tomatoes, undrained
- 1 cup vegetable broth
- ¼ teaspoon crushed red pepper flakes
- ¼ teaspoon pepper
- ½ teaspoon grated lemon peel
- 3 tablespoons lemon juice

1. Cook rice according to the package directions. Meanwhile, in a large skillet, heat oil over medium heat. Add the onion; cook and stir for 3-4 minutes or until tender.

2. Stir in chickpeas, tomatoes, broth, pepper flakes and pepper; bring to a boil. Reduce heat; simmer, covered, 10 minutes to allow flavors to blend. Uncover; simmer 4-5 minutes or until liquid is slightly reduced, stirring occasionally. Stir in lemon peel and lemon juice. Serve with rice.

PER SERVING *1 cup chickpea mixture with 1 cup rice equals 433 cal., 9 g fat (trace sat. fat), 0 chol., 679 mg sodium, 76 g carb., 12 g fiber, 13 g pro.*

FREEZE IT

Do not prepare rice until later. Freeze cooled chickpea mixture in freezer containers. To use, partially thaw in refrigerator overnight. Heat through in a saucepan, stirring occasionally and adding a little broth if necessary. Serve with rice.

Gyro Meat Loaf with Tzatziki Sauce

I love this Greek spin on meat loaf because I can sneak in spinach on my meat-and-potatoes family. And I get to make a whole other meal with the leftovers — gyros.

—MANDY RIVERS LEXINGTON, SC

PREP: 20 MIN.
BAKE: 55 MIN. + STANDING
MAKES: 8 SERVINGS

- 1 package (10 ounces) frozen chopped spinach, thawed and squeezed dry
- 1 cup dry bread crumbs
- 1 small onion, finely chopped
- 2 large eggs, lightly beaten
- ¼ cup grated Romano cheese
- 2 teaspoons dried oregano
- 1½ teaspoons garlic powder
- ¼ teaspoon salt
- 2 pounds ground lamb or beef
- 1 cup refrigerated tzatziki sauce

1. Preheat oven to 350°. In a large bowl, combine the first eight ingredients. Crumble the lamb over mixture and mix well. Shape into a loaf and place in a greased 11x7-in. baking dish.
2. Bake, uncovered, for 55-60 minutes or until no pink remains and a thermometer reads 160°. Let loaf stand 15 minutes before slicing. Serve with tzatziki sauce.
FREEZE OPTION *Securely wrap and freeze cooled meat loaf in plastic wrap and foil. To use, partially thaw in refrigerator overnight. Unwrap; reheat on a greased shallow baking pan in a preheated 350° oven until a thermometer reads 165°.*

Marvelous Shells 'n' Cheese

I switched up the mac 'n' cheese that my mother makes, and she agrees that my version is rich and heavenly. Just pop it in the oven and dinner will be ready shortly!

—LAUREN VERSWEYVELD
DELAVAN, WI

PREP: 25 MIN. • **BAKE:** 30 MIN.
MAKES: 6 SERVINGS

- 1 package (16 ounces) medium pasta shells
- 1 package (8 ounces) process cheese (Velveeta), cubed
- ⅓ cup 2% milk
- 2 cups (16 ounces) 2% cottage cheese
- 1 can (10¾ ounces) condensed cream of onion soup, undiluted
- 3 cups (12 ounces) shredded Mexican cheese blend
- ⅔ cup dry bread crumbs
- ¼ cup butter, melted

1. Cook pasta according to the package directions. Meanwhile, in a large saucepan, combine process cheese and milk; cook and stir over low heat until melted. Remove from the heat. Stir in cottage cheese and soup.
2. Drain pasta and add to cheese sauce; stir until coated. Transfer to a greased 13x9-in. baking dish. Sprinkle with Mexican cheese blend. Toss bread crumbs with butter; sprinkle over the top.
3. Bake, uncovered, at 350° for 30-35 minutes or until heated through. Serve immediately.
FREEZE OPTION *Do not prepare bread crumbs until later. Cool unbaked casserole; cover and freeze. To use, partially thaw in refrigerator overnight. Remove from refrigerator 30 minutes before baking. Prepare bread crumbs as directed; sprinkle over top. Bake casserole as directed, increasing time as necessary to for a thermometer to read 165°.*

**MARZIPAN CUPS
WITH CURRANT JELLY**
PAGE 223

Sweet Treats

Take your pick from fabulous ice cream cakes, frosty pops
and chilly treats of all kinds. Plus, savor the delicious ease
of made-ahead cookies, fruit cups and pies on ice.

Tangerine Chocolate Semifreddo

When I wanted a new frozen treat for my family, I came up with a citrusy, chocolaty version of the classic Italian semifreddo custard. For an elegant presentation, top each serving with whipped cream, tangerine and cocoa.

—CLAIRE CRUCE ATLANTA, GA

PREP: 35 MIN. + FREEZING
MAKES: 6 SERVINGS

- 8 large egg yolks
- ¾ cup sugar, divided
- 1 tablespoon grated tangerine peel
- 1 tablespoon tangerine juice
- ⅛ teaspoon salt
- ½ cup semisweet chocolate chips, melted
- 1 teaspoon vanilla extract
- 1 cup heavy whipping cream Sweetened whipped cream and baking cocoa

1. In top of a double boiler or metal bowl over simmering water, combine the egg yolks, ½ cup sugar, tangerine peel, juice and salt. Beat on medium speed until mixture is thick, frothy and holds a ribbon and a thermometer reads 160°. Remove from heat; whisk in melted chocolate and vanilla. Quickly transfer to a bowl; place in ice water and refrigerate for 15 minutes or until completely cool, stirring occasionally.

2. In a large bowl, beat cream until it begins to thicken. Add remaining sugar; beat until stiff peaks form. Fold into the cooled chocolate mixture. Pour into six freezer-safe dessert glasses or dishes. Freeze until firm, about 4 hours.

3. Just before serving, top with sweetened whipped cream and dust with cocoa. Serve frozen custard immediately.

⑤INGREDIENTS

Polka-Dot Macaroons

Macaroons studded with M&M's are easy to mix up in a hurry. That's good, because believe me, they never last long.

—JANICE LASS DORR, MI

PREP: 15 MIN.
BAKE: 10 MIN./BATCH + COOLING
MAKES: ABOUT 4½ DOZEN

- 5 cups flaked coconut
- 1 can (14 ounces) sweetened condensed milk
- ½ cup all-purpose flour
- 1½ cups M&M's minis

1. Preheat oven to 350°. In a large bowl, mix coconut, milk and flour until blended; stir in M&M's.

2. Drop mixture by rounded tablespoonfuls 2 in. apart onto greased baking sheets. Bake for 8-10 minutes or until edges are lightly browned. Remove from pans to wire racks to cool.

FREEZE OPTION *Freeze cookies, layered between waxed paper, in freezer containers. To use, thaw before serving.*

Lemony Coconut Macaroons

These chewy gems have refreshing lemon flavor. They freeze well and thaw quickly, so you can cure a craving anytime.

—KARLA JOHNSON EAST HELENA, MT

PREP: 15 MIN.
BAKE: 15 MIN./BATCH + COOLING
MAKES: 2½ DOZEN

- 4 **large egg whites**
  Dash salt
  Dash cream of tartar
- 1 **can (14 ounces) sweetened condensed milk**
- ¼ **cup lemon juice**
- 1 **package (14 ounces) plus 2 cups flaked coconut**
- 1½ **teaspoons grated lemon peel**
- ½ **teaspoon baking powder**

1. Preheat oven to 325°. In a small bowl, beat egg whites, salt and cream of tartar on high speed until stiff peaks form. In a large bowl, beat milk and lemon juice until thickened, about 3 minutes. Stir in coconut, lemon peel and baking powder. Fold in beaten egg whites.
2. Drop coconut mixture by rounded tablespoonfuls 2 in. apart onto parchment paper-lined baking sheets. Bake for 15-18 minutes or until golden brown. Cool on pans 2 minutes. Remove from the pans to wire racks to cool.
FREEZE OPTION *Freeze cookies, layered between waxed paper, in freezer containers. To use, thaw before serving.*

2. Divide the dough into four portions. Shape each into a disk; wrap in plastic wrap. Refrigerate 30 minutes or until firm enough to roll.

3. Preheat oven to 375°. For filling, in a small bowl, beat jelly and confectioners' sugar. On a lightly floured surface, roll one portion of the dough to ⅛-in. thickness. Cut with a floured 2-in. round cookie cutter. Place about ½ teaspoon filling in center of half of the cookies. Cover with remaining cookies. Press edges with a fork to seal. Place 2 in. apart on ungreased baking sheets. Repeat with remaining dough and filling.

4. Bake 10-12 minutes or until edges are light brown. Cool on pans 2 minutes. Remove to wire racks to cool completely.In a small bowl, mix confectioners' sugar and milk until smooth. Drizzle over cookies; let stand until set. Store in an airtight container in the refrigerator.

FREEZE OPTION *Transfer wrapped disks to a resealable plastic freezer bag; freeze. To use, thaw dough in refrigerator until soft enough to roll. Prepare filling and cookies. Bake and decorate as directed.*

Filled Strawberry Cookies

Because I learned to bake with my grandmother and mother, it felt like passing along a sweet new family tradition when I shared this recipe with them.

—ANDREA ZULAUF LIVONIA, NY

PREP: 45 MIN. + CHILLING
BAKE: 10 MIN./BATCH + COOLING
MAKES: 3½ DOZEN

- **1 cup butter, softened**
- **1½ cups confectioners' sugar**
- **1 large egg**
- **1½ teaspoons vanilla extract**
- **2½ cups all-purpose flour**
- **1½ ounces strawberry gelatin**
- **1 teaspoon baking soda**
- **1 teaspoon cream of tartar**

FILLING
- **¼ cup plus 2 tablespoons strawberry jelly**
- **¾ cup confectioners' sugar**

ICING
- **1½ cups confectioners' sugar**
- **3 tablespoons 2% milk**

1. Preheat oven to 375°. In a large bowl, cream the butter and confectioners' sugar until blended. Beat in egg and vanilla. In another bowl, whisk flour, gelatin, baking soda and cream of tartar; gradually beat into creamed mixture.

DID YOU KNOW?

Most vanilla comes from Madagascar and Reunion Island—formerly known as the Bourbon Islands—off the southeast coast of Africa. Bourbon vanilla is celebrated for its strong, clear vanilla flavor and creamy finish.

Coconut Ice Cream Torte

Guests will ooh and aah when you bring in a fabulous ice cream torte ringed with irresistible candy bars. Even the busiest host can deliver this summer showstopper. It's super easy, you can make it days in advance and it serves 12 of your best friends — and you.

—TASTE OF HOME TEST KITCHEN

PREP: 15 MIN. + FREEZING
MAKES: 13 SERVINGS

- 10 macaroons, crushed
- ¼ cup butter, melted
- ¾ cup hot fudge ice cream topping
- 26 snack-size Mounds or Almond Joy candy bars
- 1 quart vanilla ice cream, softened
- 1 quart strawberry ice cream, softened
- ¼ cup sliced almonds, toasted

1. In a small bowl, combine the cookie crumbs and butter. Press onto the bottom of a greased 10-in. springform pan. Freeze for 15 minutes.

2. In a microwave, heat the hot fudge topping on high for 15-20 seconds or until pourable; spread over crust. Trim one end from each candy bar; arrange around edge of pan. Freeze for 15 minutes. Spread vanilla ice cream over fudge topping; freeze for 30 minutes.

3. Spread strawberry ice cream over vanilla layer; sprinkle with almonds. Cover and freeze until firm. May be frozen for up to 2 months. Remove from the freezer 10 minutes before serving. Remove sides of pan.

NOTE *If Almond Joy candy bars are used, arrange bars with the almond side facing inward toward the center of the pan.*

Cherry Mocha Balls

My mother-in-law gave me this recipe before my wedding, and I've made mocha balls nearly every Christmas since. Because they freeze so well, I'll frequently bake some early and put them away to call on as instant holiday treats.

—JEANA CROWELL WHITEWATER, KS

PREP: 15 MIN. + CHILLING
BAKE: 15 MIN./BATCH + COOLING
MAKES: ABOUT 6 DOZEN

- 1 **cup butter, softened**
- ½ **cup sugar**
- 4 **teaspoons vanilla extract**
- 2 **cups all-purpose flour**
- ¼ **cup baking cocoa**
- 1 **tablespoon instant coffee granules**
- ½ **teaspoon salt**
- 1 **cup finely chopped pecans**
- ⅔ **cup chopped red candied cherries**
   Confectioners' sugar

1. In a large bowl, cream butter and sugar until light and fluffy. Beat in vanilla. In another bowl, whisk the flour, cocoa, coffee granules and salt; gradually beat into creamed mixture. Stir in the pecans and cherries. If necessary, refrigerate dough until firm enough to shape.

2. Preheat oven to 350°. Shape the dough into 1-in. balls; place 2 in. apart on ungreased baking sheets. Bake for 15 minutes or until the cookies are set. Cool completely on wire racks. Dust with confectioners' sugar.

FREEZE OPTION *Freeze cookies, layered between waxed paper, in freezer containers. To use, thaw before serving.*

Banana Split Brownie Cake

Brownies, ice cream, bananas, hot fudge, nuts—everything we love about a banana split is beautifully layered into the most awesome cake ever.

—TASTE OF HOME TEST KITCHEN

PREP: 20 MIN. + FREEZING
MAKES: 14 SERVINGS

- 2 packages (13 ounces each) fudge brownies
- 1 quart strawberry ice cream, softened
- 3 large firm bananas, halved lengthwise
- 1 cup hot fudge ice cream topping, warmed
- 1 quart vanilla ice cream, softened
- ¾ cup chopped pecans

1. Arrange the brownies in a greased 9-in. springform pan, cutting to fit and filling in small holes. Spread with strawberry ice cream. Cover and freeze for 3 hours or until firm.
2. Arrange bananas over ice cream, cutting to fit as needed. Spread with fudge topping and vanilla ice cream. Sprinkle with pecans. Cover tightly and freeze overnight. May be frozen for up to 2 months.
3. Remove from the freezer 10 minutes before serving. Carefully run a knife around edge of pan to loosen; remove sides of pan.
NOTE *This recipe was prepared with Little Debbie fudge brownies.*

Cherry Biscochitos

 After discovering the wonderful anise flavor of *biscochitos,* the traditional cookies of New Mexico, I created my own version using maraschino cherries and fresh cranberries.

—MARY SHIVERS ADA, OK

PREP: 45 MIN. • **BAKE:** 10 MIN./BATCH
MAKES: 11 DOZEN

- 1 cup shortening
- 1 cup sugar
- 1 large egg
- ¼ cup maraschino cherry juice
- ¼ teaspoon anise extract
- 3¾ cups all-purpose flour
- 1½ teaspoons baking powder
- ¼ teaspoon salt
- 1 cup fresh or frozen cranberries, finely chopped
- ¼ cup maraschino cherries, well drained and finely chopped
- ¼ cup confectioners' sugar

1. Preheat oven to 375°. In a large bowl, cream shortening and sugar until light and fluffy. Beat in egg, cherry juice and extract. In another bowl, whisk the flour, baking powder and salt; gradually beat into creamed mixture. Stir in cranberries and cherries.
2. Divide dough in half; shape each into a disk. On a lightly floured surface, roll each portion of dough to ¼-in. thickness. Cut with a floured 2-in. star-shaped cookie cutter. Place 1 in. apart on ungreased baking sheets.
3. Bake 7-9 minutes or until the edges begin to brown. Remove from oven and immediately dust with confectioners' sugar. Remove cookies from pans to wire racks to cool.
FREEZE OPTION *Freeze cookies, layered between waxed paper, in freezer containers. To use, thaw before serving or, if desired, reheat on a baking sheet in a preheated 350° oven until warm.*

EAT SMART
Citrus Strawberry Ice

An icy fruit dessert is perfect for summer, refreshing after dinner.

—**MARIE RIZZIO** INTERLOCHEN, MI

PREP: 30 MIN. + FREEZING
MAKES: 6 SERVINGS

- 1 **cup sugar**
- ¾ **cup water**
- 1 **tablespoon shredded orange peel**
- 2 **teaspoons shredded lemon peel**
- 1½ **teaspoons shredded lime peel**
- ⅓ **cup orange juice**
- 3 **tablespoons lemon juice**
- 2 **tablespoons lime juice**
- 4 **cups sliced fresh strawberries**

1. In a small saucepan, bring first five ingredients to a boil. Reduce the heat; simmer, uncovered, 5-6 minutes or until sugar is dissolved. Strain; discard peels. Add juices to syrup; cool.
2. Place half of juice mixture and berries in a blender; cover and pulse until nearly smooth. Pour into 2-qt. freezer container. Repeat with the remaining juice mixture and berries.
3. Cover and freeze for 12 hours or overnight, stirring several times. Ice may be frozen for up to 3 months. Just before serving, break apart with a large spoon.
PER SERVING *⅔ cup equals 173 cal., trace fat (trace sat. fat), 0 chol., 2 mg sodium, 44 g carb., 3 g fiber, 1 g pro.*
CITRUS BERRY ICE *Reduce strawberries to 2 cups and add 2 cups fresh raspberries.*

Cafe Mocha Cookies

These taste like my favorite coffeehouse drink in cookie form. They're crispy outside but soft in the middle.

—**ANGELA SPENGLER** TAMPA, FL

PREP: 20 MIN. • **BAKE:** 10 MIN./BATCH
MAKES: ABOUT 3 DOZEN

- 6 **tablespoons butter, softened**
- ⅓ **cup shortening**
- ½ **cup packed brown sugar**
- ⅓ **cup sugar**
- 1 **large egg**
- 2 **tablespoons hot caramel ice cream topping**
- 1 **teaspoon vanilla extract**
- 1½ **cups all-purpose flour**
- 4 **teaspoons dark roast instant coffee granules**
- ½ **teaspoon baking soda**
- ½ **teaspoon salt**
- 1½ **cups (9 ounces) dark chocolate chips**

1. Preheat oven to 350°. In a large bowl, cream the butter, shortening and sugars until light and fluffy. Beat in egg, ice cream topping and vanilla. In another bowl, whisk the flour, coffee granules, baking soda and salt; gradually beat into creamed mixture. Fold in chocolate chips.
2. Drop dough by rounded tablespoonfuls 2 in. apart onto ungreased baking sheets. Bake 8-10 minutes or until set. Cool on pans 2 minutes. Remove to wire racks to cool.

FREEZE IT

Drop the dough by rounded tablespoonfuls onto waxed paper-lined baking sheets; freeze until firm. Transfer to resealable plastic freezer bags; return to freezer. To use, bake frozen cookies as directed, increasing time by 1-2 minutes.

Lime Shortbread

This sweet-tart cookie just melts in your mouth and is so delicious. You can freeze the dough for up to 3 months. Bake up one log and save the other for when you need a treat.

—ABIGAIL BOSTWICK TOMAHAWK, WI

PREP: 25 MIN. + CHILLING
BAKE: 10 MIN./BATCH
MAKES: ABOUT 4½ DOZEN

- 1 **cup butter, softened**
- ¾ **cup confectioners' sugar**
- 1 **tablespoon grated lime peel**
- 2 **teaspoons vanilla extract**
- ½ **teaspoon almond extract**
- 2 **cups all-purpose flour**
- ¼ **teaspoon baking powder**
- ⅛ **teaspoon salt**
- ½ **cup chopped dried cherries**

1. In a large bowl, cream butter and confectioners' sugar. Beat in lime peel and extracts. Whisk flour, baking powder and salt; gradually beat into the creamed mixture. Stir in cherries.

2. Divide dough in half; shape each into a 7-in.-long roll. Wrap in plastic wrap; refrigerate rolls 3-4 hours or until firm.

3. Preheat the oven to 350°. Unwrap and cut dough crosswise into ¼-in. slices. Place 2 in. apart on ungreased baking sheets. Bake 9-11 minutes or until edges are golden brown. Remove from pans to wire racks to cool.

FREEZE OPTION *Place wrapped logs in resealable plastic freezer bag; freeze. To use, unwrap the frozen logs and cut into slices. If necessary, let dough stand a few minutes at room temperature before cutting. Bake as directed.*
ORANGE SHORTBREAD *Substitute grated orange peel for the lime peel and chopped dried cranberries for the cherries.*

⑤INGREDIENTS

Lemon-Poppy Seed Cutout Cookies

Even though cake mix is one of the ingredients, this recipe produces fantastically crisp cookies, not cake-like ones. You'd never guess that these poppy-speckled treats weren't made from scratch.

—CHARLOTTE MCDANIEL
JACKSONVILLE, AL

PREP: 30 MIN. + CHILLING
BAKE: 10 MIN./BATCH + COOLING
MAKES: 3 DOZEN

- 2 **large eggs**
- ½ **cup canola oil**
- 1 **package lemon cake mix (regular size)**
- ¼ **cup poppy seeds**
- ¾ **teaspoon grated lemon peel**

1. In a large bowl, beat eggs and oil; gradually add cake mix and mix well. Stir in poppy seeds and lemon peel.

2. Divide dough in half. Shape each into a disk; wrap in plastic wrap. Refrigerate for 2 hours or until firm enough to roll.

3. Preheat oven to 375°. On a lightly floured surface, roll each portion of dough to ⅛-in. thickness. Cut with a floured 2¼-in. flower-shaped cookie cutter. Place cookies 2 in. apart on greased baking sheets.

4. Bake 9-11 minutes or until the edges are lightly browned. Remove from the pans to wire racks to cool completely. Store in airtight containers.

FREEZE OPTION *Freeze cookies in freezer containers. To use, thaw in covered containers before serving.*

cookie tops and remove the center of each. Spread the marshmallow creme over the bottom of the solid cookies; cover with remaining cookies.

FREEZE OPTION *Freeze shaped balls of dough on baking sheets until firm. Transfer to resealable plastic freezer bags; return to freezer. To use, bake the cookies as directed.*

EAT SMART **⑤INGREDIENTS**

Frosty Fruit Cups

With just four ingredients, it's a snap to blend together fruit cups. Frozen in muffin cups for individual servings, they're a fun way to get kids to eat fruit.

—BETH LITZENBERGER
GOTHERNBURG, NE

PREP: 10 MIN. + FREEZING
MAKES: 16 SERVINGS

- 2 **cans (8 ounces each) crushed pineapple, undrained**
- 3 **medium firm bananas, sliced**
- 2 **packages (10 ounces each) frozen sweetened sliced strawberries, thawed and undrained**
- ¼ **cup chopped walnuts**

Place pineapple in a blender or food processor; cover and process until smooth. Add fruit; blend well. Pour ⅓ cup each into paper- or foil-lined muffin cups; sprinkle with walnuts. Freeze for at least 2 hours. May be frozen for up to 1 month.
PER SERVING *1 serving equals 88 cal., 1 g fat (0 g sat fat), 0 mg chol., 2 mg sodium, 20 g carb., 2 g fiber, 1 g pro.* ***Diabetic Exchange:*** *1½ fruit.*

Chocolate Marshmallow Cutouts

I make rich, fudgy cookies that taste like brownies with a marshmallow filling. The heart-shaped cutouts make them fancy, but to save time simply make sandwich cookies with marshmallow creme.
—KELLY WARD STRATFORD, ON

PREP: 35 MIN. + CHILLING
BAKE: 10 MIN./BATCH + COOLING
MAKES: ABOUT 2 DOZEN

- 1¼ **cups butter, softened**
- 2 **cups sugar**
- 2 **large eggs**
- 2 **teaspoons vanilla extract**
- 2 **cups all-purpose flour**
- ¾ **cup baking cocoa**
- 1 **teaspoon baking soda**
- ½ **teaspoon salt**
- 1 **jar (7 ounces) marshmallow creme**

1. In a large bowl, cream butter and sugar until light and fluffy. Beat in the eggs and vanilla. In another bowl, whisk flour, cocoa, baking soda and salt; gradually beat into the creamed mixture. Refrigerate, covered, 1 hour or until firm enough to shape.
2. Preheat oven to 350°. Shape level tablespoons of dough into balls; place balls 2 in. apart on ungreased baking sheets. Bake 6-8 minutes or until cookies are set. Using a 1¼-in. heart-shaped cookie cutter, score the center of half of the cookies. Cool cookies completely on the pans placed on wire racks.
3. Using the same heart-shaped cookie cutter, gently cut scored

Pumpkin Cake Roll

Keep one in the freezer for a quick dessert for family or unexpected guests, to take to a gathering or to give as a yummy gift.

—ERICA BERCHTOLD FREEPORT, IL

PREP: 30 MIN.
BAKE: 15 MIN. + FREEZING
MAKES: 10 SERVINGS

- 3 **large eggs, separated**
- 1 **cup sugar, divided**
- ⅔ **cup canned pumpkin**
- ¾ **cup all-purpose flour**
- 1 **teaspoon baking soda**
- ½ **teaspoon ground cinnamon**
- ⅛ **teaspoon salt**

FILLING

- 1 **package (8 ounces) cream cheese, softened**
- 2 **tablespoons butter, softened**
- 1 **cup confectioners' sugar**
- ¾ **teaspoon vanilla extract**
  Additional confectioners' sugar, optional

1. Line a 15x10x1-in. baking pan with waxed paper; grease the paper and set aside. In a large bowl, beat the egg yolks on high speed until thick and lemon-colored. Gradually add ½ cup sugar and pumpkin, beating on high until sugar is almost dissolved.

2. In a small bowl, beat egg whites until soft peaks form. Gradually add remaining sugar, beating until stiff peaks form. Fold into the egg yolk mixture. Combine the flour, baking soda, cinnamon and salt; gently fold into pumpkin mixture. Spread into prepared pan.

3. Bake at 375° for 12-15 minutes or until the cake springs back when lightly touched. Cool for 5 minutes. Turn cake onto a kitchen towel dusted with confectioners' sugar. Gently peel off waxed paper. Roll up cake in the towel jelly-roll style, starting with a short side. Cool completely on a wire rack.

4. In a small bowl, beat the cream cheese, butter, confectioners' sugar and vanilla until smooth. Unroll the cake; spread filling evenly to within ½ in. of edges. Roll up again. Cover and freeze until firm. May be frozen up to 3 months. Remove from freezer 15 minutes before cutting. Dust the cake roll with confectioners' sugar if desired.

⑤INGREDIENTS

Frozen Chocolate Monkey Treats

Fresh banana becomes an irresistibly yummy treat when you coat the slices with chocolate and dip them in peanuts, sprinkles or even toasted coconut.

—**SUSAN HEIN** BURLINGTON, WI

PREP: 20 MIN. + FREEZING
MAKES: 1½ DOZEN

3 **medium bananas**
1 **cup (6 ounces) dark chocolate chips**
2 **teaspoons shortening**
   Toppings: chopped peanuts, toasted flaked coconut and/or colored jimmies

1. Cut each banana into six pieces (about 1 in.). Insert a toothpick into each piece; transfer to a waxed paper-lined baking sheet. Freeze until completely firm, about 1 hour.
2. In a microwave, melt the chocolate and shortening; stir until smooth. Dip banana pieces in chocolate mixture; allow the excess to drip off. Dip in toppings as desired; return to a baking sheet. Freeze at least 30 minutes before serving.

NOTE *To toast coconut, bake in a shallow pan in a 350° oven for 5-10 minutes or cook in a skillet over low heat until golden brown, stirring occasionally.*

Homemade Ice Cream Sandwiches

I inherited my love of cooking from my mother, a former home ec teacher. She sent me this recipe so we could make our own ice cream sandwiches. We love them.

—KEA FISHER BRIDGER, MT

PREP: 25 MIN. + FREEZING
BAKE: 10 MIN. + COOLING
MAKES: 16 SERVINGS

- 1 **package chocolate cake mix (regular size)**
- ¼ **cup shortening**
- ¼ **cup butter, softened**
- 1 **large egg**
- 1 **tablespoon water**
- 1 **teaspoon vanilla extract**
- ½ **gallon ice cream**

1. In a large bowl, beat cake mix, shortening, butter, egg, water and vanilla until well blended. Divide into four equal parts.
2. Between waxed paper, roll one part into a 10x6-in. rectangle. Remove one piece of waxed paper and invert dough onto a ungreased baking sheet. Score the dough into eight pieces, each 3x2½ in. Repeat with remaining dough.
3. Bake at 350° for 8-10 minutes or until puffed. Immediately cut along scored lines; prick holes in cookies with a fork. Cool.
4. Cut ice cream into 16 slices, each 3x2½x1 in. Place ice cream between two cookies; wrap in plastic wrap. Freeze on a baking sheet overnight. May be frozen up to 2 months.
NOTE *Purchase a rectangle-shaped package of ice cream in the flavor of your choice for the easiest cutting.*

Marzipan Cups with Currant Jelly

These bite-size beauties look and taste gourmet, but they're easy to make and boast a delicate almond flavor. The hidden jelly surprise and pretty nut accent make them a nice addition to any treats tray.

—LORRAINE CALAND SHUNIAH, ON

PREP: 1 HOUR + CHILLING
BAKE: 15 MIN./BATCH + COOLING
MAKES: ABOUT 7 DOZEN

- 2 **cups butter, softened**
- 1 **cup sugar**
- 2 **large eggs**
- 2 **teaspoons vanilla extract**
- 4 **cups all-purpose flour**
- ½ **teaspoon salt**

FILLING
- 1 **can (8 ounces) almond paste**
- ½ **cup sugar**
- 2 **large eggs**
- ½ **teaspoon almond extract**
- 1 **cup red currant jelly**
- 84 **whole almonds**

1. In a large bowl, cream butter and sugar until light and fluffy. Beat in the eggs and vanilla. In another bowl, whisk flour and salt; gradually beat into creamed mixture. Refrigerate 1 hour or until firm.
2. Preheat oven to 350°. Using well-floured hands, press tablespoonfuls of dough onto bottoms and up the sides of greased mini-muffin cups.
3. For filling, in a small bowl, mix almond paste and sugar until blended. Add eggs and extract. Place ½ teaspoon jelly in each cup; top with 1 teaspoon of almond mixture. Place one almond on top of each cup. Bake 15-18 minutes or until golden brown. Cool in pans 5 minutes. Remove cups to wire racks to cool completely.

7-9 minutes or until edges are light brown. Cool on pans for 2 minutes. Remove to wire racks to cool.

FREEZE OPTION *Freeze wrapped logs in a resealable plastic freezer bag. To use, unwrap frozen logs and cut into slices. If necessary, let dough stand a few minutes at room temperature before cutting. Bake as directed.*

⑤INGREDIENTS

Strawberry Sherbet

This is a delightful, tasty treat for any time of year. It's perfect for kids or as an end to an elegant meal. For a special presentation, serve it in fancy dessert dishes with a pretty cookie or brownie accent.

—PAT KEY CENTRAL CITY, KY

PREP: 10 MIN.
PROCESS: 20 MIN. + FREEZING
MAKES: 1½ QUARTS

- 1 **can (14 ounces) sweetened condensed milk**
- 1 **package (16 ounces) frozen unsweetened strawberries, thawed**
- 2 **cups strawberry soda**

1. In a blender, combine milk and strawberries; cover and process until smooth. Transfer to a large bowl; stir in soda.
2. Pour into cylinder of an ice cream freezer; freeze according to manufacturer's directions. Transfer to a freezer container; freeze for 2-4 hours before serving. May be frozen for up to 1 month.

Snickerdoodle Crisps

This classic cookie from New England can be made two ways: soft or crunchy. My version spiced with cinnamon, ginger and nutmeg snaps with crisp perfection.

—JENNI SHARP MILWAUKEE, WI

PREP: 20 MIN. + CHILLING
BAKE: 10 MIN./BATCH
MAKES: ABOUT 5 DOZEN

- 1 **cup butter, softened**
- 2 **cups sugar**
- 2 **large eggs**
- 2 **teaspoons vanilla extract**
- 3 **cups all-purpose flour**
- 4 **teaspoons ground cinnamon**
- 2 **teaspoons ground ginger**
- ¾ **teaspoon ground nutmeg**
- ½ **teaspoon ground allspice**
- 2 **teaspoons cream of tartar**
- 1 **teaspoon baking soda**
- ½ **teaspoon salt**

SPICED SUGAR

- ⅓ **cup sugar**
- 1 **teaspoon ground cinnamon**
- ¾ **teaspoon ground ginger**
- ¼ **teaspoon ground nutmeg**
- ¼ **teaspoon ground allspice**

1. In a large bowl, cream butter and sugar until light and fluffy. Beat in the eggs and vanilla. In another bowl, whisk the flour, spices, cream of tartar, baking soda and salt; gradually beat into creamed mixture.
2. Divide dough in half; shape each into an 8-in.-long roll. Wrap rolls in plastic wrap; refrigerate 2 hours or until firm.
3. Preheat oven to 350°. In a small bowl, mix spiced sugar ingredients. Unwrap and cut dough crosswise into ¼-in. slices; press cookies into sugar mixture to coat both sides or sprinkle sugar mixture over cookies. Place 2 in. apart on greased baking sheets. Bake

Butter Pecan Pumpkin Pie

Whenever I serve this pie, everyone thinks I worked all day to make it, but it's actually easy to assemble. It's handy to have in the freezer when unexpected company stops in for coffee and dessert.

—**ARLETTA SLOCUM** VENICE, FL

PREP: 20 MIN. + FREEZING
MAKES: 8 SERVINGS

- 1 **quart butter pecan ice cream, softened**
- 1 **pastry shell (9 inches), baked**
- 1 **cup canned pumpkin**
- ½ **cup sugar**
- ¼ **teaspoon each ground cinnamon, ginger and nutmeg**
- 1 **cup heavy whipping cream, whipped**
- ½ **cup caramel ice cream topping**
- ½ **cup chocolate ice cream topping, optional**
  Additional whipped cream

1. Spread ice cream into the crust; freeze for 2 hours or until firm.

2. In a small bowl, combine the pumpkin, sugar, cinnamon, ginger and nutmeg; fold in the whipped cream. Spread over ice cream. Cover and freeze for 2 hours or until firm. May be frozen for up to 2 months.

3. Remove from the freezer 15 minutes before slicing. Drizzle with the caramel ice cream topping. Drizzle with chocolate ice cream topping if desired. Dollop slices with whipped cream.

EAT SMART ⑤INGREDIENTS

Sweet Potato Frozen Yogurt Pops

Once I had my little girl, I quickly became creative in the kitchen because I needed to have healthy foods on hand. These pops turned out to be a favorite.

—**JENN TIDWELL** FAIR OAKS, CA

PREP: 10 MIN. + FREEZING
MAKES: 6 SERVINGS

- 2 cartons (6 ounces each) honey Greek yogurt
- 1 cup mashed sweet potatoes
- ¼ cup fat-free milk
- ½ teaspoon ground cinnamon
- 6 freezer pop molds or paper cups (3 ounces each) and wooden pop sticks

Place the first four ingredients in a food processor; process until smooth. Pour into the molds or paper cups. Top molds with the holders. If using cups, top with foil and insert sticks through foil. Freeze until firm.

PER SERVING *1 pop equals 129 cal., 5 g fat (3 g sat. fat), 14 mg chol., 51 mg sodium, 18 g carb., 1 g fiber, 3 g pro.* **Diabetic Exchanges:** *1 starch, ½ fat.*

DID YOU KNOW?

Cinnamon comes in two basic types: Ceylon and cassia. Ceylon cinnamon's delicate, complex flavor is ideal for ice creams and simple sauces. The spicy, bolder cassia cinnamon (often labeled simply as cinnamon) is preferred for baking.

German Chocolate Cream Pie

This lovely, light-textured pie is simple to whip up and keep on ice until needed. A graham cracker crust makes it super convenient. To put a classic German accent on the dessert, top each slice with a spoonful of cherry pie filling.

—GENISE KRAUSE STURGEON BAY, WI

PREP: 5 MIN.
COOK: 15 MIN. + FREEZING
MAKES: 6-8 SERVINGS

- **4 ounces German sweet chocolate, chopped**
- **⅓ cup milk**
- **3 ounces cream cheese, softened**
- **2 tablespoons sugar**
- **1 carton (8 ounces) frozen whipped topping, thawed**
- **1 graham cracker crust (9 inches)**
  Whipped topping, fresh mint and chocolate dessert decorations, optional

1. In a saucepan over low heat, cook the chocolate and milk until chocolate is melted; stir until smooth. In a bowl, beat the cream cheese and sugar until smooth. Stir in the chocolate mixture. Fold in the whipped topping. Spoon into the crust. Freeze until firm. May be frozen for up to 3 months.
2. Remove from the freezer 10 minutes before serving. Garnish with whipped topping, mint and chocolate dessert decorations if desired.

⑤ INGREDIENTS
Pecan Roll-Ups

This recipe is so delicious it's sure to become a holiday favorite with your family. Pecans tucked inside make the cookies so rich.

—LEE ROBERTS RACINE, WI

PREP: 45 MIN. + CHILLING
BAKE: 15 MIN./BATCH + COOLING
MAKES: 8 DOZEN

- **1 cup butter, softened**
- **1 package (8 ounces) cream cheese, softened**
- **¼ teaspoon salt**
- **2 cups all-purpose flour**
- **1¼ cups confectioners' sugar, divided**
- **96 pecan halves (about 2 cups)**

1. In a large bowl, beat butter, cream cheese and salt until smooth. Gradually beat in flour.
2. Divide dough in half; shape each into a disk. Wrap in plastic wrap; refrigerate for 2 hours or until firm enough to roll.
3. Preheat oven to 350°. Dust a work surface with about 2 tablespoons confectioners' sugar. Roll one portion of dough into an 18x8-in. rectangle; cut dough crosswise into six 3-in.-wide sections. Cut each section crosswise into eight 1-in.-wide strips. Roll each strip around a pecan half; place 1 in. apart on ungreased baking sheets. Repeat with remaining dough and pecans, dusting work surface with an additional 2 tablespoons sugar.
4. Bake the cookies for 12-15 minutes or until bottoms are lightly browned. Remove to wire racks to cool completely.
5. Place remaining sugar in a shallow bowl. Roll cookies in sugar, coating well.
FREEZE OPTION *Bake and roll cookies in confectioners' sugar as directed. Freeze in freezer containers, separating layers with waxed paper, for up to 3 months. Thaw before serving; dust with additional sugar.*

Best of Both Cookies

Our kids' most requested cookies are peanut butter and chocolate chip, so I came up with this recipe combining the two. The two doughs swirled together create a lovely marbled pattern in the cookie.

—LORI KESINGER BAKER, MT

PREP: 25 MIN. + CHILLING
BAKE: 10 MIN./BATCH
MAKES: ABOUT 6½ DOZEN

- ¾ cup creamy peanut butter
- ½ cup butter, softened
- ½ cup sugar
- ½ cup packed brown sugar
- 1 large egg
- 1¼ cups all-purpose flour
- ½ teaspoon baking powder
- ½ teaspoon baking soda
- ¼ teaspoon salt

CHOCOLATE DOUGH
- ½ cup butter, softened
- ½ cup sugar
- ½ cup packed brown sugar
- 1 large egg
- 1 teaspoon vanilla extract
- 1¼ cups all-purpose flour
- ¼ cup baking cocoa
- ½ teaspoon baking powder
- ½ teaspoon baking soda
- ¼ teaspoon salt

1. In a large bowl, cream the peanut butter, butter and sugars until light and fluffy, for about 4 minutes. Beat in the egg. Combine the flour, baking powder, baking soda and salt; gradually add to the creamed mixture and mix well.

2. For the chocolate dough, in another large bowl, cream butter and sugars until light and fluffy. Beat in egg and vanilla. Combine the flour, cocoa, baking powder, baking soda and salt; gradually add to the creamed mixture and mix well.

3. Divide each portion in half. Knead one peanut butter and one chocolate portion together 5-10 times or until it just begins to swirl. Shape into a 10-in. log. Wrap in plastic wrap. Repeat with the remaining dough. Refrigerate logs for 3-4 hours or until firm.

4. Preheat the oven to 350°. Unwrap and cut log into ¼-in. slices. Place 2 in. apart on lightly greased baking sheets. Bake 6-8 minutes or until bottoms are lightly browned. Cool for 2 minutes before removing from pans to wire racks.

FREEZE OPTION *Place wrapped logs of cookie dough in resealable plastic freezer bag; freeze. To use, unwrap frozen logs and cut into slices. If necessary, let the dough stand a few minutes at room temperature before cutting. Bake as directed.*

Nutty Caramel Ice Cream Cake

Tuck this dessert in the freezer for one of those ready-anytime celebrations. A caramel, butter pecan and almond version is our favorite, but try it with other ice cream, cookie and syrup flavors.

—**DAVID STELZL** WAXHAW, NC

PREP: 30 MIN. + FREEZING
MAKES: 16 SERVINGS

- 4 **cups crushed pecan shortbread cookies (about 52 cookies)**
- ¼ **cup butter, melted**
- 6 **cups butter pecan ice cream, softened**
- 1 **carton (8 ounces) frozen whipped topping, thawed**
- ¾ **cup slivered almonds, toasted**
- ¾ **cup milk chocolate English toffee bits**
- ¼ **cup caramel sundae syrup**

1. In a large bowl, combine the cookie crumbs and butter. Press 2 cups onto the bottom of a greased 9-in. springform pan. Spoon half of the ice cream into the prepared pan. Freeze for 20 minutes.

2. Repeat layers with remaining cookie crumbs and ice cream. Spread with whipped topping. Sprinkle with almonds and toffee bits. Cover and freeze overnight or until firm. May be frozen for up to 2 months.

TO USE FROZEN CAKE *Remove from freezer 10 minutes before serving. Drizzle with syrup.*

Chai Tea Sandwich Cookies

Spiced cookies filled with creamy chai tea-flavored chocolate are sure to impress. for tea or treats.

—**LAUREN KNOELKE** MILWAUKEE, WI

PREP: 45 MIN. + CHILLING
BAKE: 10 MIN./BATCH + COOLING
MAKES: ABOUT 3½ DOZEN

- **8 ounces white baking chocolate, finely chopped**
- **⅓ cup heavy whipping cream**
- **2 chai-flavored black tea bags**

COOKIES
- **2 cups all-purpose flour**
- **½ cup sugar**
- **½ teaspoon ground cinnamon**
- **½ teaspoon ground cardamom**
- **⅛ teaspoon salt**
- **⅛ teaspoon pepper**
- **1 cup cold butter, cut into 16 pieces**
- **2 teaspoons vanilla extract**

1. For ganache, place chocolate in a small bowl. In a small saucepan, bring cream just to a boil; remove from heat. Add the tea bags; let stand for 10 minutes. Discard tea bags.

2. Reheat the cream just to a boil. Pour over chocolate; let stand 5 minutes. Stir with a whisk until smooth. Cool to room temperature or until the ganache thickens to a spreading consistency; stir occasionally, about 1 hour.

3. Meanwhile, in a large bowl, whisk flour, sugar, cinnamon, cardamom, salt and pepper; cut in butter with vanilla until crumbly. Knead until dough holds together when pressed. Shape into two disks; wrap each in plastic wrap. Refrigerate for 15 minutes or until firm enough to roll.

4. Preheat oven to 350°. On a lightly floured surface, gently roll dough to ⅛-in. thickness, lifting and rotating dough as needed. Cut with a 1½-in. round cookie cutter. Place 1 in. apart on ungreased baking sheets. Bake for 10-12 minutes or until lightly browned. Remove the cookies from the pans to wire racks to cool completely.

5. Spread 1 heaping teaspoon ganache on bottoms of half of the cookies; cover with the remaining cookies. Let stand until set.

FREEZE OPTION *Prepare dough. Transfer the wrapped disks to a resealable plastic freezer bag; freeze. To use, thaw cookie dough in refrigerator until soft enough to roll. Make the ganache. Prepare, bake and fill the cookies as directed.*

Almond Chocolate Biscotti

My neighbors like getting gifts of these white chocolate-drizzled cookies. And I like that they're a cinch to make.

—**GINGER CHATFIELD** MUSCATINE, IA

PREP: 20 MIN.
BAKE: 40 MIN. + COOLING
MAKES: ABOUT 3½ DOZEN

- **1 package chocolate cake mix (regular size)**
- **1 cup all-purpose flour**
- **½ cup butter, melted**
- **2 large eggs**
- **¼ cup chocolate syrup**
- **1 teaspoon vanilla extract**
- **½ teaspoon almond extract**
- **½ cup slivered almonds**
- **½ cup miniature semisweet chocolate chips**
- **1 cup white baking chips**
- **1 tablespoon shortening**

1. Preheat the oven to 350°. In a large bowl, beat the cake mix, flour, butter, eggs, chocolate syrup and extracts until well blended. Stir in almonds and chocolate chips. Divide dough in half. On ungreased baking sheets, shape each portion into a 12x2-in. log.

2. Bake for 30-35 minutes or until firm to the touch. Carefully remove to wire racks; cool for 20 minutes.

3. Transfer baked logs to a cutting board. Using a serrated knife, cut diagonally into ½-in. slices. Place on ungreased baking sheets, cut side down. Bake for 10-15 minutes or until firm. Remove from pans to wire racks to cool completely.

4. In a microwave, melt baking chips and shortening; stir until smooth. Drizzle over biscotti; let stand until set. Store the biscotti between pieces of waxed paper in airtight containers.

FREEZE OPTION *Freeze undrizzled cookies in freezer containers. To use, thaw in covered containers. Drizzle with baking chip mixture as directed.*

MASHED POTATO CUPS
PAGE 238

Cook Once, Eat Twice

You'll love these convenient dishes. Serve one for dinner, then pop the second in the freezer for a busy day, to share with a friend...whatever. It's like money in the bank.

Creamy Ham Pasta Casserole

Top a rich casserole with a little crunch, and you've got a dish the whole family will love.

—**MARION LITTLE** HUMBOLDT, TN

PREP: 20 MIN. • **BAKE:** 20 MIN.
MAKES: 2 CASSEROLES
(9 SERVINGS EACH)

- 10 **cups uncooked tricolor spiral pasta**
- 4 **celery ribs, chopped**
- 1 **medium green pepper, chopped**
- ½ **cup chopped onion**
- ¼ **cup butter, cubed**
- 3 **cans (10¾ ounces each) condensed cheddar cheese soup, undiluted**
- 3 **cups 2% milk**
- 1 **teaspoon salt**
- 4 **cups cubed fully cooked ham**
- 2 **cans (8 ounces each) mushroom stems and pieces, drained**
- 1 **cup crushed Ritz crackers**

1. Cook pasta according to the package directions. Meanwhile, in a Dutch oven, saute the celery, pepper and onion in butter until tender. Stir in the soup, milk and salt. In a very large bowl, combine the soup mixture, ham and mushrooms. Drain pasta; add to soup mixture and toss to coat.

2. Transfer to two greased 13x9-in. baking dishes. Top with the cracker crumbs. Cover and freeze one casserole for up to 3 months. Bake the remaining casserole, uncovered, at 350° for 20-25 minutes or until golden brown.

FREEZE IT

To use frozen casserole, thaw in the refrigerator overnight. Remove from the refrigerator 30 minutes before baking. Bake, uncovered, at 350° for 50-55 minutes or until heated through.

Spaghetti Ham Bake

My sister passed along the recipe for this convenient casserole. I appreciate being able to freeze one pan for a hectic day.

—MARY KILLION HERMISTON, OR

PREP: 25 MIN. • **BAKE:** 30 MIN.
MAKES: 2 CASSEROLES
(6 SERVINGS EACH)

- 2 packages (7 ounces each) thin spaghetti, broken into 2-inch pieces
- 4 cups cubed fully cooked ham
- 2 cans (10¾ ounces each) condensed cream of chicken soup, undiluted
- 2 cups (16 ounces) sour cream
- ½ pound sliced fresh mushrooms
- ½ cup chopped onion
- ½ cup sliced ripe olives
- 1½ teaspoons ground mustard
- 1 teaspoon seasoned salt
- 2 teaspoons Worcestershire sauce

TOPPING
- 2 cups soft bread crumbs
- ¼ cup butter, melted
- 2 cups (8 ounces) shredded cheddar cheese

1. Cook spaghetti according to package directions; drain and place in a large bowl. Stir in the next nine ingredients.

2. Transfer to two greased 11x7-in. baking dishes. Toss crumbs, butter and cheese; sprinkle over tops. Bake at 325° for 30 minutes or until hot.

FREEZE OPTION *Cover and freeze casseroles. Thaw in the refrigerator overnight. Bake, uncovered, at 325° for 50-55 minutes or until heated through.*

Chicken Tater Bake

You'll please everyone in the family with this inviting dish. It tastes like chicken potpie with a crispy Tater Tot crust.

—FRAN ALLEN ST. LOUIS, MO

PREP: 20 MIN. • **BAKE:** 40 MIN.
MAKES: 2 CASSEROLES
(6 SERVINGS EACH)

- 2 cans (10¾ ounces each) condensed cream of chicken soup, undiluted
- ½ cup 2% milk
- ¼ cup butter, cubed
- 3 cups cubed cooked chicken
- 1 package (16 ounces) frozen peas and carrots, thawed
- 1½ cups (6 ounces) shredded cheddar cheese, divided
- 1 package (32 ounces) frozen Tater Tots

1. In a large saucepan, combine the soup, milk and butter. Cook and stir over medium heat until heated through. Remove from the heat; stir in the chicken, peas and carrots, and 1 cup cheese.

2. Transfer to two greased 8-in. square baking dishes. Top with Tater Tots; sprinkle with remaining cheese.

3. Cover and freeze one casserole for up to 3 months. Cover and bake the remaining casserole at 350° for 35 minutes. Uncover; bake 5-10 minutes longer or until heated through.

TO USE FROZEN CASSEROLE
Remove from the freezer 30 minutes before baking (do not thaw). Cover and bake at 350° for 1½-1¾ hours or until heated through.

BEEF TATER BAKE *Do not make chicken filling. Cook 2 pounds ground beef with 1 cup each chopped onion and celery; drain. Add 2 cans condensed cream of celery soup, 1 teaspoon salt and ½ teaspoon pepper. Place filling in two baking dishes; proceed as directed.*

Vegetarian Lasagna Alfredo

When we were newly married, I remembered how much my husband enjoyed a white lasagna we ate at a restaurant. I decided to re-create the dish at home, but with lots of tomatoes from the garden and broccoli instead of spinach.

—JAMIELYNN GRIFFITH BUFFALO, NY

PREP: 1 HOUR
BAKE: 35 MIN. + STANDING
MAKES: 2 LASAGNAS
(12 SERVINGS EACH)

- 18 lasagna noodles
- 7 cups fresh broccoli florets
- 2 large eggs, lightly beaten
- 2 cartons (15 ounces each) ricotta cheese
- 4 teaspoons Italian seasoning
- 8 medium fresh tomatoes, chopped
- 4 envelopes Alfredo sauce mix, divided
- 6 cups (24 ounces) shredded part-skim mozzarella cheese

1. Cook noodles according to package directions. Meanwhile, place broccoli in a steamer basket. Place in a large saucepan over 1 in. of water; bring to a boil. Cover and steam for 5-7 minutes or until crisp-tender.

2. In a large bowl, combine the eggs, ricotta cheese and Italian seasoning; gently stir in the tomatoes and broccoli. Set aside.

3. Preheat oven to 350°. Drain noodles. Prepare two envelopes of Alfredo sauce mix according to package directions. Spread ¼ cup sauce in each of two greased 13x9-in. baking dishes. Top each with three noodles, 1 cup ricotta mixture, 1 cup mozzarella cheese and ¼ cup sauce. Repeat layers. Top with remaining noodles, sauce and mozzarella cheese. Bake lasagna, uncovered, 35-40 minutes or until bubbly and edges are lightly browned. Let stand 15 minutes before cutting. For each lasagna, prepare one envelope of sauce mix according to package directions; serve with lasagna.

FREEZE OPTION *Cover and freeze lasagna up to 3 months. To use, thaw in refrigerator overnight. Remove from the refrigerator 30 minutes before baking. Preheat oven to 350°. Bake, uncovered, 50-60 minutes or until bubbly and edges are lightly browned. Let stand 15 minutes before cutting. Prepare an envelope of Alfredo sauce mix according to package directions; serve with lasagna.*

PER SERVING *1 piece equals 243 cal., 11 g fat (6 g sat. fat), 53 mg chol., 384 mg sodium, 22 g carb., 2 g fiber, 16 g pro.* **Diabetic Exchanges:** *2 lean meat, 1½ starch, 1 fat.*

TOP TIP

If you don't have Italian seasoning, you can mix up your own with equal amounts of basil, thyme, rosemary and oregano. You can also add parsley flakes, marjoram, sage, savory or garlic powder.

Cheesy Kielbasa Bake

My aunt originally made this hearty casserole for family gatherings. Now I enjoy fixing it for my family any night of the week. What an awesome way to sneak in some garden veggies.

—KATE BECKMAN HEMET, CA

PREP: 55 MIN. • **BAKE:** 30 MIN.
MAKES: 2 CASSEROLES
(8-10 SERVINGS EACH)

- 12 **ounces uncooked elbow macaroni**
- 2 **pounds kielbasa or Polish sausage, halved lengthwise and sliced**
- 1 **tablespoon olive oil**
- 2 **medium onions, chopped**
- 2 **medium zucchini, quartered and sliced**
- 2 **medium carrots, grated**
- ½ **teaspoon minced garlic**
- 1 **jar (26 ounces) spaghetti sauce**
- 1 **can (14½ ounces) stewed tomatoes**
- 1 **large egg, lightly beaten**
- 1 **carton (15 ounces) ricotta cheese**
- 2 **cups (8 ounces) shredded cheddar cheese**
- 2 **cups (8 ounces) part-skim shredded mozzarella cheese**
- 2 **green onions, chopped**

1. Cook macaroni according to package directions. Meanwhile, in a large skillet, brown sausage in oil over medium heat; drain. Add onions, zucchini, carrots and garlic; cook and stir for 5-6 minutes or until crisp-tender.

2. Stir in spaghetti sauce and tomatoes. Bring to a boil. Reduce heat; simmer, uncovered, for 15 minutes. Drain macaroni.

3. In a small bowl, combine egg and ricotta cheese. In each of two greased 13x9-in. baking dishes, layer a fourth of each of the following: macaroni, meat sauce, ricotta mixture, cheddar and mozzarella. Repeat layers. Top with green onions.

4. Cool one casserole; cover and freeze for up to 2 months. Cover and bake remaining casserole at 350° for 15 minutes. Uncover; bake 15 minutes longer or until cheese is melted.

TO USE FROZEN CASSEROLE
Thaw in the refrigerator for 24 hours. Remove from the refrigerator 30 minutes before baking. Cover and bake at 350° for 35-40 minutes or until heated through.

Make Once, Eat Twice Lasagna

Our family loves this recipe accompanied with a green salad and garlic bread. It is so handy on lazy days or when guests arrive to have an extra ready-made pan in the freezer.

—GERI DAVIS PRESCOTT, AZ

PREP: 35 MIN.
BAKE: 55 MIN. + STANDING
MAKES: 2 LASAGNAS
(12 SERVINGS EACH)

- 18 **lasagna noodles**
- 3 **pounds ground beef**
- 3 **jars (26 ounces each) spaghetti sauce**
- 2 **large eggs, lightly beaten**
- 1½ **pounds ricotta cheese**
- 6 **cups (24 ounces) shredded part-skim mozzarella cheese, divided**
- 1 **tablespoon dried parsley flakes**
- 1 **teaspoon salt**
- ½ **teaspoon pepper**
- 1 **cup grated Parmesan cheese**

1. Cook noodles according to package directions. Meanwhile, in a Dutch oven, cook beef over medium heat until no longer pink; drain. Stir in spaghetti sauce; set aside.

2. In a large bowl, combine the eggs, ricotta cheese, 4½ cups mozzarella cheese, parsley, salt and pepper.

3. Drain noodles. Spread 1 cup meat sauce in each of two greased 13x9-in. baking dishes. Layer each with three noodles, 1 cup ricotta mixture and 1½ cups meat sauce. Repeat layers twice. Top with Parmesan cheese and the remaining mozzarella cheese.

4. Cover and freeze one lasagna for up to 3 months. Cover and bake remaining lasagna at 375° for 45 minutes. Uncover and bake 10 minutes longer or until bubbly. Let stand for 10 minutes before cutting.

TO USE FROZEN LASAGNA
Thaw in refrigerator overnight. Remove from refrigerator 30 minutes before baking.

Cover and bake at 375° for 60-70 minutes or until heated through. Uncover; bake 10 minutes longer or until bubbly. Let stand for 10 minutes before cutting.

⑤INGREDIENTS
Mashed Potato Cups

I came up with this recipe as a way to use up leftover mashed potatoes. It's a nice alternative to the standard potatoes or rice.

—JILL HANCOCK NASHUA, NH

START TO FINISH: 30 MIN.
MAKES: 2 PANS (6 SERVINGS EACH)

- 3½ **pounds cubed peeled potatoes**
- ½ **cup 2% milk**
- ¼ **cup butter**
- 1 **teaspoon salt**
- ⅛ **teaspoon pepper**
- 1⅓ **cups plus 2 tablespoons shredded Colby-Monterey Jack cheese, divided**
- 2 **tablespoons minced fresh parsley**

1. Place potatoes in a large saucepan and cover with water. Bring to a boil. Reduce heat; cover and cook for 10-15 minutes or until tender. Drain.

2. In a large bowl, mash potatoes, milk, butter, salt and pepper until smooth. Stir in 1⅓ cups cheese. Grease two six-portion muffin pans; divide potato mixture between pans. Sprinkle with remaining cheese; top with parsley.

3. Cover and freeze one pan up to 3 months. Bake remaining pan at 350° for 15-20 minutes or until heated through.

TO USE FROZEN POTATO CUPS
Thaw in the refrigerator. Bake as directed.

Chicken Tetrazzini

A good friend shared a version of this recipe with me 35 years ago. I pay it forward by taking the second casserole to friends when they are unable to cook.
—**HELEN MCCHEE** SAVOY, IL

PREP: 30 MIN. • **BAKE:** 20 MIN.
MAKES: 2 CASSEROLES
(3-4 SERVINGS EACH)

12 ounces spaghetti
⅓ cup butter, cubed
⅓ cup all-purpose flour
¾ teaspoon salt
¼ teaspoon white pepper
1 can (14½ ounces) chicken broth
1½ cups half-and-half cream
1 cup heavy whipping cream
4 cups cubed cooked chicken
3 cans (4 ounces each) mushroom stems and pieces, drained
1 jar (4 ounces) sliced pimientos, drained
½ cup grated Parmesan cheese

1. Cook spaghetti according to package directions. Meanwhile, in a Dutch oven, melt butter. Stir in flour, salt and pepper until smooth. Gradually add broth, half-and-half and whipping cream. Bring to a boil; cook and stir 2 minutes or until thickened.
2. Remove from heat. Stir in the chicken, mushrooms and pimientos. Drain spaghetti; add to pan and toss to coat.
3. Transfer to two greased 11x7-in. baking dishes. Sprinkle with cheese. Cover and freeze one casserole for up to 2 months. Bake the second casserole, uncovered, at 350° for 20-25 minutes or until heated through.

FREEZE IT

To use frozen casserole, thaw in the refrigerator overnight. Cover and bake at 350° for 30 minutes. Uncover; bake 15-20 minutes longer or until heated through. Stir before serving.

Debra's Cavatini

I love how this recipe makes two casseroles. I add a little something different each time, such as extra garlic, cheese or herbs.

—**DEBRA BUTCHER** DECATUR, IN

PREP: 45 MIN. • **BAKE:** 35 MIN.
MAKES: 2 CASSEROLES
(6 SERVINGS EACH)

- 1 **package (16 ounces) penne pasta**
- 1 **pound ground beef**
- 1 **pound Italian pork sausage**
- 1¾ **cups sliced fresh mushrooms**
- 1 **medium onion, chopped**
- 1 **medium green pepper, chopped**
- 2 **cans (14½ ounces each) Italian diced tomatoes**
- 1 **jar (23½ ounces) Italian sausage and garlic spaghetti sauce**
- 1 **jar (16 ounces) chunky mild salsa**
- 1 **package (8 ounces) sliced pepperoni, chopped**
- 1 **cup (4 ounces) shredded Swiss cheese, divided**
- 4 **cups (16 ounces) shredded part-skim mozzarella cheese, divided**
- 1½ **cups shredded Parmesan cheese, divided**
- 1 **jar (24 ounces) three-cheese spaghetti sauce**

1. Cook pasta according to package directions. Meanwhile, in a Dutch oven, cook beef, sausage, mushrooms, onion and green pepper over medium heat until the meat is no longer pink; drain.

2. Drain pasta; add to the meat mixture. Stir in the tomatoes, sausage and garlic spaghetti sauce, salsa and pepperoni.

3. Preheat oven to 350°. Divide half of pasta mixture between two greased 13x9-in. baking dishes. Sprinkle each with ¼ cup Swiss cheese, 1 cup mozzarella cheese and ⅓ cup Parmesan cheese. Spread ¾ cup of three-cheese spaghetti sauce over each. Top with remaining pasta mixture and three-cheese spaghetti sauce. Sprinkle with remaining cheeses.

4. Cover and bake 25 minutes. Uncover; bake 10 minutes or until cheese is melted.

FREEZE OPTION *Cover unbaked casserole and freeze for up to 3 months. To use, thaw in the refrigerator overnight. Remove from refrigerator 30 minutes before baking. Preheat oven to 350°. Bake casserole, covered, 45 minutes. Uncover; bake 10 minutes or until the cheese is melted.*

HOW TO

QUICKLY SEED A BELL PEPPER

Holding the pepper by the stem, slice from the top of the pepper down, using a chef's knife. Use this technique to slice around the seeds when a recipe calls for julienned or chopped peppers.

Simple Creamy Chicken Enchiladas

One of the first recipes I created and cooked for my husband right after we got married, these creamy enchiladas were an instant hit. He was so impressed, and now we fix them for friends regularly.

—MELISSA ROGERS TUSCALOOSA, AL

PREP: 30 MIN. • **BAKE:** 30 MIN.
MAKES: 2 CASSEROLES
(5 SERVINGS EACH)

- 1 rotisserie chicken
- 2 cans (14½ ounces each) diced tomatoes with mild green chilies, undrained
- 2 cans (10¾ ounces each) condensed cream of chicken soup, undiluted
- 1 can (10¾ ounces) condensed cheddar cheese soup, undiluted
- ¼ cup 2% milk
- 1 tablespoon ground cumin
- 1 tablespoon chili powder
- 2 teaspoons garlic powder
- 2 teaspoons dried oregano
- 1 package (8 ounces) cream cheese, cubed
- 20 flour tortillas (8 inches), warmed
- 4 cups shredded Mexican cheese blend

1. Preheat the oven to 350°. Remove meat from the bones; discard bones. Shred chicken with two forks and set aside. In a large bowl, combine tomatoes, soups, milk and the seasonings. Transfer 3½ cups of mixture to another bowl; add chicken and cream cheese.

2. Spread ¼ cup soup mixture into each of two greased 13x9-in. baking dishes. Place ⅓ cup of the chicken mixture down the center of each tortilla. Roll up and place seam side down in baking dishes. Pour remaining soup mixture over the tops; sprinkle with cheese.

3. Bake, uncovered, for 30-35 minutes or until heated through and cheese is melted.

FREEZE OPTION *Cover and freeze unbaked casseroles up to 3 months. To use, partially thaw in refrigerator overnight. Remove from refrigerator 30 minutes before baking. Preheat oven to 350°. Cover casserole with foil; bake 45 minutes or until heated through and a thermometer inserted in center reads 165°. Uncover and bake 5-10 minutes longer or until cheese is melted.*

Barbecue Turkey Meat Loaf

My family loves meat loaf, and I tried many recipes for it over the years before creating this fabulous keeper. My girls and I make several loaves at one time, then freeze the ones we don't use.

—ROBYN YOUNG INDIANAPOLIS, IN

PREP: 20 MIN.
BAKE: 50 MIN. + STANDING
MAKES: 2 LOAVES (8 SERVINGS EACH)

- 2 large eggs, lightly beaten
- ½ cup barbecue sauce
- ⅓ cup 2% milk
- 2 tablespoons Worcestershire sauce
- 2 teaspoons prepared mustard
- 1⅓ cups seasoned bread crumbs
- 1 small onion, finely chopped
- 2 garlic cloves, minced
- 1 teaspoon salt
- 1 teaspoon rubbed sage
- 2 pounds extra-lean ground turkey
- 1 pound Italian turkey sausage links, casings removed

TOPPING
- 1 cup barbecue sauce
- ½ cup packed brown sugar
- 2 teaspoons prepared mustard

1. Combine the first 10 ingredients in a large bowl.

Crumble ground turkey and sausage over mixture and mix well. Pat into two greased 9x5-in. loaf pans. Combine the topping ingredients in a small bowl; spread over tops.

2. Cover and freeze one meat loaf for up to 3 months. Bake the remaining loaf, uncovered, at 350° for 50-55 minutes or until no pink remains and a thermometer reads 165°. Let stand 10 minutes before slicing.

TO USE FROZEN MEAT LOAF
Bake frozen meat loaf as directed, increasing time to 1¼-1½ hours.

Breakfast Sausage Bread

Any time we take this savory, satisfying bread to a potluck, it goes over very well. We never bring any home. My husband usually makes it, and he prides himself on the beautiful golden loaves.

—SHIRLEY CALDWELL
NORTHWOOD, OH

PREP: 25 MIN. + RISING
BAKE: 25 MIN.
MAKES: 2 LOAVES (16 SLICES EACH)

- 2 loaves (1 pound each) frozen white bread dough, thawed

- ½ pound mild pork sausage
- ½ pound bulk spicy pork sausage
- 1½ cups diced fresh mushrooms
- ½ cup chopped onion
- 3 large eggs, divided use
- 2½ cups (10 ounces) shredded mozzarella cheese
- 1 teaspoon dried basil
- 1 teaspoon dried parsley flakes
- 1 teaspoon dried rosemary, crushed
- 1 teaspoon garlic powder

1. Cover dough and let rise in a warm place until doubled. Preheat oven to 350°. In a large skillet, cook the sausage, mushrooms and onion over medium-high heat 6-8 minutes or until meat is no longer pink, breaking up sausage into crumbles. Drain. Transfer to a bowl; cool.

2. Stir in two eggs, cheese and seasonings. Roll each loaf of dough into a 16x12-in. rectangle. Spread dough with sausage mixture to within 1 in. of edges. Roll up jelly-roll style, starting with a short side; pinch seams to seal. Place loaves on a greased baking sheet.

3. In a small bowl, whisk remaining egg. Brush over tops. Bake 25-30 minutes or until golden brown. Serve warm.

FREEZE OPTION *Securely wrap and freeze cooled loaves in foil and place in resealable plastic freezer bags. To use, place foil-wrapped loaf on a baking sheet and reheat in a 450° oven 10-15 minutes or until heated through. Carefully remove foil; return to oven a few minutes longer until crust is crisp.*

Beef Taco Lasagna

This recipe makes two big pans.
Freeze one or both to enjoy later.

—**STACEY COMPTON** TOLEDO, OH

PREP: 30 MIN.
BAKE: 35 MIN. + STANDING
MAKES: 2 CASSEROLES
(8 SERVINGS EACH)

- 24 **lasagna noodles**
- 2 **pounds lean ground beef (90% lean)**
- 2 **envelopes taco seasoning**
- 4 **large egg whites**
- 2 **cartons (15 ounces each) ricotta cheese**
- 8 **cups (2 pounds) shredded cheddar cheese**
- 2 **jars (24 ounces each) chunky salsa**

1. Preheat oven to 350°. Cook noodles according to package directions. Meanwhile, in a large skillet, cook beef over medium heat until no longer pink; drain. Stir in taco seasoning. In a small bowl, combine egg whites and ricotta cheese. Drain noodles.

2. In each of two 13x9-in. baking dishes, layer four noodles, ¾ cup ricotta mixture, half of the beef mixture and 1⅓ cups cheddar cheese. Top each with four noodles, ¾ cup ricotta mixture, 1½ cups salsa and 1⅓ cups cheese. Repeat.

3. Bake, uncovered, for 35-40 minutes or until heated through. Let stand for 10 minutes before cutting.

FREEZE IT

Cover and freeze unbaked lasagna. To use, partially thaw in refrigerator overnight. Remove from refrigerator 30 minutes before baking. Bake lasagna as directed, increasing time as necessary to heat through and for a thermometer to read 165°.

Mint Chip Freeze

I'm a retired home economics teacher and have quite a collection of recipes from my classes. My students really like this refreshing frozen dessert made with ice cream and Oreo cookies.

—**ROBERT LAMB** DALEVILLE, IN

PREP: 30 MIN. + CHILLING
MAKES: 2 DESSERTS
(15-18 SERVINGS EACH)

- 2 **packages (15½ ounces each) Oreo cookies, crushed**
- ½ **cup butter, melted**
- 1 **can (12 ounces) evaporated milk**
- 1 **cup sugar**
- ½ **cup butter, cubed**
- 2 **ounces unsweetened chocolate, chopped**
- 1 **gallon mint chocolate chip ice cream, softened**
- 1 **carton (16 ounces) frozen whipped topping, thawed Shaved chocolate**

1. In a large bowl, combine the cookie crumbs and butter. Press into two 13x9-in. dishes. Refrigerate for 30 minutes.
2. In a small saucepan, combine the milk, sugar, butter and chocolate. Cook and stir over medium heat until thickened and bubbly, about 12 minutes. Remove from the heat; cool completely.
3. Spread ice cream over each crust. Spoon cooled chocolate sauce over top; evenly spread to cover. Freeze until firm. Spread with whipped topping. Desserts may be frozen for up to 2 months. Remove from freezer 10 minutes before cutting. Garnish with shaved chocolate.

Mexican Chicken Alfredo

One family member likes Italian; another likes Mexican. They'll never have to argue when this rich and creamy sensation is on the menu.

—**TIA WOODLEY** STOCKBRIDGE, GA

PREP: 25 MIN. • **BAKE:** 30 MIN.
MAKES: 2 CASSEROLES
(4 SERVINGS EACH)

- 1 **package (16 ounces) gemelli or spiral pasta**
- 2 **pounds boneless skinless chicken breasts, cubed**
- 1 **medium onion, chopped**
- ¼ **teaspoon salt**
- ¼ **teaspoon pepper**
- 1 **tablespoon canola oil**
- 2 **jars (15 ounces each) Alfredo sauce**
- 1 **cup grated Parmesan cheese**
- 1 **cup medium salsa**
- ¼ **cup 2% milk**
- 2 **teaspoons taco seasoning**

1. Preheat oven to 350°. Cook pasta according to package directions.
2. Meanwhile, in a large skillet over medium heat, cook chicken, onion, salt and pepper in oil until chicken is no longer pink. Stir in Alfredo sauce; bring to a boil. Stir in cheese, salsa, milk and taco seasoning.
3. Drain pasta; toss with chicken mixture. Divide between two greased 8-in. square baking dishes. Cover and bake for 30-35 minutes or until bubbly.
FREEZE OPTION *Cover and freeze unbaked casserole up to 3 months. To use, thaw in refrigerator overnight. Remove from refrigerator 30 minutes before baking. Preheat oven to 350°. Bake casserole, covered, 50-60 minutes or until bubbly.*

BARLEY CORN SALAD
PAGE 70

**BAKED CHICKEN
CHIMICHANGAS**
PAGE 158

LOADED CHICKEN & GOUDA CALZONES
PAGE 150

SWEET-AND-SOUR
MEAT LOAF
PAGE 118

CHICKEN NOODLE
CASSEROLE
PAGE 152

CHICKEN ALOHA
PAGE 160

BAKED SPAGHETTI
PAGE 111

APRICOT TURKEY PINWHEELS
PAGE 38

DEBRA'S CAVATINI
PAGE 240